Social Work Practice

Social Work Practice

Religio-Philosophical Foundations

Essays in Honour of Professor Indira Patel

Edited by
CHHAYA PATEL

RAWAT PUBLICATIONS
Jaipur • New Delhi • Bangalore • Guwahati • Kolkata

ISBN 978-81-7033-527-6

Reprinted, 2016

Published by
Prem Rawat for **Rawat Publications**
Satyam Apts., Sector 3, Jawahar Nagar, Jaipur - 302 004 (India)
Phone: 0141 265 1748 / 7006 Fax: 0141 265 1748
E-mail: info@rawatbooks.com
Website: rawatbooks.com

New Delhi Office
4858/24, Ansari Road, Daryaganj, New Delhi 110 002
Phone: 011-23263290

Also at *Bangalore, Guwahati* and *Kolkata*

Typeset by Rawat Computers, Jaipur
Printed at Chaman Enterprises, New Delhi

Contents

PART III
Sites of Social Work Practice

Foreword

While writing the Foreword to this Felicitation Volume for Professor Indira Patel, an earthy and socio-culturally a rooted intellectual, one's mind goes back almost half a century to the era and social environment in which the Faculty of Social Work, M. S. University of Baroda, Vadodara was started in 1950, and the country as a whole was still in the spirit of the early days of national independence. Creativity and desire to serve could be felt all-around, pride in India's cultural values was shared at all levels. The majority of India's population lived in villages and the economy was basically agriculture-oriented. In that setting, it was pertinent that social work education be formulated to emphasize needs of rural population with understanding of their deep-seated traditions and values, at the same time utilizing modern scientific knowledge to provide basic and other necessary services.

In the years immediately following the Second World War, realization dawned, as never before: how small a universe mankind lives in is, and how closely intertwined lives are across the geographical and national boundaries. With accessibility of speedy transportation and opening up of national frontiers, students from India looked to the West to acquire scientific and technological knowledge in all fields, including social work. Those returning after studies abroad in western countries, particularly the USA and the UK, became pioneers in establishing educational programmes and welfare services offering employment opportunities to trained social workers. At the same time, it must be noted that the first institution to provide training in social work in India, presently bearing the name of the Tata Institute of Social Sciences, Mumbai, was started in the late 1930s. Prior to independence of the country, the welfare services were more in the nature of amelioration, by and large carried out by semi-religious organizations and well-intended philanthropic citizens.

The Faculty of Social Work, M.S. University of Baroda, where Professor Indira Patel received her post-graduate education in social work, had opted to concentrate on rural welfare work, in response to the evident need of the hour and its location being in very close proximity to villages of rural Gujarat. Even as a student, Professor Patel demonstrated her learning towards service to the rural population. Growing up in Gujarat, the homeland of Gandhiji and Sardar Patel, had its influence on the young and undoubtedly generated pride in deeper age-old values and culture of India. It is not surprising that as a young student Indira Patel was also charged with, and nurtured the desire to be of service to the downtrodden. Throughout her working years, Professor Patel stayed close to her home base. While serving on the staff of the Faculty of Social Work and later as the Dean, she actively participated in the development of welfare services in and around Vadodara.

Simultaneously, she had attempted to search and find for herself a deeper meaning of life in relation to the humanity as a whole and had tried consistently to synthesize these values with social work philosophy and social work education in India. Her own convictions were based in *Vedanta* philosophy and through it, the approach to human problems, perhaps remains to be consolidated into methods that can be taught in classrooms and applied on a wide scale. The challenge of it lies ahead and needs to be pursued further.

As in other fields, so also in social work, India has to find its own identity; the soil and the seeds have to match. India has to evolve approaches to human problems that would be compatible with its own psyche. Only then will it bear lasting results. Much can be said about social work philosophy and approach introduced in social work education in the early days of establishment of schools of social work in India. All that was learnt in the western setting was enthusiastically introduced with the hope of rapid development. But it remains a debatable point whether it has made the necessary impact on cross sections of the country. The pertinent question is whether it has touched the ethos of the common man in India or does it remain at the level of the elite? Having known Professor Indira Patel since her student days, I am inclined to believe that the question posed above was at the base of her search to find an answer in the teachings of Swami Vivekananda and the universal concepts of *Vedanta* philosophy.

In order to understand the problems of a society, it is necessary to understand its cultural milieu. In a broader context one can safely deduce that the common goal of peoples all over the world is to be at peace with one's self and in harmony with those around, that the basic needs are also to sustain the body, develop the mind and regulate the emotions to gratify individual drives and avoid conflicts. The moot question is how to achieve it. There can be no doubt that social development can not be conceptualized without self-development which is growth from within. Whether it is attempted through psychological and analytic methods evolved or by introspection aimed at realization that an individual is an inseparable, integral part of the universe, are but different approaches, two different paths, searching for the destination termed 'human happiness'. In one case, there is emphasis on 'ego identity', 'ego-assertion', a drive to achieve 'success'; the other sees self in oneness with the entire universe and hence strives towards the ultimate which is 'ego assimilation', i.e., ego's immersion into infinity. In highlighting some of these points here, it is not intended to debate the right or the wrong of an approach nor to say either one is more effective than the other, but to bring forth an attempt made by an individual to search within herself and examine her own convictions in the framework of her chosen profession.

Over the years, Professor Indira Patel has emphasized the concept of service and self-development based on the *Vedanta* norms of the totality of the universe and has striven to relate it to social work education in India. This effort to link the scientific learning with cultural roots deep in the Indian psyche deserves recognition and further thought which may at a future date provide a sound foundation to social work education and practice in India.

Dr. (Ms.) Parin Vakharia
Founder Dean
Faculty of Social Work
M.S. University of Baroda
Vadodara

Preface

The customary practice of saying a word or two about such a work comes as a good opportunity to tell the readers about the combination of circumstances and individuals who shaped this effort. This work is chiefly a product of circumstances all through but for timely help of a few individuals whom I gratefully remember and record here my gratitude to them. Between 1985 and 1990, I was deeply involved in exploring and choosing an area of research for my doctoral degree. As a Social Work Instructor at ICDS-MLTC in South Gujarat University, Surat, I was considerably exposed to tribal development functionaries, society and region, as I travelled extensively in tribal areas of South Gujarat. With the aim of doing Ph.D., I came back to Vadodara and again joined the Faculty of Social Work. It was in this connection that I began meeting my teachers and senior colleagues, trying to find out the possibilities of doctoral research by composing a few sketchy proposals that were in my mind. Professor Anil Navale, presently Head and Dean, Faculty of Social Work; Coordinator, UGC-DRS Programme in Social Work; and Honorary Director, National Service Scheme, M.S. University of Baroda, Vadodara, was the first person to bring me closer to Professor Indira Patel by involving me in numerous academically related activities and programmes. He convinced me that there is a lot more to learn from "Ben" (as he, like many others, called her) and she has not been adequately sourced by genuine learners. I owe a very special word of thanks to Prof. Navale, as looking back, I feel I would have missed a major lesson in my life, had I not come in contact with Indiraben. This apart, the credit for initiating me into the field of social work teaching, practice and profession goes to Professor Navale. Before taking to teaching, I worked with him in the NSS and acquired important insights into the issues that are usually encountered in the field.

My meetings with Professor Indira Patel increased and I was very happy to find in her an esteemed elderly, caring colleague and a great teacher. These meetings turned out to be a long-drawn process of unlearning and relearning the basics of social work discipline and profession. After her retirement in 1988, our meetings continued at her residence. In February 1989, I prepared a research proposal for the Ph.D. degree. It could not be considered then as the Faculty Administration was exploring the possibility of introducing an M.Phil. degree course as a pre-requisite for doing Ph.D. For next three years, the M.Phil. degree course could not be introduced for various reasons. However, during these three years, my proximity with Indiraben increased several fold. Since neither Ph.D. nor M.Phil. was becoming possible to do, I was in search of some worthwhile, academically productive and fulfilling activity, apart from usual teaching at the Faculty. Again various academic plans were conceived, discussed, debated, dropped and redrawn. During this time, Indiraben's book (1987) was generating a good deal of interest here and abroad and many readers were corresponding with her and planning to come to meet her. As she was not keeping too well, she entrusted to me the task of corresponding on her behalf with all these readers and admirers of her book and also organize their meetings with her in Vadodara if desired by some of them.

During one such meeting, Indiraben expressed her view that no such work has been taken up all these years that highlights direct or indirect contribution of Baroda School of Social Work which is quite unique and hitherto undocumented. I immediately took up the suggestion and shortly came up with an outline to do a small book on *Philosophy and Practice of Social Work: The Baroda Perspective*. She warmly and affectionately agreed to go through it in a week's time. In the next visit, I found all the labour was hopelessly lost. She threw a volley of questions on my outline which I found difficult to answer and defend to her satisfaction. She came up with the names of about a dozen books on the theme and told me first to read them well and then attempt to rewrite the outline. Ultimately, I found it difficult to prepare an outline for a full-length book on such a complex and vast theme which can satisfy her entirely. As a result, I merrily abandoned the project and stayed put for next few months but remained in touch with her.

This was also the period when some of the eminent social scientists in western India were being honoured by bringing out felicitation volumes on the themes of their life-long work in various disciplines of social sciences. It then just struck to me in one of those typical, empty, idle moments of gapping and brooding, as to why not approach the well-known social scientists and eminent social work academicians, known to Indiraben and her work, for an edited volume on "Philosophy and Practice of Social Work in India" to felicitate her. I put in everything once again to prepare an outline on this project. After gathering enough courage, on one fine morning, I gave it to Indiraben for her perusal and comments. It took a great effort to convince her that the proposed outline was well-intended and definitely did not amount to subtle form of sycophancy or partisanship in any way. She agreed to permit such an effort only if the genesis and contribution of Baroda School was also focused. On the whole, she had found it broadly agreeable but wished it to be shown to someone else who could take a more balanced view and give more objective comments on the whole project. Indiraben suggested Professor Niranjana A. Gokarn, Head, Social Work Education/Practice Cell, Tata Institute of Social Sciences, Mumbai, as one such source. I wish to record here my immense indebtedness to Professor Gokarn for finding time in the midst of her busiest schedules and various time-bound responsibilities on her hand to go through the proposal and gave very useful comments and suggestions to revise it. Later on, Professor Gokarn gave addresses of a few eminent social work academicians who could be contacted for the proposed volume. Indiraben was also quite helpful in giving us a few names of some of her teachers, students and contemporary fellow-academicians. A list of 36 prospective contributors was drawn and a call letter was posted to such luminaries as Parin Vakharia (Hyderabad), Armaity Desai (Mumbai), Ammu M. Mazumdar (USA), M.S. Gore (Mumbai), Shanker Pathak (Bangalore), K.D. Gangrade (Delhi), Dorothy Baker (USA), D.L. Sheth (Delhi), N.R. Sheth (Ahmedabad), Niranjana A. Gokarn (Mumbai), K.V. Ramana (Vishakhapatnam), C.P. Goyal (Ladnu, Rajasthan), Radha Paul (Chennai), P.D. Kulkarni (Pune), R.R. Singh (Delhi), K.K. Jacob (Udaipur and Bhubaneswar), Mirza Ahmed (Lucknow), S.N. Ranade (Delhi), Kalindi Mazumdar (Mumbai), S.P. Punalekar (Surat), Lancy Lobo (Surat) and Bharati Sharma (Aizwal, Mizoram) among others. As the responses began to come from far and wide, we were greatly delighted by the good words written for Baroda School and Indiraben; and this increased my enthusiasm.

Despite having made persistent efforts to receive the contributions from several eminent scholars in the profession by spending almost a fortune in long distance telephoning (including ISD calls), corresponding by registered and speed posts (several times over), personally visiting some, as and when possible, and waiting to hear or after hearing to receive their articles for the volume, I register here a partial failure on my part and disappointment for not having succeeded in receiving them. A somewhat similar experience is recorded by Vimala Thangavelu in her book. It is possible that some either did not receive the communications or having received chose to ignore them. Others were appreciably frank in conveying their inability to write due to advanced age, ill-health or sheer paucity of time. A few could not write despite genuinely willing to do so for understandable reasons of pressing commitments of very active academic life. It is unfortunate that this volume is published without the contribution of several eminent scholars. A word on delay in publishing this volume is quite due. Between 1993 and 1996, a combination of personal and family circumstances diverted my attention and energies considerably, and disengaged me from this work. During the period from 1996 to 1998, we withheld the publication despite the entire manuscript being ready as we were trying to receive a write up in form of a biographical sketch on Indiraben from one of the most outstanding fellow-academicians and the closest friends of hers. The worst shock of my life came when all of a sudden Indiraben passed away on 21 December, 1995. Today, I feel absolutely heart-broken and sad that Indiraben is no more to see this work being published. Her sudden demise changed the whole complexion and character of the effort. What had begun as a felicitation volume has now got transformed into a commemoration volume. Well, I can't be too sure but it seems this is what the fate had it in store for us !

Parin Vakharia has done us a great honour and favour by writing a Foreword for this volume. We are extremely grateful to her for having first promptly agreed to write it and then very quickly sending it along with very useful, critical and corrective comments on the project. Indiraben's eyes had welled up when the Foreword was read out to her. She was simply overwhelmed and beholdened in sheer joy and gratitude to her teacher and mentor. I wish to place on record my sincerest thanks to all the contributors of the volume and offer my profound apologies for sitting on their valuable articles for so long. Needless to even state, but for their efforts this volume would not have got composed. I thank the editors and publishers of the journals for permitting me to reprint in this volume the already published articles by D.L. Sheth and Harsh Sethi in *Voluntas*, 2(2), 1991 (Manchester, UK), TISS Social Work Educators' Forum in *The Indian Journal of Social Work*, 58(2), April 1997 (Mumbai) and by Chhaya Patel (Chap. 15) in *The Journal of the M.S. University of Baroda* (Vadodara), 41-42 (Social Science No.) 1992-93. Satya P. Agarwal's contribution was originally published in his book (1993) and out of admiration and appreciation of Indiraben's interest and work on the same lines, he graciously allowed us to revise and publish it in this volume. I thank him sincerely. I thank Indubhai Shelat, Former Dean, Faculty of Social Work, M.S. University, Vilasben Patel, a housewife and Indiraben's closest friend and Chimanbhai Patel as well as Prakashbhai Joshi of Shri Ramkrishna Mission, Vadodara, who among others have helped me time and again while collecting biographical details and the photograph of Indiraben. Pravin R. Chalke is a multi-job hand and commands remarkable proficiency with various computer applications and deserves very special mention. He has prepared the manuscript by typing, type-setting and composing it extremely meticulously, painstakingly and efficiently. I extend my sincere thanks to him for doing the job with interest and cheer. I thank the publishers for having done an extremely good job of planning the production of this volume.

It is again a matter of happy coincidence that the volume is being published in the Golden Jubilee Year of the Baroda School of Social Work. It gives me a great joy for setting a small milestone of glory in an institute's Golden Jubilee Year. My loving daughters, Prachi and Bhoomi, have bore the most brunt of my rather long-drawn involvement in bringing out this publication. There is indeed no way to compensate them adequately for the intermittent losses of their rightful time with their mother, and yet I make here a modest attempt to retrieve some lost ground. My mother, Anandiben Rambhai Patel, has been a constant source of immense support and help all through my life. They are my perennially sustaining backward and forward linkages with the past and the future. I feel I am singularly most fortunate to receive a great deal of encouragement, guidance and support in my this and other works from Priyavadan, my husband, who despite having his own pressing academic commitments has ungrudgingly found time for extensive and insightful discussions with me.

Finally, I humbly place this volume in your hands with a hope that it will serve some useful purpose in reinforcing and enhancing the frontiers of various concerns of social work education, practice and profession in India that were so dear to Indiraben.

Chhaya Patel

Indira Patel: Philosophy and Social Work Practice

by Chhaya Patel

AN EARTHY AND ROOTED INTELLECTUAL

Professor Indira Muljibhai Patel was affectionately known as 'Indiraben' or simply as 'Ben' to many of her students, colleagues and friends, spread in every nook and corner of the country and in a few countries abroad. Though unmarried and single all her life, Indiraben had become almost a family member to a large number of her admirers, colleagues, friends and institutions in all parts of the country, ranging from Kerala, Tamil Nadu, Andhra Pradesh to West Bengal, Sikkim, Orissa, Mizoram, U.P., neighbouring states of M.P., Rajasthan and Maharashtra as well as a few countries in Asia, Europe and America. Despite not having had her own family, she knew the institution of Indian family so well that she possessed complete grasp of all aspects of family life and always had up her *pallu* relevant advices, counsels and remedies for all, be they children, married women, widows, estranged wives or husbands, demanding mothers-in-law or foot-loose teenagers in the families. Everyone of such vast number of estranged categories of social life-mosaic, who approached her or whom she regularly met either as a neighbour, relative, family friend, teacher or simply a senior citizen, found a rare depth of warmth, trust, regard and love. I believe these close encounters with multi-splendoured aspects of family and social/community life kept her authentically abreast with the changing dynamics and dimensions of family life in modern times. Her close association with families helped her obtain first-hand insights into the dynamics of family life and equipped her with original and convincing solutions to numerous small and big problems that the increasing number of joint as well as nuclear families faced. After her retirement from the service, the same vast network of families came handy to fill the momentary void that was created in her life. All her life, she remained an active member of a women's group, comprising literate, semi-literate and illiterate women, known as *Ekadashi Bhajan Mandali* (which met twice in every month of the Hindu calendar on the eleventh day). The *Mandali* sang devotional songs (of Vaishnava sect) with music in which Indiraben sang and played either *dholak* (a drum-like musical instrument) or *vajapeti* (harmonium).

Indiraben was born on 4 September, 1928 in Vadodara. She was a Leuva Patidar Patel from Sojitra in Kheda district which is one of the six socially highest ranked villages of Charotar region in Kheda. Swami Anand (1965:6-7) has described Charotar Patidar community as one of the two 'head-strong' communities of Gujarat (the other being Anavils of South Gujarat). This is originally a peasant caste and well known for its community traits like----fearlessness, bitter tongue but soft, caring and kind heart, unbending, rebellious, courageous, hardworking, straightforward and outspoken, faithful and traditional. Indiraben was a repository of many of these community traits. While making a point, she was loyal only to the truthfulness of her conviction and point and not to any other partisan consideration whatsoever. She cannot be put down or brushed aside in any meeting chaired or attended by such dignitaries like the Mayor, ministers, city politicians, UGC representatives, government secretaries or officials and senate/syndicate members, or Vice-Chancellor of the University. In one such meeting, her words exploded in the face of the Vice-Chancellor when she shot back in the midst of a discussion saying, "...you mean to say, was I drunk in the previous meeting when I heard you say..." There are many other instances of her unbending and uncompromising temperament when she worked as an administrator of the Faculty in her capacity as either the Head or the Dean.

One more incident, though unpleasant and bitter but worthy of recall, needs to be briefly sketched in order to highlight the quality of forgiveness and rancour-free heart she had. During her deanship at Vadodara, one of her administrative decisions was challenged by one of her colleagues in the Court of Law as unjust, biased and violative of the rules. The colleague won the case but after some time resigned and left. The ordeal of the court case had shattered Indiraben and made her quite unhappy, bitter and wounded. She momentarily developed utter contempt, dislike and disgust about that colleague and nursed this wound for quite some time. After many years, Indiraben went to attend a Selection Committee meeting as its external expert member in one of the most reputed institutions of higher learning in West Bengal. One of the candidates was no other than the same old colleague who had dragged her to the Court of Law in Vadodara. Seeing Indiraben enter the Selection Committee room alongwith the other members, this candidate was totally nonplused and crest-fallen, thinking that her opportunity of selection is foreclosed as Indiraben will surely take revenge of old bitter legal battle at Vadodara. Contrary to this apprehension, Indiraben made the whole situation relaxed, comforting and rancour-free. She immediately rose to the occasion and did not misuse the opportunity for settling petty individual scores at the cost of the interest of the host institution and the individual scholar. Such lofty acts of nobleness are fast becoming rare and forgotten.

Another highly distinguishing quality she had was of maintaining a dignified distance from structures of authorities and positions of power in the institutions. She never ran after positions of power and status. On the contrary, she firmly believed that one's work should be of such level, quality and utility that recognition and honours should come to you rather than your chasing them and in the process becoming a pauper as you, she believed, inevitably lose your self-respect, dignity, soul, pride and values of self-worth. This is not to raise her to the heights of divinity or create around her some kind of a halo of super human mysticism as is often the practice, but to state that Indiraben was very much an earthy and this-worldly person.

She developed and shaped her *weltanschauung* and personal life on the highly appreciable commitments to the ideals of ancient text—the *Gita*—and on the life messages of *Karma Yogis* like Vivekananda and Gandhiji. She lived a simple life and gave all her earnings, savings and post-retirement benefits back to the society in numerous ways through donations and contributions to a number of institutions. She wore *khadi* all her life and used bicycle for local conveyance during most of her working life. Although an oriental to the core, she was herself a great admirer of many aspects of western culture such as education, work ethics, etiquettes, mannerisms of day-to-day exchanges, small tea-parties, layout of her drawing room and of course the game of cricket. Truly, Indiraben was a woman of immense substance, veritable fountain of ideals of good life and living as well as a visionary of a good, enlightened, equal and just society based on principles of religio-philosophical foundations of *Vedant* as practised by Ramkrishna Mission and propounded by Swami Vivekananda.

Recalling her childhood days, spent in an elite locality of Pratapgunj of Vadodara and at a twilight time of Vadodara's famous Gaekwad rule, British rule in general and Gandhi's national freedom movement, she once stated that there was a distinct impact of all these tumultuous historic periods (co-existing at the same time) on the elitist, advanced and progressive families of Vadodara. Her family being a doctor's family was no exception to this. Like others, it was also split between the pulls and pushes of acceptance and rejection of western versus oriental values of life. Some members in her family preferred western education and discipline while others admired and adopted Gandhian values of nationalism, simplicity, social service, social reform, regular prayers, etc. These formative years of childhood phase of life instilled in young Indira a good blend of Gandhian and western values. She grew up to become a seeker of ultimate truth through the discourse and doctrines of *Vedantic* religious philosophy and used them as a base to achieve national goals of reconstruction of rural Indian society by creating a good mix of modernity and tradition.

Indiraben had her entire education in Vadodara. She obtained her Bachelor of Arts degree in Psychology in 1950 and Master of Social Work (MSW) degree in 1953 in the maiden batch of the course at the M.S.University of Vadodara. During 1953-55, she joined Gandhi Ashram in Koba, Ahmedabad and also became a member of Bharat Sevak Samaj with great excitement, enthusiasm and hope of doing some good work on the basis of what was newly learnt at the MSW course. She soon got disillusioned at Koba and rushed to her teachers at the M.S.University and discussed with them her experiences in the field threadbare. She told them that the goal of national reconstruction and social transformation cannot be realized with the highly personalized, myopic and merely idealistic approach of the people in the voluntary sector. She felt there was too much of pettiness over small matters, subjective and partisan decision-making and narrow vision. More importantly, she also realized that there was a great paucity of committed, talented and trained cadre of young professionals to work as social workers. She, therefore, decided to adopt a modest two-pronged personal professional strategy to achieve the national goals. On one hand, she decided to teach, train and produce select batches of young people to take a plunge in activities of rural social reconstruction and welfare, and, on the other hand, to keep in constant touch with the relevant agencies involved in this work. So that important lessons can be learnt from their experiences and critical feedback can be obtained to tailor and alter the curriculum of MSW course accordingly.

The Baroda School of Social Work had chosen to be a generic course with a fair blend of theory and practice right from the beginning. In the initial stage, the vision for academic planning of the Faculty was done by Parin Vakharia and shared with her by S.N. Ranade and late Perviz Bhatt. The Faculty owes a lot to their convictions and fortitude in building the foundation. Others such as Indira Tayal, Ammu M. Muzumdar, G.G. Dadlani and Indiraben Patel strengthened this foundation by joining the Faculty later and made valuable contributions to establish the Faculty as a reputed academic centre for teaching and training in generic social work. A great deal of emphasis was placed on field work, field contact, field exposure, and interacting with the field functionaries for both the teachers and the students of social work. From these convictions she had joined the Faculty of Social Work, M.S.University, Baroda, as a lecturer in 1955. She obtained her Master of Social Sciences degree from Adelphi College, School of Social Work, New York, USA in 1960-61. In 1971, she became Professor of Social Work. During 1969-75, she served as the Dean, Faculty of Social Work, Vadodara. In 1975, she had the most deserved and privileged honour of being the President of Association of Schools of Social Work India (ASSWI). In the same year, she participated in the International Association of Social Work Conference held at Hong Kong. She wrote her self-guided doctoral research on *A Study of the Contribution of Swami Vivekananda: An Oriental Approach to Social Work* which was submitted to and approved by the M.S.University, Baroda in 1983.

Alongwith the teaching of the papers on History and Philosophy of Social Work and Social Group Work Method to the students of MSW, she also kept herself actively involved in all those social processes that were going on in the wider society beyond the campus and were relevant to her profession and institution. The National Cadets Corps was one such agency whom she served as Teacher Officer for some time. She was closely associated with the activities of V.T. Krishnamachari Institute of Rural Development in village Samiyala, Vadodara. She established Child Guidance Clinic for the children with special needs at the Faculty for creating a better opportunity of field work training in social work education for the students. Besides, she was a moving spirit behind introducing National Service Scheme (NSS) programme at the University and housed it in the Faculty. Through the activities of NSS, she maintained a close contact with the young girls and boys, offering a wide spectrum of specializations and subjects in various colleges/faculties of the University ranging from Arts, Commerce, Science, Technology and Engineering, Polytechnic to Fine Arts, Performing Arts (then known as Music College), Home Science, Law and the Medical College. Throughout the seventies, the NSS made a major contribution in channelizing the University youth for rural reconstruction and numerous social services in urban need-centres such as slums, central prison, homes for physically and visually handicapped, remand homes for boys and girls, sick and ill in the hospitals etc.

Her association with Ramkrishna Mission Kendra at Vadodara, Rajkot and Belur Math has become legendary. Her devotion and commitment to Mission's goals and activities was complete and unflinching. She first worked as Vice-President of Vadodara Kendra and later on worked as its Secretary. She contributed a great deal in the Mission's activities of rural reconstruction and upliftment known as '*pallimangal*'. She was instrumental in initiating the nation-wide celebration of Youth Week by the NSS on Swami Vivekananda's Birth Anniversary on 12 January every year since 1985. She remained a life-long devotee of the Mission and struggled to synthesize the goals of the Mission with that of her profession's. Her only book, *Vivekananda's Approach to Social Work* was published in 1987 that was developed from an originally written doctoral thesis by her in 1983. This book is well-received here and abroad (Agarwal, 1993). Her real and seminal contribution lies in filling the long-existing void of a firm philosophy for motivating and sustaining a social worker who encounters and faces the toughest and most trying situations while actually practising social work.

Her views and position on written printed words were that

of an orthodox, conservative and conventional academic. She did not believe in writing on social concerns for the sake of writing. Indiraben further believed that a written word without some remote or immediate context of practice or relation with action was hollow ('*bodo*' as she called it in Gujarati) and often misleading. Therefore, she placed a great value on the aspect of practice of social work rather than merely producing an impressive-looking diarrhoea of words neatly composed into futile and sterile theorizations. Her consistent advice throughout the life to all her students and colleagues who wanted to teach and to undertake research on the issues of social work concerns was first and foremost to acquire an experience, proximity and familiarity with the field of the subject of teaching or area of research, at least for 3-5 years and then get initiated. She herself took almost the entire lifetime, first to compose her doctoral thesis and then publish it. On this count, she was widely misunderstood by her students and colleagues, especially those who were under the academic impact of American/western credo of 'publish or perish'. Many thought that she was turning them down from taking to teaching and excelling in research by doing doctorate as a part of the usual strategy of the politics of selections and promotions with which the higher learning centres are replete with. She was extremely strict, uncompromising and demanding from her quota of research students, writing dissertations under her guidance as a part requirement of the course on MSW. Some students and colleagues misunderstood her this concern as authoritarianism of a sort whereas others saw it as an inevitable and the worthiest quality of a good teacher and a worthy colleague who was committed to the ideal of bringing out the best in every student and colleague. As a result of her these views on the subject of research she could register with her only one doctoral research student who completed it in 1988, the year of her retirement from the service as teacher.

After her retirement, Indiraben chose to reduce her involvement in the academic activities that required outstation travelling to remote places. However, she continued to remain concerned with the major developments and premises of the discipline. During these years, she kept her doors open for all the former students, colleagues, visiting academicians from here and abroad, who periodically came to the Faculty and the University on different assignments. She once again resumed rather vigorously her role of an honorary, informal and intimate 'consultant' on various academic or semi-academic matters. On the other hand, despite her failing health, her involvement in the activities of the Ramkrishna Mission in and out of Vadodara increased. Her participation in *Ekadashi Bhajan Mandali* also increased and became regular till her passing away on 21, December 1995.

RELIGIOUS PHILOSOPHY AND HER VISION OF SOCIAL DEVELOPMENT

As we have mentioned in the previous section, Professor Indira Patel was not much of a writer although she was an avid and keen reader of wide-ranging philosophical, literary and social science works. She was, as she often said, a deliberate *kanjus* (parsimonious) with words while she either spoke or wrote them. As a result, she has left very little by way of academic writings in form of articles in the journals or published books except one book (1987) and a few articles. Hers was, thus, truly an oral scholarship. In this section, it is intended to discuss the religious philosophy that shaped her vision of social development as contained in her only but seminal book (1987) and also as obtained from the multiple sittings with her, discussing her position on this aspect. However, some of the citings are of recent dates as those works are relevant to and supportive of her thinking. The idea is to acquire an insight into the making of an earthy, rooted and indigenous social work academician who has spent a lifetime in striking a balance between the demanding callings of the field, discipline and community/society.

The themes of linkage, relevance and utility between religious philosophy, individual and social development not only fascinated Professor Indira Patel but preoccupied her throughout the life. From her early formative years, as young graduate and post-graduate student, she was involved in an intensive and deeper search for a true meaning of life and a social order which should be founded on ethico-moral resources contained in religious philosophy. She was committed and devoted to the ideal of developing a vision of society in which the religious and social spheres were not viewed as divorced from each other. Both had a mutually complementary social role to play in order to uplift the man to spiritual heights as well as fulfil his material needs. She was in search of a correct balance between temporal and spiritual aspects of life. These were the years when the national mainstream (comprising such great leaders as Rabindranath Tagore, Gandhiji, Sardar Patel, Rajendra Prasad, Sarojini Naidu, Kaka Kalelkar, K.M. Munshi, Vinoba Bhave, Zaverchand Meghani, U.N. Dheber etc.) before and after independence, was greatly concerned with the cherished ideal of removing rural poverty, social backwardness and fear from the minds of the masses. To her, physical aspects of social development such as education, health, housing, drinking water, sanitation, food and family and spiritual aspects of ethical conduct by individual and institutions formed important sites of social work education and practice. These were the areas of action or what is now known as praxis or social advocacy. She began her work in life from these island-like small areas of action and progressively went on to raise them and link them to the crucial questions of ethico-moral aspect of religious philosophy and individual conduct (Mukherji, 1971).

Social development was her life-long central concern and academic mission. She had objectively analyzed and acknowledged the social gains of freedom struggle in form of heightened popular consciousness, social reforms like removal of untouchability and superstitious beliefs, increased participation of women in freedom and social movements and their education. At the same time, she was fully aware about the limitations and insufficiencies of these social gains of freedom movement to further reshape "...the society for the good of the individual and the society as a whole" (1987:12). She believed that strong measures were needed for further consolidation of these gains. She was an ardent and bitter critic of the legislative approach which was recklessly followed by the new nations as a major mechanism to usher in a new social order without understanding the complexities of a plural, traditional, poor, multi-religious and predominantly rural society. She was confident and sufficiently convinced that acts, laws and legislations will not succeed in issues, spheres and sites of social development. For instance, the problems of beggary, prostitution, child labour, atrocities on women and weaker sections cannot be solved by mere legislations and laws. Legislative approach can yield results only if some preparatory and supportive grounds are readied by well-directed, conscious social efforts. She believed that social changes aimed at being brought about by reservation policy, consumption-oriented welfare measures for upliftment of weaker sections cannot really yield positive results of long-term value. She thought that "...these very efforts have weakened many of our basic institutions like education, family and religion, accompanied by violence and a slow but visible process of moral weakening" (1987:12). Such failures create a moral vacuum in society which the public services and agencies are incapable to fill. She was against the breakdown of family, community, religious institutions and loss of human (individual) freedom at any cost (Peck, 1978:185-97).

She was convinced that in view of these conditions, the very concept of social development needs to be redefined to suit country and society-specific context. She had realized that it is a nebulous concept open to wide-ranging interpretations and definitions. However, she viewed it as a "... cohesive and balanced process that enhances the viability of society to function for the well-being of all its members as understood and perceived by the state and which safeguards the rights of the individuals to an equitable share in the goods and service of the society" (1987:15). To her, social development was not a target once achieved and then shelved phenomenon. The prime concern of social development is to shape the complete man and it is a continuous project (Gore, 1985). She was quite worried and deeply concerned with the vulgarizing and dehumanizing effects of western brand of modernity on man, family, community and society. Consumption-driven, hungry, unsatiated and materialistic man is increasingly being reduced to animal instincts, feeble-minded existence and continued to be subjected to that state of life from generation to generation by a perverse system of education. Sophisticated technology has further dehumanized him. Drug addiction, premature pregnancies, destitution, delinquency, divorces, alcoholism, prostitution or sex working, abortions, child abuse are the products of vulgarized and corrupted western popular mass culture which is unabashedly promoted by TV and other electronic media (now in non-western societies like India too). Crimes, mental illnesses, emergence of zero tolerance zones, neglect of sick and aged, all-pervasive violence in family, community, neighbourhood, films, fiction, etc., are the fall-out effects of the western, capitalist, consumption-driven, so-called free society, which continuously chains and enslaves the man by sinking him from one baser indulgence to other and give him a false feeling of having had the fruits of his individual freedom (Thangavelu, 1978). She firmly believed that only a life-long, lasting and continuous educative process can produce and shape a complete man. Man-making knowledge cannot be terminal but a continually evolving body of knowledge all through the life of a man. What she meant was that up to a phase in life, one receives education as a measure of acquiring multiple proficiencies to generate awareness, income, wealth and services for the self, family and society through one of the myriad forms of wealth generation and then as a growing and ageing adult he has to be educated on ethico-moral doctrines preached in various religious philosophies by such indigenous forms of mass religious discourse of varying frequency, scale, periodicity and size of gathering as *katha* (an instituted or installed form of mass congregation for religious public discourse, that is addressed by a religio-spiritual leader or a saint and attended by children, young and old and completed within a fixed period usually a week) or *satra* (a sacrificial study session lasting from 13 to 100 days). Behind this innovative thinking, she had the contribution of *Swadhyay* movement led by Pandurang Shastri Athavale and *Swadhyay Parivar* in her mind (Sheth, 1998 and Roy, 1993) as well as *kathas* by Morari Bapu and Dongare Maharaj in Gujarat.

This redefinition of social development is shared by social workers alongwith other disciplines of social science such as political science, sociology, psychology and economics. She believed that "the profession of social work with its recent orientation to development in general and to social development in particular has a long background in terms of its goals which has moved from curative to preventive and then to development... which has in turn necessitated broadening of the value base of social work" (1987:15). This broadening of the value base is directly related to various philosophical positions and multi-culturality that exists in a plural, multi-cultural and multi-religious democratic society. The unique approaches of each of these multi-religious philosophical traditions and perspectives that have enriched Indian and global human civilization necessitates their incorporation in the very understanding of social work and its practice. The *Vedantic* tradition of Indian philosophy would need consideration in the same manner as the Chinese or Japanese religio-philosophical tradition would need with their distinct cultural and philosophical viewpoints. The concept of values and its importance and relevance in cross-cultural or multi-cultural situations continuously needs to be examined. Such a comparative religio-philosophical index is necessary to understand the experience of varieties of human deprivations, as the conditions of poverty, disabilities and malfunctions on one hand and potentialities on the other are cognitively as well as incognitively not the same.

She argued that there are fundamental differences in oriental and occidental thinking. The oriental philosophy places the individual, the self or *atman* at the centre and views it as one with the universe whereas the occidental philosophy views society as supreme and the individual good becomes subservient to collective good. The oriental philosophy stresses on individual self-realization in a manner which does not negate but complement the collective societal/community good. Social service and spirituality, which primarily involves discipline of body and mind are the twin means of self-realization. The concept of morality contains judgemental value about good and bad, virtue and vice and a feeling of intellectual superiority that, "I am the doer. I know and control right and wrong doings; for my doing I shall get rewards or punishments" (1987:19). Whereas, spirituality is beyond this kind of judgemental valuation of human or institutional conduct or behaviour. It is a moral valuation in the sense that it does not seek value judgements of something being high or low, good or bad, virtuous or vicious and righteous or wrongful. She believed that "spiritual activities are more or less spontaneous and generally spring from love and self-effacement... (They) are not purposeful, planned or otherwise volitional" (1987:19). Spirituality actually goes beyond morality. According to Vivekananda, spirituality originates from joy, bliss or cosmic love as concepts like mine and thine then melt away. Self is viewed as a tiny atom of the entire creation or universe. Therefore, she believed that in social work perspective, there are no substantive differences between helper, intervener, client, giver or receiver as they all are components of one universal amplitude.

It is quite ironic that Indian philosophical thinking, till recently, was continued to be viewed as idealistic, static and purposeless. These deficiencies usually surface when we compare Indian philosophy with western philosophy which is heavily loaded with its nationalist, scientificist and empiricist perspectives. She unreservedly admired the conquest of western man on nature which is punctuated by his struggle for survival and securing material good for the largest number of fellow beings through immense scientific and technological advances.

But her core concern was where to go from there? What course the further development should take? It is against such backdrop that she sought "... avenues, values and means for further development" by examining and evaluating the potential of various approaches to social work in leading us to further development. She viewed social work from three broad philosophical premises of idealism, utilitarianism and spiritualism. Idealist and utilitarian schools are essentially western and they viewed service to others as an intrinsic value and purposive acts for collective good. The secular character of modern social work stems from these premises. Whereas, according to Patel, the spiritual view is indigenous in origin. It views social service as instrumental and a form of *sadhana* (a spiritual pursuit for attaining emancipation) which enriches the self that gives and benefits the one who receives. It is primarily a process of melting one's ego in a manner that does not leave a vacuum of inactivity, renunciation, nothingness or alienation from society. On the contrary, it binds him more strongly with his society and fellow beings. Vivekananda's spiritual man is no different than any other ordinary individuals living the worldly material social life.

Patel found Indian philosophical thought unique in such respects as (1987:21):

> ... idealism, attitude to life and its problems and in its method of search for the ultimate truth. There is no sharp distinction between philosophy and religion as both seek for the central meaning of human existence. They supplement each other in search for truth or reality as a whole. Philosophy is a rational attempt to integrate knowledge and unify experience whether religious, aesthetic, social, moral or just scientific. Hence, the dichotomy between faith and reason is superficial if not meaningless.... Philosophy activates personal growth and training makes man what he was not before. Philosophy has twin goals to discover and root out personal biases so that the society could be reconstructed in terms of accepted ideals and values.

Thus, she was greatly fascinated by the Indian philosophical doctrines (Chattopadhyaya, 1964 and 1976) which preached symbiosis of thought and action through a rigorously disciplined mind of an intuitively engaged philosopher-seeker of truth. Such a state of mind leads one to purity of soul which gives them the right to speak for those beyond one's own self, i.e., on behalf of the mankind. Introspection of self within is the first step to knowledge. The central message of *yoga* is "to see the self" first. Primary task is to transform the inner self and secondary goal is to change or control the external world. One who desires to change the world has to first change himself in a credible manner otherwise he has no scriptural, ethical, religious or philosophical mandate to do so.

While assessing the contemporary philosophical Indian scene, she noted that such philosophers as Tagore, Aurobindo, Ramkrishna, Vivekananda, Gandhi, Radhakrishnan and others are of the view that the heritage of Indian philosophy and culture has a distinct continuity. The spiritual synthesis has some kind of eternality which links the glorious past with the potential present and promising future (Jain, 1994). Tradition and modernity co-exist and flourish at the cost of neither. The middle ages in Indian history had seen the fruitful interface between Islam and Hinduism, Buddhism, Jainism and other religious sects giving rise to the ideas of unity, fraternity, puritanism and silent prayer. This multi-religious interface produced a synthesis of thought and culture which further enriched it by adding a much missing dimension of humanism of the Sufis. A plurality of divergent viewpoints in these religions created a new scope of peaceful co-existence, mutual respect and tolerance (Chaudhari, 1979). According to her, a major challenge to this synthesizing process came from west as science and liberalism influenced the Indian intellect profoundly. Science became a new creed of liberation of the socio-economically deprived people and spearheaded a humanistic reconstruction of society. Yet, Indian philosophical tradition withstood these onslaughts of materialism and rationalism and continued to be rooted in its soil with necessary periodic modifications.

Patel was firm in her conviction that in India, religion had a special relevance and place. Its role can be ignored only at the peril of individual and collective loss of spiritual and material interest. Her following words reflect this thinking (1987:28) amply:

> In India, religion has always played a fundamental role in all reform movements. Even in the modern quest for social and political rectitude, the influence of religion is significantly evident. Any attempt, therefore, to interpret the economic, social and political environment ignoring the religious and spiritual foundations of Indian thought would not only be incomplete but pointless too. Vivekananda, among others, though inspired by the past was firmly rooted in the present... he developed a theory of action, an outlook which modern social engineering can rely on to its advantage. He... always had an eye on the sufferings of the poor and the disadvantaged.

All her life, Patel has laboriously worked to argue, establish and justify Vivekananda as the modern prophet and path-finder of modern India, providing comprehensive guidelines to social work practitioners and professionals. Accordingly, the needy fellow men and women must be served as a mission or *sadhana* and not as patronizing acts of self-gratification or salvation. Social service should be an act of adoring the latent divine in every soul. She has upheld and propagated the doctrine of "*Jiva* is *Shiva*". Her this doctrine eliminates the dichotomy of individual good and social good as well as the futile question of the primacy of one over the other.

It is sufficiently clear by now that Patel's primary concern was not in religious philosophy *per se* but in its linkage to the actual, evident, real issues of this-worldliness. The roots of this linkage lie in the prominent emergence of humanistic philosophical school of thought in nineteenth century as a synthesis of three divergent streams of God-centred view, a man-centred view and a world-centred view of the history of the western thought (Hick, 1994). Humanism rejected domination of man by the world around him and by God. Instead, it stood for the value of man as man and tried to give him the central place in western social agenda and order. Thus, man came onto the centre stage.

The origin of social work profession, to which she was committed, lies in the welfare-oriented humanist approach to man. Man has traversed a long history through such phases as nomadic, feudal and capitalist. Man faces maximum problems in the modern-capitalist phase which has created affluence for a select few and misery for the most through its 'wholesale industrialization'. Such problems as child labour, exploitation of the disadvantaged, dispossessed and deprived sections, oppression by the rich, stress, alienation, family disintegration, etc., call for new science, techniques and institutions to solve them. Social welfare and charity measures were essentially of personalized, corrective, short-term measures but they proved to be the genesis of modern-day social work concern, practice and institutions. Emergence of welfare state and social democracy widened these concerns and broadened the scope of social work practice (Ranade, 1974 and Sharma, 1985). It has today established itself as a helping, humanitarian profession. Its aim is to help the needy at all stages and situations of life by changing the attitudes of man and environmental set-up. Issues like health, economic upliftment, psycho-social well-being and planned change are on agenda of social work profession in India (Luthra and Oommen, 1987).

Patel has summarized as follows the major philosophical value premises and assumptions on which education and practice of social work profession are based (1987:32-34):

1. Humanitarianism is the basic philosophical value premise of social work. It views individual on his or her inherent worth. Theory and practice of social work is based on this conviction.
2. Human suffering should be eliminated in all respects as it is the essence of scientific humanitarian approach to social work.
3. Man's inherent creativity is assumed as lying latent within

him and all that is needed to be done is to help him help himself in shaping his destiny by activating that silent pool of creativity by external interventions.

4. All that the human beings need to bring out their inherent potentialities is a set of appropriate institutions and timely opportunities.
5. Human behaviour is an end product of his interaction with social institutions and environment. Many complex forces influence his behaviour which is often violative of social norms.
6. A behaviour of an individual or a collectivity is purposive. Social work intervention has to remain non-judgemental and accept the individuals and groups as they are. The history of an individual's behaviour is first obtained, studied, understood and thereafter modificatory or rectificatory strategies of intervention are planned by the social workers.
7. Social workers enter the scene on an assumption and faith that the clients have dynamic capacity to change their behaviour.
8. An individual is an integral part of the basic social institutions like family, community and society. It must be clearly realized that there is a mutually interdependent relationship between the individual, community and society. He receives advices, support, assistance and opportunities for growth and development and in return he contributes to the overall good and health of the community and society.

These values determine the practice and education of professional social work as espoused by the occidental approach. Social work seeks to assist individuals, groups and communities with a view to reaching the highest degree of mental, physical and social well-being. The helping process requires that the social worker's own personal value judgements remain checked and facilitate evolving of an effective and dispassionate helping relationship with the client.

It is highly relevant and pertinent to recall here that a few years hereafter, the TISS Social Work Educators' Forum did a great service to the fraternity of social work educators across the country by preparing a long overdue: "Declaration of Ethics for Professional Social Workers". It has become a landmark piece of labouriously done collective work. All the members of the SWEF Sub-Committee for Code of Ethics richly deserve to be congratulated and praised for their such a painstaking collective effort. The Declaration Charter provides for broad ethical principles to guide the conduct with respect to: (1) self and the profession; (2) work with the marginalized needy people; (3) the state and society; (4) co-workers and employing organizations; and (5) social work education and research. This Declaration should prove to be a torch-bearer for long to all those who wish to use social work knowledge, philosophy and skills through essentially a humanistic value framework (see Appendix I).

Patel's life-long mission was to search for an alternative approach from the internal religio-cultural and philosophical sources. She believed that understanding man necessiates understanding his relationship with God and the world around him. Man's relationship with society is only one of the aspects of his being as he also lives a life unto himself, dissociated from a given social milieu. Thus, any social work intervention cannot confine itself only to the externalities of social bondages of a man----a client, alone but his internalities also need to be focused and considered while he is being helped by a social worker. She posed a big question as to: "Can we say with adequate justification that the social work approach as we have in the West has in any way developed an acquaintance with the inside of man?" (1987:35). Despite certain efforts by Plato and Freud, the depths of an individual's inside remained ungauged and unknown to West. It is this fact that led Patel to explore and develop an oriental approach to social work which assumes that there lies in every man a bountiful, abundant and infinite capacity for development, provided his inner self is adequately known through discipline, meditation and *sadhana*. Interestingly, there was no bitterness or pinch of usual, derogatory or dismissive positions or comments in her thinking and writings on western civilization or way of life, which one often comes across in a discussion like this, viz., relevance of West to East and *vice versa* or superiority of one over the other. She derived her religio-cultural and socio-philosophical perspective from the works of Vivekananda. His following words influenced and shaped her thinking to a great extent:

> To the oriental, the world of spirit is as real as to the occidental is the world of senses. The oriental ideas are as necessary for any progress of the human race as are the occidental (1971:154).

> We want to lead mankind to the place where there is neither the Vedas, nor the Bible, nor the Koran, yet this has to be done by harmonizing the Vedas, the Bible and the Koran. Mankind ought to be taught that religions are but the varied expressions of *THE RELIGION* which is oneness, so that each may choose the path that suits him best (1971:416).

She was fully convinced that like any other discipline, the discipline of social work must have a definite value-base as one of the strongest prerequisites to achieve the status of a profession. Call it a value base or code of conduct or professional ethics, they are a must as they provide a base to the client and professionals to evaluate and modify their knowledge, organization and practice. These evaluative standards are simply inevitable, though they may change from time to time as the need may arise (TISS, 1997; also refer to Appendix I). In her book (1987), she analyzes and describes Vivekananda's thinking on various aspects of human development and its implications for contemporary social work institutions, interventions and activities. Besides, all her life, she remained in constant touch with the members of the Ramkrishna Mission by intermittently visiting its various centres and continuously discussed these issues and their activities for evolving a clearer and clearer perspective on these aspects. In sum, hers was a life of mind and praxis which she so purposefully spent in evolving a synthesis of occidental and oriental approaches to social work but primarily showing the relevance of oriental religious philosophy in redefining the goals and practice of social work.

REFERENCES

Agarwal, Satya P. (1993), *The Social Role of the Gita: How and Why*. Delhi: Urmila Agarwal.

Chattopadhyaya, Debiprasad (1964), *Indian Philosophy: A Popular Introduction*. New Delhi: People's Publishing House.

— (1976), *Two Trends in Indian Philosophy*. Mysore: Prasanga.

Chaudhuri, Nirad C. (1979), *Hinduism: A Religion to Live By*. New York: Oxford University Press.

Gore, M.S. (1985), *Social Aspects of Development*. Jaipur: Rawat.

Hick, John H. (1994), *Philosophy of Religion*. New Delhi: Prentice Hall.

Jain, Girilal (1994), *The Hindu Phenomenon*. New Delhi: UBS Publishers.

Luthra, Prem Nath and Oommen T.K. (1987), *Professional Social Work: As I See It* (Fifty Years of Professional Social Work in India. Commemorative Lectures). New Delhi: Department of Social Work, Jamia Millia Islamia.

Mukherji, Santi L. (1971), *The Philosophy of Man-Making: A Study in Social and Political Ideas of Swami Vivekananda*. Calcutta: New Central Book Agency.

Patel, Indira (1987), *Vivekananda's Approach to Social Work*. Madras: Sri Ramkrishna Math.

Peck, M. Scott (1978), *The Road Less Travelled: A New Psychology of Love, Traditional Values and Spiritual Growth*. London: Rider.

Roy, Ramashray (1993), "Swadhyaya: Values and Message" in Ponna Wignaraja (ed.), *New Social Movements in the South: Empowering the People*. New Delhi: Vistaar Publications.

Sheth, N.R. (1998), "Children of the Same God: A Spiritual Approach to Social Transformation" in Ghanshyam Shah (ed.), *Social Transformation in India*, Vol. 2, Jaipur, Rawat.

Swami Anand (1965), *Dhartinu Lun* (reprinted in *Dhartini Aarti* (in Gujarati). Bhavnagar: Lok Milap Trust, 1971.

Swami Vivekananda (1971), *The Complete Works*. Mayavati Advaite Ashram, 12th Edition.

Thangavelu, Vimala (1978), *The Samsar Model of Social Work Practice*. Mangalore: Preeti Publication.

TISS Social Work Educators' Forum (1997), "Declaration of Ethics for Professional Social Workers", *The Indian Journal of Social Work*, 58(2) April.

Introduction

by Chhaya Patel

This chapter is attempted and composed with an admission and confession that the original intentions and objectives of the effort have been fulfilled only partially. The nature of responses that were received, has influenced the content, composition and character of the volume. Originally, we had drawn a very detailed and extensive outline for inviting scholars to contribute articles for the volume but retrospectively it is felt that it was too ambitious a blueprint to be materialized and achieved in single endeavour of this nature. At one point, it was suggested to us that the respective contributors be clearly requested to contribute their articles on a specifically assigned topic or theme, so that internal logic and theoretical cohesiveness of the volume can be retained. Whereas we thought that eliciting responses by offering a veritable menu-like outline of themes for contributors to make pickings from is a better course to follow as it would leave them free to decide about the topic of their liking. Ultimately, good and bad both have resulted from this course. For good, because so many well-wishing scholars whom we approached unfortunately could not join us in our effort due to their various prior or continuing commitments (as can be seen from the contents of Appendix II). Some such gaps in responses would have definitely disturbed the plan of solicited contributions and disturb the composite, unifying theoretical framework. All the contributions which were ultimately received could not neatly fit into our original framework that had sought to identify points of convergence, interaction and interdependence between religion, philosophy and social work. It is bad in the sense that the whole outline was widely open-ended and finally has thus defied to some extent the logic of our attempt for thematic structuration and integration of the volume. It must also be recalled that we had received one more suggestion from Parin Vakharia that such practising religions as Sikhism, Judaism and Zoroastrian be included in the outline to enrich the interface between religious philosophy and social work practice in a multi-religious society like India. There is no second opinion on the importance of this suggestion and it was honoured despite the dispatches of the call letters were already made. However, it is regrettable that we could not get expected and favourable responses from those whom we approached. It is hoped a future attempt will rectify this imbalance and cover all major religions in an exercise like this. While our initiative was well-received and encouraging messages came, they did not quite always materialize into concrete contributions for understandable reasons. However, we are immensely indebted to all those contributors who made it possible to join us, despite all odds at their end in honouring and commemorating the pioneering contribution of one of our most committed intellectuals as Prof. Indira Patel. We offer our profound apologies to all those scholars whose contributions could not be accommodated for various factors beyond us.

We are fortunate in receiving favourable responses and contributions from a total of fourteen scholars in the disciplines of Social Work, Sociology and Philosophy. Except for two, all the writers knew Patel and her work quite well. Some scholars like Parin Vakharia, K.V Ramana, D.L. Sheth, K.D. Gangrade, C.P. Goyal, Kalindi S. Mazumdar, Sandhya Joshi and Bharti Sharma had varying levels of intimate personal and professional relationship of mutual respect and regards. All these contributors have written their articles on the themes that were part of Patel's life-long concerns in one way or other, with varying degrees of treatment of material and so on. This is not to suggest that all of them agreed to her method, thesis, argument and position on those issues lock, stock and barrel. They do not necessarily subscribe to Patel's ideas on role of religious philosophy and social work education, practice and profession *in toto*. The only thread that runs through them all unanimously is regarding their admiration of her wider concerns of social transformation, social development and ethics in social work profession and appreciation of her commitment, intellectual integrity and dedication.

All the papers that we received are organized here into three broadly defined parts. Part I is titled as "Religio-Philosophical Foundations of Social Work". It comprises of five subsequent chapters by Lancy Lobo, Kalindi S. Mazumdar, Nitin J. Vyas, Chhaya Patel and Satya P. Agarwal, which deal with the questions of linkages between religious philosophy and general as well as social work perspectives. As the title suggests, Part II, viz., "NGO Sector and Disciplinary Concerns" deals with the disciplinary concerns of social work profession and aspects of practice in NGO sector of India. It comprises of three chapters by D.L. Sheth and Harsh Sethi, C.P. Goyal, and Sandhya Joshi. Part III, titled as "Sites of Social Work Practice", comprises of discussions on various sites of social work interest and practice such as rural social work, age-care policies, female casual labourers, community mental health and women's development. It contains five contributions by K.D. Gangrade, K.V. Ramana, S.P. Punalekar, Bharti Sharma and Chhaya Patel.

Lancy Lobo, in his opening essay on "Social Vision and Concern in Christianity: A Historical Perspective", argues that every religion has a vision and it is expressed through a variety of outlets. More often than not, the basic tenets of original religious doctrines get bypassed or 'clouded' and what is left or added as religion becomes a ready, handy tool in the hands of powerful detractors. This process is perennial. Mankind has to constantly struggle for rediscovering these frequently lost original contents of religious wisdom, ethics and philosophy. Lobo feels that the contemporary Indian society is on the brink of communal divides as violence is unleashed on the innocent in the name of religion. He has employed hermeneutic approach in order to profile a social vision that is contained in the Christian scriptures and in social teachings of the Catholic Church as developed historically. In the process, Lobo discusses origin and causes of liberation theology. In Latin America, where liberation theology originated, the unequal socio-economic order, glaring poverty, tight grip of the church and ruling classes on masses, injustice, hunger, illiteracy resulted in loss of original religious values of God's kingdom and hence people, priests and nuns got provoked to raise the banner against system's tyranny on poor, helpless, hungry people. It tried to heighten the critical social awareness of the people about their rights and role of the church to aid the poor effectively. Lobo's account insightfully captures the broad contours and provides important glimpses into the working of Indian Catholic Church which is moving from social work to social action. He has argued that church in India is committed to the central and crucial issues of liberation, mobilization and conscientization and undertakes such empowering activities as fighting for the rights of children, women, fishermen, tribals, dalits and the deprived. He concludes his article by quoting famous words of advice by Mahatma Gandhi on keeping the face of the poorest man in mind while in doubt about self or an act to be undertaken.

Kalindi S. Mazumdar's paper on "Hinduism: A Social Work Perspective" is an account of personal experience of social work practice. She first discusses the main tenets of Hinduism and then relates them to her experiences as social work practitioner. She makes no claims of having cultivated authentic scholarship on religious philosophy of Hinduism but undertakes the exercise from a generalist perspective. She describes her efforts of achieving a synthesis of religious philosophy of Hinduism and social work profession throughout her working life as a social work educator and a practising professional. She further shows how she derived inner strength and spiritual sustenance from this process of synthesizing to pursue the difficult profession of social work education and practice. According to her, the basic tenets of Hinduism and the cardinal values of social work converge on one meeting ground of upholding the dignity of the human being. She explores the main principles of Hinduism to various field practices which flow from and in return enrich the core concerns of social work philosophy, theory, education and practice.

Nitin J. Vyas in his essay on "Non-Violence and Man-Making in Buddhist Philosophy" argues that violence is the real bane, a curse, a blot, a stigma on otherwise a noble species of human beings. He is deeply concerned about the man's ever-growing instinct for violence which subsequently continues to take more and more lethal forms. He is skeptical about the potential of local as well global processes that are presently engaged in humanizing society. He is in search of a philosophical discourse which can wean away man from a life of violence to a life of peace and non-violence. His hopes are pinned on the fact that as against the ignominious and brutal history of wars, bloodsheds, killings, tortures and sufferings at various levels of human existence in form of family, clan, community, religious or ethnic collectivity, there also exists a glorious history of peaceful, harmonious, cooperative and communitarian, caring co-existence between the people's widely diversed religions and regions.

He then pleads for an evolution of a non-violent global social order by comprehensively tapping the higher spiritual resources of man which can keep the basal instincts of violence under tight leash. He looks at Buddhist religious philosophy to outline its conception of man-making process, social vision in general and tenets of non-violent social order. According to Vyas, Buddhism has probed the problem of violence with utmost sincerity and seriousness by locating and examining it in the problem of man to man and man to universe mutual relationships. He has attempted to rediscover and reinterpret this collective human heritage in order to face the issues of mutual distrust and disharmony among men and nature.

Chhaya Patel's paper on "Ethics, Individual and Society in Islamic Philosophy: A Hermeneutic Exploration" begins with a brief introductory narrative on major methodological and philosophical developments in social sciences in late twentieth century, namely, positivism and hermeneutics. She argues that hermeneutic or interpretative model of social inquiry is more suitable for 'reading' classical and scriptural texts as a rich source of insights, knowledge, information and understanding of human experiences of life, and the aspirations and affairs of a particular socio-religious community within a larger human society. Such classical texts as *Rig Veda, Upanishads, Puranas*, epic texts like the *Ramayana, Mahabharata* and *Gita*, texts containing Buddhist, Jain, Sikh or Zoroastrian philosophies, the *Bible*, the *Quran*, and the *Arthasastra* are to be viewed as rich treasures of socially useful wisdom, understanding, knowledge and insights into a life-world of a given society at a given time or for all time to come. These texts depict civilizational and religio-cultural histories of regions, communities and societies. Patel has viewed looking at Islamic philosophy and tradition from this perspective as most timely task on hand of a socio- philosophic student-investigator. Her article aims at understanding basic teachings and philosophical conceptions in Islam regarding various aspects of ethics, individual and society. She tries to reveal Islamic conception of man, various man-making processes and ethical principles guiding individual conduct and evolution of an Islamic social organization. Her discussion provides a bird's eye view of main philosophical tenets of Islam, a glimpse into its origin and development and finally profiles ethics, individual and society as conceived in Islamic religious philosophy.

Satya P. Agarwal's essay on "Vivekananda's Socio-Spiritual Approach to India's Social Problems" originates from his interest in studying religious responses to the social challenges of the modern age. He describes the life and work of Vivekananda in order to illustrate how he developed a reformist-modernist perspective and formulated a socio-spiritual approach to tackle India's social and economic problems by basing it on harmonious synthesis of *Karmayoga* and *Vedanta*. He also captures the processes and struggles that led to the foundation of Ramkrishna Mission and also assumes that solutions to India's many social problems must be hidden and rooted in its rich religio-philosophical traditions of long standing. The first part sketches a brief biographical profile of Vivekananda. Thereafter, the social problems of India as perceived by Vivekananda are discussed. The third part contains a plan of action as devised by him and based on practical *Vedanta*.

The paper by D.L. Sheth and Harsh Sethi titled as "The NGO Sector in India: Historical Context and Current Discourse" attempts to sketch a historical context of development of the NGO sector in India. They have composed a very detailed, insightful and in-depth historical narrative of voluntarism in India before and after independence beginning from Raja Ram Mohan Roy and *Brahmo Samaj*. They state that the once vibrant Gandhian voluntary organizations are on a steady decline since 1960s, whereas the Christian and non-Christian religious organizations have continued voluntary activities in education and health and relief work in floods, famines, droughts, etc. With the growing disenchantment of the people with the formal institutions of planning, politics and development between 1960s and 1980s, the field was open for new entrants to come and take charge. Thousands of disillusioned young people came to the fore and took up the issues of poverty, human rights, inequality, injustice, ecology, gender and peace. Mobilization, conscientization and empowerment became the new credo of non-formal, non-political social activism. Yet, the conventional developmental concern for harnessing the energies of the young, through programmes like NSS and Nehru Yuvak Kendras, continued to dominate the mainstream academic imagination. They have subsequently categorized the available literature on NGOs in India into five broad types: (a) morphological studies; (b) intra-organizational studies; (c) efficacy studies; (d) relationship studies; and (e) impact studies. According to authors, the social science research community has not shown as much interest in the NGO sector as the developmental social activists have shown. They raise number of questions pertaining to their definition, classification, implication on state and society, political parties, popular participation. They conclude their illuminating paper by suggesting to explore all these issues by detailed and rigorous empirical studies.

C.P. Goyal's paper on "Social Work in the Changing Scenario" cautions the community of social work practitioners and educators regarding the necessity of keeping constantly rolling so as not to gather the proverbial moss. In other words, Goyal argues that the phenomenon of change is all-pervasive and its impact on individuals, collectivities, institutions, organizations and wider social processes is inescapable. It is upto us to respond to the process of change adequately by perceiving it correctly so that the socio-economic and political institutions can be sufficiently altered and geared to retain their relevance and utility in such moments of flux, drift and shift. Social institutions must develop sufficient resilience to adjust to new situations. An attempt is made here to examine the prospects and potential of profession and discipline of social work in India to meet with the challenges of changing scenario in the country. The author reflects on general processes of social transformation and their impact on social work education. He also discusses its likely impact on social workers. Then, he reviews the changing scope of governmental socio-political policies *vis-a-vis* the needy groups of workers or clients. He re-establishes the relevance of social work profession and makes an earnest plea for tapping the growing scope of its role in new contexts. The professional associations, according to him, have a special role to play and, therefore, they need to be strengthened.

Sandhya Joshi, in her essay on "Field Training for Social Development" examines the question of social development of a historically and socio-economically most backward Harijan community in Vadodara city. She links the question of nation-wide poverty scene to the ongoing concerns of social work educators who are conscious of imparting a relevant training to developmental professionals. Her essay is an outcome of an experience and insight that she has gained from a larger. She dwells upon at length on development constraints and limit situation of urban poor which manifest in form of self-imposed limits, psycho-social oppression and lack of information and low competencies. Development perspective in social work is also discussed alongwith devising of a package of social work training inputs for honing specialized skills for the field training of development workers. She concludes her essay with a note of caution that morally and ideologically taxing field conditions can cause rapid 'burn out' in students and therefore social work educators must be careful in organizing open community placements.

As the title suggests, K.D. Gangrade's paper on "Gandhi Through Five Generations: A Personal Account of Rural Social Work" is an autobiographical tale, weaving up major issues, concerns and questions of social work practice over as long a stretch of time as five decades of an actively spent lifetime. Gangrade begins on a very pessimistic note as he is profoundly perturbed by the loss of character in post-independence era. Corruption and failure of mass politics are the other two issues bothering him. Politics of his times used to arouse hope but today it has got degenerated and has become a chief means to capture public power for personal and partisan ends. Political parties are increasingly failing in meeting the basic needs of the people and revelling in ever-increasing levels of corruption. He laments the fact that today's child has neither his parents, teachers, neighbours, religious leaders nor political leaders of character who can inspire him and serve as an ideal model. Gangrade conducts a critical assessment and demonstrates the downfall of our value system by narrating comparative case studies of two villages. His rather long paper is divided into eight sections. The first section narrates Gandhi's influence on him through family and school. The second section profiles the ideal of *bhaichara* (brotherhood) model of communitarian village life, led by the first and second of the five generations covered here. The third section deals with Quit India Movement and his participation in it. The fourth section describes his work of Gandhian rural reconstruction and college studies. The fifth section is a commentary on arrival of independence but departure of Gandhian values and Gandhi himself. The sixth section is a mixed bag of good developmental work and subsequent collapse of the whole work due to complete erosion of values with the arrival of CDP. The seventh section discusses the impact of mass media, western culture and unprincipled life of political leaders and political parties. The final section raises important ethical and political questions as a moral of the two case studies. He severely criticizes the *neta-babu* (politician-bureaucrat) brand of socialism which has cheated the poor people by keeping them poor and made the rich people richer. He makes a very passionate plea to all social work professionals for continuously asking the questions on the sudden downfall in our moral and social standards and their role in retrieving the lost ground.

Age-care has always been an important site of social work concern and practice but its importance has significantly risen in last few decades due to the processes of urbanization, modernization, industrialization and nuclearization of families in rural as well as urban areas. Ageing is emerging as an issue of great socio-demographic concern in all societies----be they developed or developing. K.V. Ramana's article on "Age-Care Policies and Programmes: Challenges Ahead" is very timely and immensely relevant to the academic concerns of social work, sociology and policy sciences. The scholars in these fields are bracing themselves to develop the field of gerontology as a part of their responses to emerging social problems and disciplinary concerns. The issue is delicately poised between the two basic institutions, viz., the family and the state. There is a debate about who should care for the aged. Historically, the onus of age-care was always on family but changing times have altered its values, character, composition and structure and the onus is gradually shifting on the shoulders of the state. However, from the analysis of the role of state, it is learnt that the state is really no substitute to family so far as the question of elderly care is concerned and hence it should be given back to family. This is further objected to by the feminist school which argues that when age-care comes back to family, it essentially means the women of the family will carry the burden of care. So, finally after some tossing of this issue between family/women and state, it is coming back to the domain of state.

The Casual Labour Market (CLM) in urban India is a product of the lopsided growth of economy and has emerged as a major site of social work, sociological and economic analysis. Extremely limited opportunities in organized sectors like industry, service and trade compel them to swell the CLMs. It is casual in terms of erratic nature of work and wage. The terms and conditions are arbitrary, casual and vague. The condition of casual labourer is pathetic. It is highly segmented market which tends to diffuse consciousness of workers and keep them under tight leash as the prospects of continuous work and good, regular, wage are linked to the primordial ties of village, caste and community. It is uncertain to such an extent that the manner of recruitment, training, retention or dismissal of a casual labourer vary from one type of employment sector to another and it may also vary within a single sector such as construction labour or domestic support services. They are the lowest, most exploited and miserable stratum of urban working class. S.P. Punalekar's paper on "Gender, Market Segmentation and Marginalization in Urban Gujarat" focuses through case studies on female casual labourers in the fast growing cities of Gujarat. He argues that any CLM is sociologically an interesting site to visit and observe. These case studies reveal the socio-economic conditions of the families; how they meet their needs and live in highly adverse urban setting; how they view their work, coworkers and employers; and how they look upto their future. On the whole, these case studies are so authentically documented that they have become an extremely interesting material for multipurpose academic, research and policy uses. Punalekar's concluding observations are quite disturbing as he notes that these households are perennially embroiled in a cyclical processes of unemployment, underemployment, poverty, ill-health, physical debility, absenteeism and low income. It is frustrating to note that despite being in cities for a long period ranging from 10 to 15 years and hard work, their own material life has not improved. Nor are they served in any way by so many urban service institutions. They are almost like castaway citizens with increased sense of alienation, marginalization and helplessness. The case studies have vividly illustrated that their survival and existence is very delicately poised. With a little push from the market and society, so many can be on the brink of starvation. It is ironical that these casual labourers contribute through their sweat and flesh for mere subsistence wages in building housing complexes, hotels, plazas, multi-storey buildings, offices, roads, gardens and numerous other urban assets for convenience and comforts of the elitist, well-placed and propertied classes in the cities, but they remain casually rewarded for a casual existence. After narrating these four cases, he summarizes the major themes of the argument and discusses various macro and micro level action plans as a socio-political intervention to change their conditions in whatever possible way.

Bharti Sharma's paper on "Community Mental Health: An Appraisal" is based on an assumption that comprehensive and complete well-being of all the individuals at all levels and in all respects is vital for social development and happy, balanced, productive and meaningful life. Health is defined as a state of complete physical, mental, social and spiritual well-being. It is more than merely the absence of disease or infirmity. Obviously, thus, mental health is an inseparable component of individual health, public health and social welfare programme. Sharma first discusses definitional aspects of mental health and then goes on to discuss mental health as bio-psycho and sociocultural phenomenon. She observes that community participation has a great role to play as a preventive strategy. Community itself is a vast dormant, untapped, idle resource which can be activated and used for generating greater involvement of one and all. She pleads for a comprehensive community mental health legislation, developing various prevention-oriented perspectives, and correct imparting of mental health education. She summarizes various service interventions such as direct services, supportive services, out-patient services, day-care services, friendly visitors' services, telephonic services for parents and various consultative services so that the problem of mental health can be tackled on a more sound footing. She concludes with an observation on social work professionals' role in the field of mental health.

Various issues of gender justice are gradually acquiring a centre-state position in contemporary social theory. There is an explosion of literature on each and every aspect of women's development. The last article by Chhaya Patel on "Women's Development, Voluntary Organizations and Social Work Concerns" is founded on an assumption that "feminism is a politics" and it seeks to redefine relations and responsibilities between man and women in society. This is an ultimate goal. In order to inch forward towards that goal the issue of women's development has to be addressed step by step so that a major feminist socio-political movement can emerge, get strengthened and take a concrete shape and definite direction. Some of the steps that Patel undertakes to delineate are explored by way of a set of questions such as: what exactly is women's development and it refers to development of which strata of women in society; what is the goal of women's development and what opportunities are available; which options strategically suit more; how sound, viable and effective they are; how can the structural and systemic blocks be overcome; what alternative social and ideological visions are available to us etc. It assesses the potential of voluntary sector and links the question of women's development to major concerns and ideological perspectives of the discipline of social work.

On the one hand, the essays in this volume are written by the scholars belonging to different disciplines and on the other hand, they are also written from different theoretical and empirical orientation within the discipline of social work. While the contributors so widely differ in conceptual, ideological and methodological orientations in their writings, they are concerned with one common goal of creating a socio-economically a well-developed, balanced humane Indian society in which man, socio-spiritual institutions, human community and nature operate in harmony with each other in attaining the ultimate religio-philosophical and socio-spiritual goals which were so dear to Professor Indira Patel all her life.

PART I

Religio-Philosophical Foundations of Social Work

I

Social Vision and Concern in Christianity: A Historical Perspective

by Lancy Lobo

Each religion has a social vision. It gets expressed through a variety of social concerns. Unfortunately, this social vision often gets clouded and 'religion' tends to become a tool in the hands of the powerful. When a social vision of a religion gets clouded, its inner contents languish. This vision has to be rediscovered from time to time. In India, it is all the more important at a time when communal violence is let loose in the name of religion.

This paper follows hermeneutic approach and attempts to outline a social vision in Christianity arising from the scriptures, its historical development especially in social teachings of the Catholic Church, the emergence of liberation theology and a glimpse of the Indian Catholic Church moving from social work to social action.

SCRIPTURAL BASIS

The first book of the *Bible*, *Genesis* notes that God created the sun, the moon, the earth, the skies, the oceans, the living beings of all kinds and finally He created man in His own image and put the rest of the creation at his disposal. The Biblical anthropology is homocentric. Man is at the centre of everything. He is to master everything for his well-being. Man is precious. The survival of this concept is largely attributed to charismatic, prophetic persons that surfaced from time to time before the birth of Christ such as Moses, Amos, Mica, Jeremias and others. These prophets severely condemned the erstwhile ruling groups and classes for the miseries they heaped on the poor, the exploitation and subjugation of the masses, the pathetic conditions of the widows and so on. Most of these prophets paid for their stance by laying down their own lives. In the *Old Testament* part of the *Bible,* God is projected basically as the God of the poor (*Anawim*) for whom He demands justice from oppressive rulers and the leaders.

Weber, the famous sociologist, has classified prophets into two categories, viz., exemplary and emissary. The former advised people to be devout, pietistic and to avoid vices. The latter stood before kings, oppressors and exploiters and condemned them. In most cases, the emissary prophets were martyred or eliminated. The word 'emissary' means the one who is sent with a message or a mission. Prophets mentioned above were emissary types and Jesus was also an emissary prophet. His death on the cross was a consequence of the stand he took against the oppression of the religious leaders of those days, viz., Pharasees, Saducees and so on. He called them hypocrites, serpents, whited graves, preachers who did not practise what they preached and so on. He was an anti-establishment prophet and called for total transformation.

The social concern of Jesus is revealed in a number of healing miracles. For instance, Jesus cured the people of every disease and sickness (Mt. 4:23), to the paralytic Jesus said, "Stand up, take up your bed and go home" (Mt. 9:2-8), Jesus opened the eyes of a blind (Jn. 9:1-38), He cured those possessed by the unclean spirits (LK. 6:17-19) and so on. The miracles of healing were not so much to establish an aura and power of Jesus but were signs of the Kingdom of God or God's reign in the world. Through the miracles of physical healing Jesus wanted inner healings to take place. Lepers, paralytics, blind and sick were marginalized by the society. By healing them Jesus showed that they too were human beings and deserved to be treated as such. The indicators of God's reign in the world were peace, love, justice, health, harmony, concern, sharing, equality, fraternity and so on.

In *Lukes's Gospel* there is a passage known as the manifesto of Jesus: "The Spirit of the Lord is upon me, because he has anointed me to preach good news to the poor. He has sent me to proclaim release to the captives and recovering of sight to the blind, to set at liberty those who are oppressed, to proclaim the acceptable year of the Lord" (LK. 4:18-20). This manifesto sums up Jesus' mission and all that he said, and did. Jesus was not a magician. His healing miracles always called for an inner healing that accompanied with external healing. For instance, for the adulterous woman He said, "Go, sin no more." To the blind he said, "Go, your faith has healed you." He repeatedly healed the sick. He took compassion on the hungry multitude and multiplied fishes and loaves. Jesus gave just one rule to live, "Love your neighbour as yourself." The story of good Samaritan is too well known to be repeated here. St. John, another prominent disciple of Jesus, writes:

> We love because God first loved us. If someone says, "I love God," yet hates his brother, he is a liar, for he cannot love God, whom he has not seen, if he does not love his brother, whom he has seen. This, then, is the command that Christ gave us: He who loves God must love his brother also (1 Jn. 4:19-21).

In the *New Testament* part of the *Bible,* God is declared to be the Father and all human beings as His children. There is to be no inferior, superior or distinctions of Greek, Jew or Gentile among them. The key Christian prayer, "The Our Father" taught by Jesus himself testifies to the belief in the equality of all humans. This prayer advocates forgiveness, "forgive us our sins as we forgive others". Elsewhere mercy, love and compassion are advocated. The words, "Thy kingdom come" are interpreted to mean a kingdom where love, charity, peace, fraternity, sharing, caring and concern exist and not a political kingdom or Christendom.

On the last judgement day, writes the *Gospel of Mathew*

(25:32-46), God will divide earth's peoples into two groups and place one of them on the right and another on the left. He will offer the Kingdom of Heaven to those who complied with when "I was hungry and you fed me, thirsty and you gave me drink; I was a stranger and you received me in your homes, naked and you clothed me; I was sick and you took care of me, in prison and you visited me." Those present said, "When, Lord, did we ever see you hungry and feed you..." The Lord will answer, "I tell you, indeed, whenever you did this for one of these poorest brothers of mine, you did it for me."

The seemingly paradoxical situations highlighted by Jesus are: (1) in giving you receive; (2) to save your life you have to lose it, or in dying you live; and (3) in loving you live. These paradoxes have shaped much of the social concern in Christianity.

The twelve disciples of Jesus began to preach, teach and heal whose records are found in the Acts of the Apostles, a part of the *Bible*. The early Christians lived communitarian lives (Acts 2:44-47). This passage has been cited as an illustration of primitive communism... mine is thine and thine is mine, sharing, brotherhood, and solidarity:

> All the believers continued together in close fellowship, and shared their property and possession with one another. They would sell their property and possessions and distribute the money among all, according to what each one needed. Every day they continued to meet as a group in the temple, and they have their meals together in their homes, eating the food with glad and humble hearts, praising God and enjoying the good will of all the people.

St. Paul, one of the great apostles of Jesus, writes in his letter to the Corinthians regarding Christian giving:

> The believers of Macedonia have been severely tested by the troubles they went through; but their joy was so great that they were extremely generous in their giving, even though they were very poor. I assure you, they gave as much as they were able, and even

more than that; of their own free will they begged us and insisted on the privilege of having a part in helping believers in Judea (2 Cor: 8:2-4).

The followers of early Christianity during this period were largely people marginalized by society such as slaves, fishermen, poor and the rejects.

THE SUBVERSION OF CHRISTIANITY

The acceptance of Christianity by King Constantine of Rome in the fourth century was the starting point of the subversion of early Christianity. The religion of the poor masses became the religion of the ruling elite. In this process religion of slaves became the slavish instrument of the state. Power, politics, triumph and glory began to invade Christianity. The Kingdom of Heaven was displaced for the earthly or worldly kingdom. The power of service was displaced by the power of authority. The servant Jesus was made into a royal personage.

This is not to deny that there were no voices that belonged to the emissary prophets. A number of such prophets (saints) arose from time to time to rekindle the spirit of early Christianity. These saints such as Chrysostom, Basil and Benedict raised voices of protest. Chrysostom said in a sermon: "The earth is for all. What is surplus belongs to the poor. While you adorn the temple, do not despise your brother in distress. Do not honour Christ in church clothes, i.e., in silk vestments and then pass him by unclothed and frozen outside. I am not saying you should not give golden altar, vessels and so on, but I am insisting that nothing can take the place of alms-giving. The Lord will prefer the second. No one was ever condemned for not adorning his house, but those who neglect the poor were threatened with hell fire for all eternity and a life of comment with devils. Adorn your house if you will, but do not forget your brother in distress."

The religious orders and monasteries of males and females took care of the poor, the diseased and the rejects of society. Benedict started a religious order (organization) to take care of the poor. But, over a period of time, these orders themselves became so rich that they lost sight of the early Christian spirit. During the Middle Ages other saintly figures arose such as Peter Valdo and Francis of Asissi and began new religious orders to reestablish the early Christian spirit.

SOCIAL TEACHING OF THE CHURCH

The sixteenth century witnessed the rise of early capitalism, industrialization and amassing private property and wealth. It placed profits before people. Massive exploitation of workers, marginalization of the masses and sharpening of inequalities marked the rise of capitalism. Socialism came as a challenge to capitalism.

The Popes voiced their concern officially through documents known as 'Encyclicals' such as *Rerum Novarum* (1891), *Quadragessimo Anno* (1931), *Mater et Magistra* (1961), *Pacem in Terris* (1963), *Populorum Progressio (1967), Octogessima Advenient (1971), Loborem Exercens (1981), Solicitudo rei Socialis* (1987) and *Centissimus Annus* (1991). This body of teaching is known as "Social Teaching of the Church". The context of this teaching is the rise of capitalism and its ills, deterioration of social and economic order, deprivation and marginalization of masses and disparity between the rich and the poor. The social teaching was an appeal for the reconstruction of the social order based on the values of God's Kingdom or God's reign of equality, justice, brotherhood, human dignity and peace. Schultheis *et al.* (n.d.: 5-9) have grouped these Encyclicals into two: (1) from *Rerum Novarum* (1891) to the Second Vatican Council (a religious parliament of Church officials from all over the world); and (2) after the Vatican Council, viz., *Populorum Progressio* (1967) onwards.

From *Rerum Novarum* to the Second Vatican Council: Reconstructing the Social Order

The Church's social teaching in the 'modern' period dates from

1891, when Pope Leo XIII in the Encyclical letter, *The Condition of Labour* (*Rerum Novarum*), spoke out against the inhuman conditions which were the normal plight of the working populace in the industrial societies. He recognized that the three key factors underlying economic life are workers, productive property and the state. He also indicated that their just and equitable interrelationship is a crucial issue for Catholic social teaching. Because of the principles which he set forth to guide in the formation of a just society, this document has become known as a *Magna Carta* for the reconstruction of the economic and social order.

On the occasion of the fortieth anniversary of *Rerum Novarum* in 1931, Pope Pius XI composed the next major social Encyclical entitled, *The Reconstruction of the Social Order* (*Quadragessimo Anno*). Writing in the midst of severe economic depression, Pius XI addressed the issue of social injustice and called for the reconstruction of the social order along the lines set forth by Pope Leo XIII. Pius XI reaffirmed the right and the duty of the Church to address social issues. While condemning capitalism and unregulated competition, he also condemned communism for its promotion of class struggle and the narrow reliance for leadership on the working class (the dictatorship of the proletariat). He stressed upon the social responsibilities of private property and the rights of the working people to a just wage and to organize them to claim their rights. He also pointed out the positive role of the governments in promoting the economic good of all individuals in a society. Economic undertakings should be governed by justice and charity as the principal laws of social life. Moreover, the Church was opposed to socialism and with its critique of capitalism being half-hearted did not radically opt out of capitalist ideology.

Thirty years later Pope John XXIII wrote two major social encyclical letters on the central issues of the day. In *Christianity and Social Progress* (*Mater et Magistra*, 1961) and *Peace on Earth* (*Pacem in Terris*, 1963), Pope John set forth a number of principles to guide both Christians and policy-makers in addressing the growing disparity between rich and poor nations and the threats to the world peace. In these letters Pope John addressed the global dimensions of social justice and Catholic social teachings. He called on committed Christians and "all people of good will" to work together in order to create local, national and global institutions, which would both respect human dignity and promote justice and peace. Pope John emphasized that the growing interdependence among nations in a world community called for an effective world government which would protect the rights of the individual human person and promote the universal common good. Thus, Pope John was credited with seminal thinking towards structural transformation.

The Church After the Second Vatican Council: The Faith that Does Justice

Since the Second Vatican Council, statements by Popes Paul VI and John Paul II, by *Synods* (a meeting of Bishops called by the Pope periodically) of Bishops and by regional and national conference of Bishops, have clarified the role of the Church in meeting this new responsibility in a rapidly changing world. The Pope and the Bishops are acutely aware that the search for God's word in the events of history is not a simple task. They also recognize that the Church has neither immediate nor universally valid solutions to the complex and pressing problems of society.

Three documents in particular have contributed to the Church's present understanding of this new responsibility. In 1967, Pope Paul VI in the document, *The Progress of Peoples* (*Populorum Progressio*), responded to the cries of the world's poor and hungry and addressed the structural dimensions of global injustice. He appealed to both the rich and the poor nations to work together in a spirit of solidarity to establish an "order of justice and the renewal of the temporal order." In order to encourage this noble enterprise he set up a Pontifical Commission on Justice and Peace.

The second document was the apostolic letter, *The Call to*

Action (*Octogesima Adveniens*), which Pope Paul VI wrote in 1971 on the occasion of the eightieth anniversary of *Rerum Novarum*. In this letter Paul VI stressed on the difficulties inherent in establishing this new order and pointed at the role of Christian communities in meeting this responsibility:

> It is up to the Christian communities to analyze with objectivity the situation which is proper to their own country, to shed on it the light of the *Gospel*'s unalterable words and to draw principles of reflection, norms of judgement and directives for action from the social teaching of the Church (para 4).

In effect, Paul VI insisted that God calls all Christians and communities to be both hearers and doers of the word. Christians who are faithful to the *Gospel* will be engaged in an ongoing 'incarnational' process which involves three separate moments:

1. evaluation and analysis of their contemporary situation;
2. discernment and reflection, bringing the *Gospel* and the teachings of the Church to bear on a particular situation; and
3. action which fights injustice and works for the transformation of society. This is to make the 'reign' of God a reality.

In the same year the world's Bishops prepared the statement, *Justice in the World*. In this third document which illustrates the influence of a truly world Church, the Bishops identified the dynamism of the *Gospel* with the hopes of people for a better world (para 5). In what has become a frequently cited statement, they asserted:

> Action on behalf of justice and participation in the transformation of the world fully appear to us as a constitutive dimension of the preaching of the *Gospel*, or in other words, of the Church's mission for the redemption of the human race and its liberation from every oppressive situation (para 6).

This vision of the social mission of the Church or a particular Church that 'does' justice as an integral element of its faith, is slowly influencing the universal Church. Such a vision and trend is manifest in the activities and teachings of regional and national conferences of Bishops. It is being proclaimed in the faith and actions of countless individuals, communities and local Churches throughout the world.

Shifts in Attitude

The Second Vatican Council marked a new period in the life of the Church. One fundamental aspect of this new period was a change in the Church's attitude toward the world. Father Land (1981) has identified four distinct aspects in this attitudinal change which are as follows:

1. *An Assault on Political Apathy*

Many Church leaders, theologians and loyal critics continue to ask how it was possible for the Church to be largely silent and passive in the face of the atrocities of the Second World War. The answer at least in part is that the Church and religion were confined to the private arena. The Council leaders recognized that the Church shares responsibility for secular as well as for religious history.

2. *A Commitment to the 'Humanization' of the Universe*

The Second Vatican Council affirmed the Church's responsibility for the world, a world which God created and Jesus walked upon. Moreover, as the Council leaders affirmed and as Pope John Paul II stated in his Encyclical letter, *On Human Work* (*Laborem Exercens*, 1981), people "can justly consider that by their labour they are unfolding the Creator's work" and contributing "to the realization in history of the God's plan." From these attitudes a respect develops for rightful autonomy of secular world.

3. *A Commitment to World Justice*

The Bishops, in their 1971 *Synod* statement, *Justice in the World*, urged that justice be sought at all levels of society but especially between rich and powerful nations and those that are poor and weak. The Bishops declared that the "doing of justice" is a "constitutive dimension of the preaching of the *Gospel*".

4. *Preferential Option for the Poor*

The Church has always understood that Christ identified with the poor and underprivileged, but looks at this option now with a new urgency. In reading the "signs of the times", the Christians see God's face above all on the face of suffering and marginalized people. Consequently, fidelity to Christ requires an identification with and an 'option' for the poor. In the last few years this conviction has become a priority for the Church in its theological reflections and pastoral actions.

SOCIAL ACTIVITIES OF POST-WAR CHURCH

The Church continued its activities of preaching, teaching and healing during the industrial revolution, especially through its well-organized religious orders of males and females. Alms-giving and charity continued. Compassion on beggars and poor was stimulated for the future of one's own soul as if it would store up merits for one's safe passage to heaven. Help and charity given unconditionally was glorified. Seeing the image of Christ in poor was advocated. Thus, one finds behind charity a curious mix of self-interest.

During the twentieth century, especially after the Second World War, two tendencies were visible within the Church: one, a widening of the range of the Church's responsibility, both geographical as well as substantive and institutional, and two, a continual displacement of the very idea of help. Help appears more and more as a conceptually unsuitable means of promoting development. This idea develops along with the understanding of development in the world at large, informed by Marxism and socialism. Besides, the Church also makes shifts from social service to social action; away from personal piety to a concern with the problem of justice; away from particular institution to the worldwide ecumenical plane; away from inside to beyond mere help and to the transformation of structures and transcending the *status quo*. Only a Christianity that is fully conscious of its social responsibility can be adequate to a dynamic, changing society.

In other words, the Church increasingly realized that help (charity) did not help and that it was counter-productive. Help symbolized the shame and degradation of the receiver and the arrogance of the giver (Sachs, 1992:65).

Liberation Theology

The term 'liberation theology' was popularized in Latin America. Most of Latin America is Christian or Catholic. However, it was far from realizing the indicators of God's Kingdom or an equitable social and economic order. The Church was largely with the ruling classes dishing a pietistic kind of religiosity to the masses who in turn also had their indigenous beliefs and rituals inherited from pre-conversion times. The irrelevance of the Church in such iniquitous situations provoked some lay people, priests and nuns to comprehend the anguish caused by hunger, chronic diseases, illiteracy, impoverishment, injustice and the hopes for liberation, participation and union through the help of Marxian analysis and religious experience. The Puebla Bishops' conference critiqued as follows:

> Analyzing this situation more deeply, we discover that this poverty is not a passing phase, instead it is the product of economic, social, and political situations and structures, though there are also other causes for the state of misery. In many instances this state of poverty within our countries finds its origin and support in mechanisms which, because they are impregnated with materialism rather than any authentic humanism, create a situation on the international level where the rich get richer at the expense of the poor, who get ever poorer (Puebla, 30/128).

The main interest of the liberation theology is to generate activity on the part of the Church that will aid the poor efficaciously. The emphasis is placed on heightening critical social awareness and fighting for one's rights leading to structural changes.

One of the concrete manifestations of fight for the structural changes is the increasing political awareness and mobilization at grass roots level in Latin America among marginalized people. The number of priests, nuns and countless lay persons killed or murdered in this process has been increasing.

THE INDIAN CHURCH

Christianity in India was largely concentrated in Kerala from the first century. But, during the colonial period, it spread in coastal areas and some parts of north and north-eastern India, especially in its tribal regions. The Christians in India are said to be largely belonging to Scheduled Castes and Scheduled Tribes. This meant that the missionaries worked with their proverbial missionary zeal through healing (health), teaching (education) and preaching (Christianity) largely among the lower social strata of Indian society. Not that they did not work among the upper segments, but they did not find substantial response from them in terms of subscribing to Christianity.

In the twentieth century, the Church has continued its mission of healing, teaching and preaching which is obvious from the nature of institutions that are operating under its auspices. It is estimated that nearly 25 per cent of the work done in the voluntary sector in India is in the hands of Christians who form 2.5 per cent of the total population of India (D'Silva, n.d.:115). It is a remarkable feat indeed. Mother Teresa's work is well known to be mentioned here.

However, lately, the Church in India has been shifting its approach to poverty. It is moving away from alms-giving, charity, help, service and poverty alleviation programmes to development, self-help, critical social awareness, organizing people at the grass roots levels to fight for their rights. It feels that it is not enough to give people fish to eat but it is necessary to teach them as to how to fish. The Church in India is involved in the issue of liberation, mobilization and conscientization and in the activities such as fighting for children and women's rights and fighting for the rights of fishermen, tribals, dalits, as well as address the cause of ecology and environment. To say in one word, it is getting more and more interested in human rights for individuals cutting across the boundaries of religion, caste, region and language. Not social work but social action is a key word today. There are very many illustrious examples of Christian missionary NGOs operating along these lines. These NGOs are largely governed by the following norms or principles:

1. needs of the poor take priority over the ones of the rich;
2. freedom of the weak takes priority over the liberty of the powerful; and
3. participation of marginalized groups in society takes priority over the preservation of an order which excludes them.

These are fairly radical principles. And yet, it seems that they are the direct translation of what a genuine "option for the poor" means. If these principles or rules of thumb are too complicated, one can think of no better way of simplifying them except by quoting a very brief passage from a letter written to Pandit Nehru by Mahatma Gandhi, who was assassinated forty-nine years ago for his commitment to the poor. It sums up what "preferential option for the poor" should be as follows:

> I will give you a talisman. Whenever you are in doubt or when the self becomes too much with you, apply the following test: Recall the face of the poorest and the weakest man you may have seen and ask yourself if the step you contemplate is going to be of any use to him. Will he gain anything by it, will it restore him to a control over his own life and destiny? In other words, will it lead to fulfilment for the hungry and spiritually starving millions? Then, you will find your doubts and your self melting away.

REFERENCES

Avila, C. (1983), *Ownership, Early Christian Teaching*. New York: Orbis Books, Maryknoll.

Boff, Leonardo and Clodovis (1988), *Salvation and Liberation*. New York: Orbis Books, Maryknoll.

Desrochers, John (1981), *The Social Teaching of the Church*. Bangalore: Sidma Press.

D'Silva, Louis (n.d.), *The Christian Community and the National Mainstream*. Poona: Spice College Press.

Gutierrez, Gustavo (1988), *A Theology of Liberation*. New York: Orbis Books, Maryknoll.

Germillion, J. (1976), *The Gospel of Peace and Justice*. New York: Orbis Books, Maryknoll.

Land, Philip (1981), *Catholic Social Teaching, 1891-1981*. Centre Focus, No.43.

Lobo, George (1993), *Church and Social Justice*. Anand: Gujarat Sahitya Prakashan.

Sachs, Wolfgang (ed.) (1992), *The Dictionary of Development*. London: Zed Books Ltd.

Schultheis, Michael, De Berri P. Ed and Henriot Peter (n.d.), *Our Best Kept Secret: The Rich Heritage of Catholic Social Teaching*. Washington: Centre for Social Concern.

2

Hinduism: A Social Work Perspective

by Kalindi S. Mazumdar

Throughout my working life, as a social work educator and a professional practitioner, it has been my humble and modest preoccupation continuously to reflect on and try to achieve a modest synthesis of religious philosophy of Hinduism and the social work profession. Consequently, I have derived a great deal of personal and professional strength from these reflections and synthesizing efforts. The basic tenets of Hinduism and the cardinal values of social work flow from one common premise, e.g., upholding the dignity of the human being. This paper then is of an autobiographical nature and attempts to focus on the similarities between these two aspects and the strengths derived from them by the author. This exercise is more directed towards identifying practical implications of Hinduism to the profession of social work rather than conducting an academic analysis only. In other words, this paper explores and examines the scope for applying the main tenets of Hinduism to numerous field practices which constitute the core concern of social work theory, method and practice.

Main Tenets of Hinduism

It must be clarified at the outset that no claim is made here about this being a scholarly and an authentic study in the sense of treating the relevant material within the tradition of a specialized discipline. Interpretation and understanding of

Hinduism is a tall calling. It requires specialized training in hermeneutic approach. I am aware that properly trained students of philosophy would look at this theme from different perspective which definitely could be more systematic, rigorous, intensive and enriching. I wish to illustrate here the intrinsic worth of an inherent relationship that objectively exists between the doctrines of religious philosophy of Hinduism and practical goals of social work education and action. I am so much convinced from my personal pursuits and a vast and varied body of experiences in the field of social work education and practice that this combination has proved to be immensely insightful, potent and rewarding. All I wish to highlight here is that such an approach not only benefits the clientele but also to the teacher and student of social work discipline. There is a scope to extract a great deal of rich theoretical insights from this combination, benefiting the both, i.e., the religious philosophy and the social work practice. With this caveat, I proceed to examine the main strands of this relationship.

The Hindu saints, while meditating on the meaning of life, i.e., the interpretation of *atman* (soul), simultaneously observed the nature around them very closely. The plant and animal life assumed a sanctity in their eyes since it was the reflection of the omnipotent and omnipresent *Brahman* (the Supreme Being). In their efforts at self-realization, the saints learnt the importance of keeping the body and the mind healthy through *yogic* living. They observed the various postures of animals which make them agile and flexible and from these observations they devised the *yogic asanas* (postures), e.g., *bhujangasan* (serpent posture), *gomukhasan* (cow-head posture) etc. They simultaneously concentrated on breath-control, hence the *pranayamas* (exercise of breath-control by means of inhalation, suspension and exhalation) which culminate in meditation. The *asanas* and the breath-control form a prelude to meditation. In their meditation, they realized certain intrinsic values so very essential for a healthy, stress-free, harmonious and peaceful life. They understood that a peaceful co-existence was the only way to happiness, i.e., harmonious co-existence with nature and with other human beings. A cardinal message of Hinduism like *Vasudhaiva Kutumbakam* (the world is my family), undoubtedly the need of the hour for the whole world today, is of central importance in such an exercise. This philosophical truth can only be realized when we accept that every part of this universe is the ultimate reflection of the *Brahman* which is encapsuled in the doctrine of *Tatvam Asi*, i.e., that thou art. Cognitive acceptance of these philosophical truths is relatively easy.

The chief difficulty and a tremendous one too, is faced while operationalizing them. The personality of the human being consists of the body, mind, intellect and the soul. The tendency is to give a great deal of importance to the body followed by the mind. The discriminating powers of the intellect are not fully utilized when one is confronted with a host of evils in society. Hence, the need to be *gunatita* (beyond the limits of a trait or quality), i.e., transcending the *tamasic* (inertness/lethargy), *rajasic* (passionate), and *satwic* (pureness) *gunas* and reach the state of equanimity, objectivity and peace of a *sakshi* (detached observer). The *sakshi* is a silent witness to the entire panorama of life. This stage of life is reached only when one has striven towards the goals of *Bahujana Hitaya, Bahujana Sukhaya*, i.e., the greatest good of the greatest number of people. In the process of achieving this goal one feels the gratification, tranquillity, equanimity and oneness with the universe.

This is, to put it very briefly and in an encapsuled form, how I have understood and interpreted Hinduism both in my personal and professional life.

Application to Social Work

Let us begin with the principle of *Tatvam Asi*. If the human, plant and animal life, in fact all material and biological aspects of life are, in essence, an embodiment of the *Brahman*, it logically follows that they deserve the utmost attention and respect. What then is the justification for the discrimination against the *dalits*, women, delinquents, aged, homeless, handicapped and certain religious communities? Where are the religious or philosophical sanctions for violence in forms of ethno-caste-communal riots, terrorism, bride-burning, child-abuse and exploitation of vulnerable groups?

As social work educators and practitioners, we ourselves should practise introspection regularly. The practice of retreat for Catholic nuns and priests and the *maun vrata* (vow of silence) of Hindu and Jain saints facilitate this process of looking within. Students also should be regularly assisted to examine their misconceptions, prejudices and biases against people as also the community and environment. Field work camps and class discussions offer a good opportunity for a dialogue with the self and society. It helps to review one's prejudices also. The assignments written by our students after the 1992-1993 Bombay riots brought out many of their misconceptions to the fore, e.g., one student wrote that he was very much afraid to enter a Muslim community dominated locality as he had been told that Muslims are a dangerous lot. Over the time, this misconception disappeared as he came in closer contact with this community. He said that his field work during the riots proved to be extremely rewarding as now he has gained new insights into the whole problem of communal questions. I should like to state one more instance of change of heart and vision. Another student from a different college of social work agreed to donate blood to the victims of riots on the condition that it would be given to a Muslim. He was counselled by the concerned faculty of the college and he realized the futility of his unnecessarily hardened communal dogmatism. He emerged a changed person from this process and experience.

The doctrine of *Tatvam Asi* has another significance for social work educators and practitioners. The educator should start with the premise that the student has innate capacities and the educator's job is to provide opportunities to the student to manifest his/her abilities. To quote Swami Vivekananda: "Education is the manifestation of the perfection already in man."

Similarly, the client too has specific capacities which have to be brought out through a process of gradual and systematic empowerment. This implies that both the educator and the practitioner consider the student/client as an equal. The distinction between the giver and the receiver is absent. Swami Ram Tirtha has established the divinity of the human being in the following words: "You are not the child of the soil and dust. You are the child of Heaven, nay, Heaven itself."

Bahujana Hitaya, Bahujana Sukhaya

According to this doctrine, the ultimate objective of life is happiness but more important question is happiness of whom? Is it ethically enough to make oneself happy at the expense of others? Can we be so myopic as to ignore the poverty of the masses? Swami Vivekananda has expressed his feelings most strongly on this matter. He states: "So long as the millions live in hunger and ignorance, I hold every man a traitor who, having been educated at their expense, pays no heed to them." Vivekananda emphasizes the importance of empathy as he said that: "Him I call a *Mahatma* whose heart bleeds for the poor." And for a social worker, empathy is an indispensable prerequisite. It was in the academic books of social work that I read about raising our sensitivity to fourth degree.

However, I realized it only in my work with victims of drought in Maharashtra, gas leak tragedy in Bhopal, communal riots in Bombay and earthquake in Latur. Reading about manmade and natural calamities is one thing and being with the victims of these calamities and sharing their grief is quite another. I could feel the anguish, despair, guilt, anger and hostility of the father, a victim of a natural calamity, who said that he watched helplessly his wife and children being buried alive under the mass of debris. It is said that Sant Tukaram, a saint of Maharashtra, felt the lashes of the whip which the bullock (pulling a cart) outside his home was being given. It is only such sensitivity which makes us reach out to the poor, vulnerable, victimized and exploited individuals and groups. It is such kind of sensitivity which proves our oneness with others in this universe. It then acts as a driving force to strive for the greatest good of the greatest number.

Indian social reformers, freedom fighters and some social activists amidst us now depict this force in their struggle against social injustice. The truth which stares us in the face is that we cannot be happy if others amongst us are not. Gyaneshwar, another saint of Maharashtra, prayed: "*Duritanche Timir Javo, Jo Jey Jey Vancho Te Te Labho, Pranijat.*" Or, "Let the pain of those suffering vanish and let each one fulfil his wishes." Although this sounds like an impossible task, social workers should work towards social justice (which leads to happiness) in specific areas, e.g., women's issues, child labour etc.

In our work for social justice and human rights, we often face failures; our ego may be bruised and our spirits dampened. Nevertheless, negative thoughts and pessimism have no place in social work. "*Aa O Bhadra Kratavo Yantu Vishwata*," i.e., "Let noble thoughts come to us from every side" (*Rig Veda*). The power of positive thoughts can never be underestimated. It was this very power which galvanized our freedom fighters to achieve the objective of independence. In social work, we need to make a conscious effort to think positively about our client, agencies, society and more importantly, about our own abilities. Faith in ourselves is equivalent to faith in God. While expounding the concept of faith, Swami Vivekananda gives us this insight: "If you have faith in the three hundred and thirty million of your mythological gods, and in all the gods which foreigners have introduced into your midst, and still have no faith in yourselves, there is no salvation for you." This exposition follows logically from the premise that each one of us is divine.

In social work the dignity and worth of the human being has been continuously emphasized. However, we need to extend this concept to social justice, social policy and social change and make the human being the pivotal point of all such transactions. The government is planning to rehabilitate the quake victims by building quake-proof houses for them. Social workers through the good auspices of the TISS (Bombay) have conducted a comprehensive survey of these victims. However, there is an urgent need for social work intervention in the plan for housing. The people themselves, especially the women, should be involved in this process. We saw a model quake-proof house built in one of the villages by a foreign charity/donor agency. But, the local people told us that it was not useful for them and therefore they tie their cattle in these homes for the fear of them being stolen or killed.

Most government programmes fail or partially succeed because the human beings for whom these programmes are initiated are not consulted or involved in the planning and implementing stages of these programmes such as the ICDS, IRDP and the family planning programmes. The social work profession should make meaningful interventions to change the attitudes of the government and the NGOs so that the human being is not lost sight of in the heap of policies and programmes. The beneficiary or receiver should be always at the centre of all developmental activities and focus.

Karmanye Vadhikarasthe, Ma Phaleshu Kadachan

Work in itself is a worship if performed according to this doctrine, i.e., like a *yogi*. Work according to *Vedanta* is rest, i.e., rest from the strife of doer and the expected results. When a human being works under the influence of his/her ego, it ceases to be work and becomes the pursuit of self-gratification. Ramdas of Maharashtra describes this aptly in his *Manache Shloka*, "*Aham bhav jya manasicha virena, tya gyana he anna potti jirena.*" In other words, those whose egos are not eliminated will never acquire knowledge or *gyana*.

Working without the expectations of results is extremely difficult. The ego conflict is evident among some social workers which makes team work and networking virtually impossible. We can eliminate ego problems by making our work a spiritual goal in itself. Savta Mali, yet another saint of Maharashtra, has embodied this truth in his *shloka* as "*Kanda Mula Bhaji, Heech Vithai Mazi*," i.e., "onions, radish and vegetable, that is my God." Savta Mali was a gardener and he saw God in his work with onions and radishes. In intense work the human being's mind and body work in union, i.e., *yoga*. The attention is not on the doer but on the work itself. Therefore, the results are positive. In the profession of social work, much would have been achieved if one did not bother as to whom the credit of good work and success goes. The social work educators and practitioners should aim at creating a second line of functionaries, so that the knowledge and the skills acquired are not only perpetuated and passed on but also cumulatively enhanced.

The Concept of *Gunatita*

In order to achieve goals of social justice for the underprivileged, vulnerable, exploited and victimized masses, we, the social workers need to be disciplined in the mind, body and intellect. Lethargy (*tamas*) has no place in our life. *Rajas* is a step further than *tamas*. It is an achievement-oriented activity which should lead us to a *satwic* stage of mind. Efforts should be made to see that the achievements in the *rajasic* stage are not the end in itself and that in our zeal for accomplishment, others in our midst are also given space to develop. The *satwic* stage symbolizes peace, equanimity and a balanced view of life. Yet, it is still influenced by the materialistic milieu and efforts should be made to transcend this stage. This is a herculean task and most of us may never be *gunatita* in which case, a *satwic* state of mind is the only option.

Our relationship with students, clients, colleagues, agencies and various social sub-systems should reflect the *satwic* perception of life. Humility, openness to learn from others whether young or old, poor or rich, comfort in admitting one's mistakes, spontaneity in one's work and endless energy characterize the *satwic* stage. There is a yearning for peace within oneself and in the environment as a whole. The inner peace is a prelude to outer peace in the world. It facilitates team work and networking among the agencies. Under these conditions only, can the *Vedic* truths be realized, e.g., "*Om Sahana Bhavatu, Sahana Bhunakta, Sahaviryam Karvav Haihee*," i.e., all should meet, partake of food and work together.

Sakshi: The Silent Observer of the Panorama of Life

The *sakshi* (detached observer) or the *sthitaprajna* (equanimity or steady wisdom) is the ultimate objective of human life. Contrary to the common belief, the *sakshi* is not rendered useless in the world, as he or she is not affected by the sensory stimuli. Such capers of the mind and body do not obstruct the transaction in the world. Yet, the inner strength of the *shtitapragna* is powerful enough to galvanize the entire universe. Social workers may never be able to realize the state of *sakshi*, yet one could work dispassionately to achieve the goals of social work, i.e., social justice, fulfilment of human rights and the empowerment of the exploited, victimized and marginalized individuals and groups in our midst.

India has had a glorious tradition of spirituality. Unfortunately, this century has witnessed events which stained this image of India. The communal inferno in Bombay, the terrorism in the north and north-east, atrocities on backward castes and tribes, etc., are ample evidences to tarnish our spiritual heritage. The unbridled materialistic, consumerist market economy and international multi-channel visual media invasion in the 1990s has further strained our cultural resources and spiritual heritage in general. Man's mind and body are under constant glare of media focus. Modernity is challenging the glorious traditions of this great land and its people. The intellectual, philosophical and religious heritage of India seems to have ceased to play any resistive role.

In these circumstances, the onus of creating a cultural rejuvenation of traditional values based on religious sources is on the shoulders of all those concerned with social work ethos, values, practices and commitments. The fiery optimism of Swami Vivekananda expressed in the following words should strengthen us and the generations of social workers to come:

> Shall India die? Then from the world all spirituality will be extinct, all moral perfection will be extinct... such a thing can never be... the power of love is infinitely of greater potency than to the power of hatred... India will be raised not with the power of flesh but with the power of the spirit.

REFERENCES

Argyris, Chris (1969), "Explorations in Consulting-Client Relationships" in Warren Bennis, *et.al.* (eds.), *The Planning of Change*. New York: Holt, Rinehart and Winston.

Brown, Brian (1921), *The Wisdom of the Hindus*. New York: Brentano's.

Chennakeshvan, S. (1974), *A Critical Study of Hinduism*. Bombay: Asia Publishing House.

Hick, John H. (1994), *Philosophy of Religion*. New Delhi: Prentice Hall of India.

— (1989), *An Interpretation of Religion*. New Haven: Yale University Press.

Morgan, K. W. (1953), *The Basic Beliefs of Hinduism*. Calcutta: YMCA Publishers.

Patel, Indira (1987), *Vivekananda's Approach to Social Work*. Madras: Ramkrishna Math.

Pincus, Allen and Minahan, Anne (1973), *Social Work Practice: Model and Method*. Illinois: F. E. Peacock Publishers.

Radhakrishnan, S. (1927), *Indian Philosophy*, 2 Vols. London: George Allen and Unwin.

Sen, Guru Prasad (n.d.), *An Introduction to the Study of Hinduism*. Calcutta: Thacker, Spink and Co.

Sharma, D. S. (1971), *Essence of Hinduism*. Bombay: Bharatiya Vidhya Bhavan.

Smith, Wilfred Cantwell (1978), *The Meaning and End of Religion*. New York: Harper and Row.

Warren, Roland L. (1971), *Truth, Love and Social Change and Other Essays on Community Change*. Chicago: Rand McNally.

Williams, George M. (1990), "Swami Vivekanand" in Robert D. Baird (ed.), *Religion in Modern India*. New Delhi: Manohar.

3

Non-Violence and Man-Making in Buddhist Philosophy

by Nitin J. Vyas

MAN AND VIOLENCE

Man's instinct for violence is as old as the life itself and it continues to persist by taking ever improving, more and more lethal and myriad forms. Violence has somehow remained an inseparable part of the man's existence. This basal instinct has extracted a great cost over the millennia. On the flimsiest provocation, pertaining to a conflict of interest in the family, community, caste, village, region, race, religion, language or culture, man turns violent and ends up paying through his flesh and blood. This goes to show that the process of humanizing our local and global society is incomplete.

This is not to state that the efforts to wean man away from violence are not made. In fact, these efforts too are as old as life of violence itself. The phenomena of violence and non-violence have co-existed. Man is at times violent and at other times non-violent. Human nature and social conditions influence his behaviour and instinct for violence. As against the ignominious history of wars, bloodshed, killings, tortures and sufferings at various levels of human existence---say in family, clans, communities, tribes, religious, ethnic groups, castes, villages, states or nations---there also exists a glorious history of peaceful, harmonious, cooperative and communitarian co-existence between widely diverse peoples and regions. Peace and non-violence have been the main spheres of moral philosophy. It is indeed very ironical that the twentieth century has seen the worst forms of violence. Two world wars, nuclear holocausts, continuous recurrence of ethnic cleansing by various fascist regimes, religious violence, political violence in form of suppression of human rights, fabricated and false encounter killings, drowning of people by the state and its strong arm agencies like police and army, and long drawn wars such as Vietnam, Korea, Iraq, Israel-Arab, etc., have surpassed all previous records of violence and killings. We have moved into the time of advance form of increased violence where scientifically, technologically and electronically developed and chemical weapons are used. This form of violence is more lethal and consequential than all those conventional forms so far known to us. The speedily spreading cult of violence once again needs to be stemmed if some social order and sanity is to prevail and human existence is to continue and flourish without undue cost in terms of human flesh and blood.

It is high time for evolving a global social order that is based on non-violence. More effective and useful non-violent methods of resolving disputes and differences among people and regions have to be evolved. Already the human civilization, in its stride, has reached the level of resolving disputes and conflicts through peaceful and non-violent means like negotiations, dialogue, discussion, persuasion, debate, exchange of views, opinions, etc. Other examples of non-violent means of dissent are strikes, *dharnas*, *gheraos*, boycott, tool down, pen down, fasting, *satyagraha*, economic sanctions, disarmament efforts, green peace and so on. In all these forms, there is an inherent presupposition and preparedness for suffering, sacrifice and understanding. The idea is to appeal to the noble and good qualities that are inherent in all human beings. The good in man should be given a chance to emerge and prevail. The moral chords should be stirred to bring about amicable settlements. The purpose of non-violent forms of resolving disputes is to soften the hardened feelings, attitudes and sentiments in the adversaries. For, violence begets violence. It is only the higher spiritual resources of man which can appropriately deal with the basal instincts for violence. Man has to be civilizationally and culturally re-made to bring out the best and the divine from within. Such man-making processes have to be accorded due primacy and continuous vigilance needs to be kept. Unity of mankind can result only from such a persistent non-violent course.

The Present Challenges

Through the mastery of scientific and technologically specialized methods and result-oriented techniques, man has made great advances in all spheres of life. These achievements have bridged the physical distances and made the world look as one externally. International friendships, cooperation, charities, cultural exchanges, aids, disaster management and philanthropic activities in general do take place in a great measure. Despite the intense modern quest for attaining the twin goals of rationalistic humanism and egalitarian social order, the entire humanity is gripped in all kinds of pathos of deepening frustration. The human society is locked in its own horns. On one hand, it continues to scale newer heights of scientific and technological advances to generate unheard variety and mass of material wealth. And, on the other hand, the hopes of good life for all, peaceful co-existence and just global order are receding in oblivion like a desert mirage. Newer and subtle forms of totalitarianism, dominance and deprivations in socio-economic, cultural and political realms continue to persist and rise.

The most common problem of all of us is effective security and decent survival for one and all. The existing mechanisms for redressal of grievances are so superficial, *ad hoc* and compartmentalized that they do not seem to take us far as the existing grievance of humanity is so deep and widespread. The crisis is total as it concerns man in all aspects of his life. Therefore, without an integral philosophy of man-making and practical experience of non-violence to guide, all efforts shall prove ineffective and relative. Where lies the way out? It is precisely the aim of this paper to explore and consider various alternatives. We can neither, of course, expect any miracles nor any supernatural agencies to do anything here. If that were to happen, it would have happened in the past so many times over, at every savage act of violence and war. The non-violent method and procedure could go a long way in making man realize his destiny as an end in itself and as an urge for integral fulfilment of his total personality.

It is mainly in this context of contemporary world that the understanding of Buddhist philosophy, its conception of man-making, vision in general and its pursuit of non-violent social order, in particular, assumes immense significance. Continuing the age-old tradition of Indian culture and thought, Buddhism probed sincerely and seriously the problem of mutual relations between man and man and the universe. Reinterpreting this past collective human heritage can contribute in a great measure to the issues faced by us.

THE BUDDHIST CONCEPTION OF MAN AND PHILOSOPHY

Buddha, the great revolutionary thinker, had challenged the authority of the established religions prevailing during his times. He had protested against barren ritualism and philosophical abstractions of the earlier *Vedic* and *Upanishadic* philosophy. To him, man is at the centre of everything and hence advocated the cultivation of the moral and spiritual character of such a man. Buddha argued that all phenomena, including the ethical and spiritual realms, are conditioned by causal laws. This causal genesis is the basic source of all laws of continuity and moral retribution. To know the essential nature of this reality and following it virtuously is the sure way to achieve fulfilment of human life.

Impermanence (*anichhas*), egolessness (*anatter*) and suffering (*dukha*) are the three fundamental principles of Buddhism. According to Buddha, the whole universal phenomenology is based on the conception of reality which is in a state of constant flux. The source of righteous living does not lie in any theological dogma or supernatural beliefs. Being atheist, he denies the Brahminic concepts of universal soul (*brahman*), individual soul (*jeeva*) or the identity of these two (*ekatva*). To him, the human self is not a metaphysical substance but the subject of all experience in the practical sense.

In other words, Buddha's concern is man's moral life, here and now. Buddha had a deep conviction in the efficacy of man's moral will. Through right efforts and enlightened, free and responsible choice, man could bring about a new non-violent existence for himself. It means that man must constantly know the objective reality openly and deal with it dynamically. In spite of its such concerns, it is very likely that Buddhism may not appear to be an authentically comparable philosophical system to its counterparts in the western philosophical traditions. It is more of a faith, a way of life and the path to be walked on. According to it, the universal laws are governing human existence and it can be examined by reason. Without accepting any centralized, rigid and traditional authority, Buddha, however, consistently grants that reason can examine these universal laws.

Thus, the human life is a constant experiment and experience. It is a gradual gaining of knowledge and training oneself accordingly. To Buddha, the worldly life is full of sorrow and suffering. Remaining indifferent towards the sufferings of the world or adding to it through one's latent or manifest deeds amounts to committing violence. Man has to be harmless and compassionate for all sentient existence. The very nature of the world is such that it presupposes the practising of non-violence by man *a priori*. Through its practice and consequent love and sympathy, the man would be able to liberate his 'will' truly. This way he can free himself from the sorrowful and conditional existence. The detailed course of his liberation and salvation is discussed in the subsequent text.

The Buddhist Philosophy

The Buddhist philosophy aims at the enlightened experience

(*nirvana*) through (i) ethico-moral discipline of body, senses and mind (*shila*); (ii) with the help of meditation (*samadhi*), and (iii) insight into the nature of reality (*prajna*). It is a path that crosses the worldly life of spiritual ignorance (*avidya*); craving (*kaam*) and suffering to a realm of transcendental wisdom (*vidya*). Thus, for Buddhism, the human suffering is virtually one with transience. Everything that takes birth dies necessarily and inexorably. The Buddhist law of dependent origination (*pratityasamutpadavada*) means that birth is the cause of suffering as well as of decay and death. It is the ignorance of this eternally valid truth which produces will-to-action (*karmic formations*). Buddha saw and realized that the materialistic and self-centred beliefs during his time had clouded and stagnated this wheel. He set the wheel in motion anew (*dharmachakra-parivartan*) for the suffering mankind. The following three are the steps to enlightened experience as propounded by Buddhist philosophy:

1. *The Conception of Self*

It is the three types of desire, viz., the desire for self-gratification (*kaam tanha*), self-preservation (*bhav tanha*) and desire for destruction (*vibhav tanha*) which impel the human mind to act. The human self as a psycho-physical entity is a dynamic continuum of body (*roop*), sensation (*vedana*), perception (*sangnya*), predisposition (*sanskaar*) and consciousness (*vignan*). It is when one makes an extreme identification of the subjective experience with this ego as the centre of observation, it leads to all the tension and sorrow of the world. For, with this comes the finite, limited and mortal self. It is a separate individual which ever passes into something other than itself in the ceaseless flow of becoming. Man, grasping things other than himself, falls into the endless chain of cause and effect. He becomes a helpless tool to forces outside oneself.

More than this, Buddha neither affirms nor denies the existence of self (*atman*). He remained silent about it and meant to accord the limits of philosophical reasons. He did not agree to many superstitions and empty views regarding self which prevailed during his time. However, as seen earlier, Buddha does accept the self as a practical postulate, as the subject of actions in moral sense. It is realized when one acts according to universal norms of human existence. These constantly operative universal norms could be applied in infinitely varying circumstances of man as they do not encroach upon the moral autonomy of the individual in any way.

2. *The Golden Mean*

Buddha could see that the vast majority of the people being sense-bound and spiritually-blind, would not be able to digest his message. Hence, he preached the doctrine of Golden Mean (*madhyam pratipaad*). Accordingly, man must choose a middle path between two extremes of hedonistic self-indulgence and ascetic self-mortification. He should make a steady pursuit of truth with his full capacity of body and mind. It is a normal psychological path that gives the seeker a firm grip on his experience. It aims at strengthening the inner freedom of man and protect him from becoming the prisoner of his irrational desires and empty illusions. Buddha presents a humanistic ethics wherein man has to have faith in himself and in his upward growth.

The way out of this worldly suffering for Buddha is making for a proper balance in the activities of the world. Here he lays down a comprehensive integral ethics of eight-fold path. The true ethical action is a spiritual regeneration attained by right moral conduct and meditation. Through it man can dissolve his existence into various components and thus get rid of the notion of ego. Only thence, one can have a limitless expansion of the self in a practical sense. With it will result the positive goodness in each with a perfect harmony of body and mind. This is indeed *ahimsa* (non-violence), for it is the very harmony with the great universe as such.

3. *Nirvana*

This highest state of spiritual realization is described as uncaused (*asankrut*), unborn (*aprabhav*) and imperishable (*ashramaran*). The cessation of ignorance is the cessation of the whole chain of causation. For Buddha, it is a refuge in one's genuine practical self which is a state of complete health and supreme felicity (*purnam sukham*). It is a radical and enlightened state of existence which is beyond any theorizing and investigation. For here there is a complete extinction of desire and hence results a total emancipation from the cycle of birth and death. This ecstatic state of highest meditation is imbued with saturating compassion for all beings. Thus, all human behaviour must be subdued and guided by this latent and genuine self. One should be earnest in performing the duties in accordance with this true self.

The Ethical Philosophy and Buddhist Schools

From among the two main schools of Buddhism, the ethical commitment of *Hinayana* restricts itself to a general attitude of compassion. It is a subjective intellectual orientation towards ethics. It did not give concrete plan of action in alleviating the suffering of others. As against this, the *Mahayana* school goes further. It also emphasizes the compassionate participation in the miseries of others as well as freeing them from those miseries. It is a distinct and new Buddhistic ethical consciousness. For, it is thence, that it grew from purely subjective ethical and ascetic form of existence to an organized religion. There is an increase in ethical commitment. There is an active response in minimizing the sorrow and suffering of the whole world through the spiritual guidance and love. It is with this development that a complete ethics of non-violence comes to be developed both as a philosophy of religious beliefs and rituals of social actions.

Moreover, the *Mahayana* school denies the existence of ego. It means that all sufferings without exception have no personal or individual owner as such. Hence, it is one's duty to minimize sufferings and get freedom from it. This means, in other words, that Buddha supports the ethics of non-violence not only in negative structures and ascetic duties but he also gives a positive meaning of it in altruistic love, compassion and welfare of human sufferings and obtain freedom from it.

However, it may be maintained that both these Buddhist schools emphasize the sublimation of worldly desires and not its total denial. Both point out that to understand the emptiness of the ego is one thing and to realize and live it actually as an egoless life is another thing. Again, both have a fundamentally humanistic conception of *nirvana* as it is not grasped in superhuman sense.

The Nature of Compassion

It is referred to earlier in this paper that Buddhism denies the notion of the individual soul. Ethically it means that the destiny of the individual soul is communal and collective living. Redeeming personal but the feeling of compassion is a sympathetic participation in the sufferings of others. This is seen in history that Buddhism as faith in general has proved as a missionary faith.

Thus, the Buddhist follower has to cultivate an ethics of inner perfection with the help of the principle of love. It is a spiritual regeneration achieved by right moral conduct and meditation. The moral and spiritual values, viz., compassion and benevolence are the fundamental bases of social life. The barriers of individual self as separating them from others break away to a wide world at once.

It means that compassion is not merely a negative action of non-killing but a mental projection synthesizing the sufferings of others. The principle of life negation is an ethical goal for preventing the 'will to live' to go on ceaselessly. There is a subjective recognition of the ethics of non-violence in this sense. But the same results in spiritual transcendence of man which makes him look at the whole universe with a feeling of kindness. Such a person is accompanied by four sublime states of conditions as (a) love, (b) sorrow at the sufferings of others, (c) joy in the happiness of others, and (d) equanimity regarding one's own happiness and suffering.

BUDDHA'S LIFE, WORK AND ITS IMPACT

By continuous travelling far and wide and organizing religious orders (*sangha*), Buddha preached his message of universal compassion for the goodness and happiness of all the people in the world (*Bahujan Hitaya*, *Bahujan Sukhaya*, or greater welfare, greater happiness). He laid down ethical norms for both monks and laymen and non-killing of a life occupies an important place. Observing *ahimsa* or non-killing is regarded indispensable in day-to-day social dealings and behaviour. Further, for Buddhism, mutual love and gratitude are declared as basic norms in familial relations.

For both Buddhist schools, right will, devoid of egoism and a sublime cultivation of moral virtues are considered as the positive aspects of non-violence. They nurtured and developed these ideas in the course of their history. Both schools considered non-violence as an integral ethics of moral norms, right behaviour and spiritual compassion.

The Contemporary Scene

As stated in the earlier part of this paper, the existence of entire mankind is threatened by the ever increasing violence and destructive capacities in the world. So long as there is no fundamental and total approach to non-violence in resolving various conflicts and tensions, no lasting peace and permanent settlement can result. The half-hearted and *ad hoc* attempts at non-violence approach of various types listed earlier *vis-a-vis* the conflicting struggle of the apparent and subtle self-interests resulting into further violence do not take us far. These attempts are still not enough to totally banish suspicion, distrust and hatred from the human society and open a path for permanent peaceful co-existence and harmony.

The present population explosion has assumed a menacing proportions. This has resulted in severe strains in many spheres of life, including ecological and social spheres. Inequality and injustice in many spheres of life threatens the very existence of sentient life in the world. It is here that the role of the Buddhist philosophy of non-violence acquires substantial relevance. Through its fundamental moral and spiritual efforts, it redesigns and reshapes man's future, as it advocates the birth of a new consciousness for man.

Goals and Objectives

As argued earlier, the average man still shuns violence. By nature man is both violent and non-violent but impulses of violence in man need to be tamed. It may be that his understanding is feeble as he is easily swayed by selfish and fanatic leaders of various shades who thrive on his ignorance. Moreover, groupism in the form of group-action is passed on as a virtue of communitarianism and collective communal concern which does greater harm to immediate as well as wider society as a whole. Leadership, guided by partisan interests often resorts to war, violence, hatred, suspicion and intolerance of the other. It doubtfully promises to attain peace, prosperity and unity for its narrowly mobilized 'collective' interest. Hence, the main problem that stands out is whether we should place our individual as well as collective future in the hands of such forces. The contemporary modern man is caught in the vicious circle of living an actual life of fragmented and truncated existence, while continuing to cherish and crave for peace and harmony along the lines of an integrated philosophy of life. The most agonizing fact is that the general human response to the ills and warnings of the world has been one of apathy and inaction.

Although, it is quite right to say that the world is independent of man in a way, yet it is also dependent on man. The whole civilizational progress in science and technology is meant for the human use and betterment of the conditions of his existence. It is meaningful only in the context of man. This implies that there has to be a totalistic and comprehensive perspective of one world and one family, freeing us thereby from narrow reasoning and goals.

THE RELEVANCE OF THE BUDDHIST VISION

Buddhism as a religion and an order can help us achieve individual and group or collective purposes today. Our future hope of achieving the type of world we want presupposes our sense of unity despite all our differences. First of all, Buddhism rejects any centralized authority. In fact, Buddha proved and practised in his own life the precepts of his philosophy. It is the actual response of the heart that counts more than mere logical status of the doctrine. Such an attitude of liberalism and egalitarianism can release a great enthusiasm and energy for a new non-violent world order.

There are some situations of life which are as crucial as of life and death. Mere ethical supremacy of non-violence over violence is not appealing at all then. In such matters, the philosophy of non-violence, man-making and social harmony needs to be practised here and now. Some degree of just selfishness without malevolence and with a touch of benevolence has to be conceded. The Buddhist concept of man and self can contribute significantly in this context.

The Buddhist emphasis of the transient character of reality includes not only what man may observe, but the man himself. Thus, even if violence comes in insoluble dilemmical situations, the choice of the individual takes the nourishment from the subjective scale of values. This would give a considerable weightage to the dignity of human personality and thinking. It is believed that forced occupation of a region or people is one thing, whereas actually conquering them is quite different. Violence can conquer physical and material man but not the heart and spirit of the man. This truth conveys a great sense of human moral saga, particularly in the face of dire violence. This truth must subdue the dominating ambitions and terror techniques of men desiring violence as a means to an end.

This means a thorough revolution and readjustment in our

life must come in all our socio-economic and cultural spheres. Initial cooperation may be a difficult task but each one of us has to be a witness to one's own inward light through a ceaseless search with purity of thought, word and deed. It is redefining and reasserting the moral and spiritual outlook which characterize our identity.

This may be done primarily with reference to many prevailing notions about success and happiness of human life. From what prevails, one can easily see a direct relationship between an easy life and violence. Non-violence regards the life of simplicity, self-restraints, body-labour and service as of more significance than pompous and luxurious life. After all, the integrated non-violent philosophy aims at one's unity with the whole universe including the non-human forms of lives and existence. It rules out self-aggrandizement of any type whatsoever. It calls for a great moral and spiritual regeneration. One of the immediate ways of achieving such a moral and spiritual regeneration is through imparting the education, training and practice of social work ethos, concerns, values and goals.

Realizing the Buddhist dictum of suffering as the base of all existence, one has to follow and continue to do beneficial deeds and thus show a higher level of consciousness towards one and all. We have to be constantly awake and conscious of the world issues. It is not saying fetishly that Buddhism is the end all and be all panacea of all ills. Still it can be concluded from the above account of philosophical discussion that it is a burning lighthouse to the suffering world of today. Buddha rightly did not give any instant effect formulae. But his message that 'meditate' experiment and experience is a timeless torch-bearer to all of us.

REFERENCES

Basak, R. G. (1961), *Buddha and Buddhism.* Calcutta: Sambodhi Publishers.

Diwakar, R. R. (1960), *Bhagwan Buddha.* Bombay: Bhartiya Vidya Bhavan.

Dumoulin, Heinrich (ed.) (1976), *Buddhism in the Modern World.* London: Coller Books.

Gangulee, N. (1957), *The Buddha and his Message.* Bombay: Popular.

George, Grimm (1957), *The Doctrine of Buddha: The Religion of Reason.* London: Allen and Unwin.

Humphreys, Christmas (1954), *Buddhism.* London: Pelican.

Kirthisinghe, Buddhadasa P. (ed.) (1984), *Buddhism and Science.* New Delhi: Motilal Banarsidass.

Law, B. C. (1966), *Concepts of Buddhism.* Holland: Kerne Institute.

Nakamure, Hajime (1975), *Buddhism in Comparative Light.* Bombay: Current Book House.

Suzuki, D. T. (1947), *The Essence of Buddhism.* London: The Buddhist Society.

Unnithan, T.K.N. and Yogendra Singh (1973), *Traditions of Non-Violence.* New Delhi: Arnold Heinnmann (India) Ltd.

4

Ethics, Individual and Society in Islamic Philosophy: A Hermeneutic Exploration

by Chhaya Patel

POSITIVISM AND HERMENEUTICS

The World War II is considered to be the turning point in the development of most of the social sciences. The positivist tradition became a major methodological force in the field of social science research. Under its impact most of the social science disciplines such as sociology, psychology, political science, etc., became impatient for achieving natural science-like methodological sophistication and status. In other words, their major goal was to achieve scientific objectivity and as a consequence of this, value-neutrality became their ideology. This development almost dismissed nearly two thousand years old normative tradition of theorizing socio-political life.

The traditional approach of studying social sciences became suspect for various reasons of substance and method. The positivist conception of social science research took the much well-known form of behaviouralism. It was an instant success, and its emergence was celebrated as a great watershed event. These developments brought about certain desirable changes in the scope, objectives and methods of studying social sciences. As a result of these developments, an empirical validation of certain theoretical and conceptual attributes of social sciences became possible. However, for about 2-3 decades, i.e., between 1950 and 1975, behaviouralism reigned supreme, but along with its success and popularity, signs of its failure and dissatisfaction also began to be noticed. Despite claiming to be scientific, objective and value-neutral, it could not predict, explain or solve certain major problems faced by the contemporary society. It was overemphatic about methodology and neglected the vital role of values, ethos, norms, culture and tradition in society. Besides it was also excessively focused on micro-realities and overlooked macro aspects. The limitations of positivist methods have led the contemporary social theorists to think about the alternatives. The role of values in organizing the public and social spheres of life has begun to be increasingly recognized (Baviskar, 1995:3-4).

The post-empiricist philosophical developments since the 1970s have tried to restore the old tradition of inquiry to its original status (Yadav, 1986). The emergence of hermeneutics as a method is a major and leading development. More generally it is referred to as an art, skill or theory of interpretation and of understanding the significance of human ideas, actions, utterances, products and institutions. Thus, from different directions, the cry has gone up for the development and application of hermeneutic approach to the study and understanding of human society. It is an acceptance of the authority of tradition and an approach to recover and interpret the meanings of social thought and social actions from the point of view of the text-composers or the agents performing the actions. Hans-Georg Gadamer, the German philosopher, published his famous work *Truth and Method* (1960) which was translated into English in 1975. It brought forth the interpretative approach to social inquiry and created a new scope for bringing under focus those texts which were kept out of the purview of sociological-philosophical interpretations.

Gadamer contends that for hermeneuticians, there are no standards of objectivity which can be recognized independent of the attainment of inter-subjective agreement by the partners in the dialogic process. The scientist's interpretations must be based on understanding held in common with their subject-objects and expressed through the mutual satisfaction of expectations on both sides, that is, through continuing agreement on the level of both interpretation and practice. To Gadamer, the ideal of a neutral, detached observer is a myth (Held, 1980:312). This interpretative model of social inquiry insists that an overzealous search for universal laws and generalizations is not necessary in order to understand the human life-experiences, actions and institutions. As we know, the social phenomena are fundamentally different from natural phenomena in the sense that they are intentional and they express the purposes and ideas of social actions. However, understanding such aspects does not require generalizations or causal laws. Rather it calls for an interpretation in which the meanings of an action are uncovered by analyzing the experience and action in the light of the agent's particular situation and in the light of the conventions, practices and values of his society.

Hermeneutic or interpretative model of social inquiry views classical and scriptural texts as a rich source of information, insights, knowledge and understanding of experiences of life, the affairs and aspirations of a particular human society or a community within a larger society. The classical texts such as *Rig Veda, Upnishads, Puranas,* the epic texts like the *Ramayana, Mahabharata* and *Gita,* texts containing Buddhist and Jain philosophies, the *Bible*, the *Quran* and the *Arthasastra* are considered to be the treasures of socially useful wisdom, understanding, knowledge and insights into the life-world of a given society at a given time or for all time to come. Some of these texts cover socio-philosophical aspects of life, whereas others cover religio-cultural and spiritual aspects. These texts are considered basic and fundamental to the understanding of organization of any societal life-world. Civilizational and cultural histories of societies or distinct communities within a given society can be studied very well on the basis of these texts. This approach is also extended to the study of literary texts and the profiles of the life-world contained therein. Instances of such scholarships are evident in the works of Chandra (1987), Suhrud and Bhagat (1994), etc., in western India. *The Subaltern*

Studies (Vols. I-IX) as an academic/intellectual movement have thrown fresh light on many hidden aspects of life lived in different periods and struggles organized for one or the other cause which remained unnoticed or scantily noticed.

In this sense, looking at the Islamic philosophy and tradition and interpreting relevant parts of its primary and secondary texts is the most timely task of inquiry. In other words, hermeneutic approach is adopted with a view to forming a correct understanding and achieving almost a complete communicability of correct interpreted meanings of life-experiences of a society or a section within a society.

This paper aims at understanding the basic teachings and philosophical conceptions in Islam regarding various rational aspects of ethics, individual and society. It attempts to reveal Islamic conception of man, various man-making processes and ethical principles guiding individual conduct and evolution of an Islamic social organization. We shall first have a bird's eye view of its main philosophical tenets which is followed by a peep into its origin and development. The rest of the text profiles ethics, individual and society as conceived in Islamic philosophy.

ISLAMIC PHILOSOPHY: ORIGIN AND DEVELOPMENT

There are various misconceptions prevailing about Islam. Some observers view Islam as a religion concerned only with divine services and statutes of personal conduct. This is incorrect. It is actually a comprehensive philosophy of life. From its inception, the central focus of Islamic philosophy has been to evolve a social organization (in wider sense) based on ethico-religious foundations. It has exhibited an inherent flexibility of allowing periodic reforms within the system to take account of specific circumstances of time and space. Islam is thus, contrary to popular belief, a flexible philosophy of life which originally conceived of a society based on such civilized principles as justice, equality and human rights (Abulala, 1990:120). The early Islamic civilization incorporated these principles and operated in accordance with dynamism and flexibility (Engineer, 1981). Social progress, religious enlightenment and scientific achievement came to be the integral features of the Islamic revolution (Wellhausen, 1972:15). When Islam was emerging, the tyrannical and tragic policy of divine right, authorizing kings and emperors to rule against the will of the people, was predominant in the world. The early Islamic rule, carrying out the Islamic instructions, put on the mantle of liberty and equality on its shoulders. It toiled hard to emancipate neighbouring people and regions who were tyrannized by the human gods of the Persian and Roman empires (Hamiduallah, 1975:73-79). However, due to static-minded and self-deceptive administrators, the Islamic state did not remain wholly active and did not progress continuously but experienced a gradual decline in the later period.

Some recent critics, on the other hand, have concluded that the major force retarding both the development and dynamism in the present-day Islamic societies is Islam itself. Islam, Rosenthal claims, is afflicted with lethargy and superstitions (1962:217). Despite purported objective and scientific analysis, both Muslim and non-Muslim writers have based their conclusions on improper and biased selection of quotations from the Islamic Holy Revelation (the *Quran* and *Hadith*). They have failed to acknowledge that Islam is far more than just a historical consequence represented by those who act officially in the name of Islam.

At the outset, Islam comprised of influential divine instructions which are first to be understood, and in the light of such an understanding, interpretations of historical events and consequences have to be inferred. Despite its rich heritage, Islam is the most misunderstood religion of today, for the simple reason that all that is good and great in it is credited to its past account. Its own votaries have not done much at present to sustain the tempo of its intellectual, moral and material development that had made Islam the silver lining to the dark skies of the middle ages.

Knowledge and understanding of history can certainly play an important role in raising the consciousness of a society that has lost its identity. The study of character, contributions and historical role of Islam is necessary in order to form a correct judgement about Islam. Any religion need not be taken merely as a point of contact or a medium between the ultimate reality and the individual. It also must be viewed as a source of inspiration for ushering in a new and desirable social order, the ethical standards for individual conduct, cultural ethos and all that is fine and lofty in a scriptural treasure of any given religion, community or society.

The word 'Islam' is derived from the Arabic root 'slm' which means among other things peace, purity, submission and obedience (Al-Marwardi, 1977:25). In the religious sense, the word 'Islam' means submission to the will of God and obedience to His Law. The connection between the original and the religious meaning of the word is obviously clear. Only through submission to the will of God and by obedience to His Law one can achieve true and lasting peace. Islam above all may be defined in terms of its original setting. It is a theology and movement directed against such human failings as immorality, excessive materialism, political and ecclesiastical tyrannies (Asad, 1970:370). The main emphasis of the Islamic philosophy is acknowledgment of sovereignty of the God as the absolute power over all human beings. The term 'Islam' stands for total and complete submission to God alone and to none other by one and all.

Having all afresh the Holy Revelation as their guide and source of inspiration for organizing the society, the Muslims of the first generation came to understand its ethical and social instructions more profoundly. The early followers constructed a civilized state and society without the guidance of Islamic law which did not emerge until the advent of Abbasid dynasty from 750 A.D. (Mohamad, 1975:11). Subsequently, the fist generation of followers of Islam understood and extracted their jurisprudence directly from the Holy Revelation, which later became an Islamic law (Ahmad, 1976).

One of the most prevailing misconceptions is regarding the nomenclature of Islam that equates Islam as 'Mohamedans' (Gibb, 1955). This is grossly incorrect. The Muslims reject and protest against the use of these terms. Referring to or calling Islam as Mohamedanism and its followers as Mohamedans causes serious offence to the sensitivity of its followers. It also amounts to an interpretative error. It must be clarified and restated that this religion cannot be named after a mortal being who was only an agent of God. Mohamed is not Allah. Allah is higher than the mortals like prophet Mohamed. Secondly, the usual practice in social science of naming a body of thought after a thinker's name like Gandhism, Marxism, Buddhism, etc., does not apply to Islam. Furthermore, the usage also erroneously implies that the Islam was founded by Mohamed and therefore it takes its name after the founder. Islam is not just another 'ism' nor do Muslims worship Mohamed or look upon him the same way as Christians, Jews, Buddhists, etc., look upon their respective founder leaders.

The Muslims worship God alone. Mohamed was only a mortal being chosen by God to teach this word to the world and lead an exemplary life for others to emulate. He is a living proof for Muslims of what man can be and of what he can accomplish in the realm of ethical excellence and virtuous living. Thus, the true name of the religion is Islam and those who follow it are to be known and referred to as Muslims. The basic concept of God in Islam is humanitarian. Man's well-being is the central concern of Islam; from that it follows that all the laws originate from God must be good and in the utmost interest of individual and society.

Islam originated in the beginning of the seventh century of our era, i.e., A.D. 612 in the Arabian peninsula as a man-making or man-shaping and socially regenerative, integrative philosophy. It can also be referred to as an ideology for evolving a new social order. It is a body of doctrine, myths, symbols, etc., of a social movement, class or similar large group. Understanding the complex forces operating on the eve of Islam's birth is a difficult task. Historical study of any society as a whole encompassing all its structures, attitudes, systems of values, cultural idioms or institutions is onerous task. It becomes all the more difficult when the society involved is a religious social formation, encumbered with its own dogmas, values and attitudes. Thus, Islam is a religious philosophy as well as an ideology which transformed the old society in which it was born, while yet retaining those of the old society's essential features which did not clash with Islam's new value system.

Islam was born in a highly commercialized milieu of Mecca, which was an international centre of commerce, trade and high finance. In fact, neither in the nomadic tribes of the Arabian desert nor in the commercial town of Mecca were any traces of the feudal mode of production or of feudal relations. It is also not correct to say that inter-tribal wars were fought in order to seize land or for territorial expansion. Agricultural production was totally unknown in and around the area where Islam was born (Ryder, 1952:187). However, in order to understand the religio-ideological spirit and philosophy of Islam, one has to avoid biased stereotypes or the mechanical applications of any evaluative system of thought or theory, ideology or model (Iqbal, 1975). Be it a social, political or ideological reality, it is much more complex than the approaches to study them seem to assume. It calls for an extremely careful analysis. This is more so in the case of a religious ideology, as the issues are more confused, and various beliefs much more steadfastly and dogmatically held than in any other ideologies. Montgomer W. Paper (1968:31) makes a very profound and realistic observation regarding the origin and growth of a religion. His following words capture the essence of his this argument:

> A religion, both in its origin and its growth, is a social phenomenon. The prophet preaches to the people belonging to a society with a distinctive structure, the sociologist can study the class in the society to which the prophet appeals immediately, to those whom he appeals at a later stage in his preaching and the class changes brought about by the acceptance of his preaching.

A sociologist studies the relations between the ideas proclaimed by the prophet and the distinctive interests of each class. Thus, the sociologist is concerned with a complex phenomenon of a way of life which is embodied in a society and its interdependent values and social structure. The sociologist is thus operating with something like a 'coherence theory', except that he is not dealing solely with ideas and beliefs but also with various social facts, such as those of religious, cultural and psychological nature.

However, the rise and spread of Islam forms a unique chapter in the history of the world civilization. Within a hundred years after its rise, it spread over three of the five continents, viz., Asia, Africa and Europe. It stretched from Spain in the west to Sindh in the east, an empire bigger than any that had ever been seen before. Today, it has more than 900 million adherents living in all parts of the world. In its formative period of the first four centuries (*Hijra* era), Islam displayed remarkable dynamism and intellectual excellence which resulted in a civilization of a very high order.

The religion of Islam is based on the cardinal principles of monotheism, equality and brotherhood. It absorbed the peoples of different races, regions and religions into one coherent religio-cultural unit, stretching from Spain to Central Asia and India. For the sake of convenience, we may divide the history of Islam into three periods: the classical (7th-12th century), the medieval (12th-18th century) and the modern period (18th century onwards). In the classical period, the religio-social order founded by the prophet made steady progress and exhibited the finest elements of its culture and cardinal values. The classical period is the most noteworthy, since it witnessed the life and living of Mohamed. This period witnessed the religion he propounded, the social and political order he established and the foundation of the culture he laid, besides the several Caliphates that arose after his death. The Umayyad Caliphate (A.D. 661-747) continued to practise many of the social and political principles of Islam but also made rapid progress in political expansion of Islam. The rule by Abbasid Caliphate (A.D. 748-1258) was the longest and the most glorious, as Baghdad became the hub of world trade and commerce. The sack of Baghdad in 1258 by the Mongols was the darkest hour in the history of Islam----a tragedy that ended the classical age.

The medieval phase witnessed the rise of several great Muslim empires that challenged the European expansion and built up distinctly local cultural zone in the place of the original monolithic cultural unity of the classical period. The political disintegration of the Islamic states began in the seventeenth century and became more apparent at the end of the eighteenth century. However, some attempts at renewal and reform of Islam were made periodically from the eighteenth century. Abdal Wahab in Central Arabia and Shah Walliullah in India were two noteworthy names of that century. Their attempts to discard traditionalism and assert the supremacy of the Islamic law are remarkable in the medieval period.

The modern period is a record of dismal failure which began from the eighteenth century and continues to the present day, as the Muslim empires have collapsed. Their social, religious, economic, political and cultural institutions have come under severe criticism from the Europeans and other non-Muslim societies in Asia (Hippler and Lueg, 1995). Their sacred lands have been overrun, occupied and colonized by the westerners. The masses in Islamic societies, as a result, got reduced to utter poverty and ignorance. However, the position began to improve slightly after the World War II when most of the regions gained their independence and European imperialism lost its teeth. Thereafter, various attempts were made for quick economic, social and political recovery. During this entire period, however, the Muslims continued to cling to the spirit of their faith which inspired them. Even during this dark period, Islam produced leaders who could challenge the west, such as Tipu Sultan of Mysore, Abdul-Kadir of Algeria, Jamaduddin Afghani of Persia, Mohamad Abduhu of Egypt, Sir Syed Ahmed Khan, Allama Iqbal and Maulana Azad of India.

ETHICS AND ISLAMIC HOLY CONSTITUTION

Ethics is the study of human conduct. It relates to certain basic ideals and norms. Moral philosophers consider these ideals and norms to be the expression of certain fundamental presuppositions that every individual accepts as valid. For this particular reason, ethics is usually called a normative science, as distinct from such positive social sciences as psychology or sociology. Although, the latter concern themselves with human behaviour, psychology focuses on an individual mental process while sociology and social work addresses ethics in relation to the physical and social environments in which an individual is placed. For psychology, all the studies of human behaviour are the same, whether the subject of the cases of study are completely different. The saint, for example, exemplifies and illustrates the ideal pattern of conduct while the criminal is expected to correct his behaviour to that of a given ideal pattern. Most moral philosophers assume that ethics specify current moral conceptions to unfold their ultimate presupposition of proper human conduct. However, the still unsettled controversies among moral philosophers started with differences in their conception of the greatest good and the ideal of happiness. Those who advocate the greatest good for happiness try to confine the study of ethics to the following four basic questions:

1. What is the greatest good in human conduct?
2. What are the sources of man's knowledge of right and wrong?
3. What are the sanctions of moral conduct?
4. What are the motives of factors which encourage an individual to perform moral acts?

The moot question that arose initially among the philosophers of ethics was regarding the concept of human happiness as an ultimate goal. However, it posed a greater challenge as to what type of happiness should be pursued—egoism or altruism; hedonism or utilitarianism? Even today no clear choice has emerged. Advocates of each of these 'isms' of human happiness have strongly supported their own doctrines, evolved from some subjective premises and much to the cost of other similar subjective premises.

Islam considers ethics and moral conduct as important aspects of one's own as well as collective societal life. Since ethics and moral conduct are extremely vast topics, this section attempts to outline only the basic elements of the concept. Ethics and moral conduct in Islam have been situated midway between the two extremes of presuppositions and actual constitution of the greatest good and happiness (Dar, 1969). The Islamic Holy Constitution proclaims: "He will not be a believer who does not love for his brother what he loves for himself." This verse contains a conception of what is right or wrong. The verse attempts to give some answers to the four questions listed above. It defines the greatest good, the source of man's knowledge of right and wrong, the sanctions of moral conduct, and finally the motivation behind man's performance of that conduct. To explain these phenomena, the verse recognizes that reason must be the only source for determining the greatest good. What is 'right' for one's own self must likewise be 'right' for another and *vice versa.* At this point, the verse does not define any right or wrong itself because of the implicit assumption of universal standards. These common rights and wrongs serve as antidotes for mankind in various circumstances. Moreover, every Islamic society would maintain certain of its own norms and traditions which do not contradict the overall framework of the Islamic Holy Constitution and which would have to be accepted as ethical norms peculiar to each specific society. So, the behaviour which seems right for someone and which may seem wrong or atleast uncomfortable for another must be measured by such universal standards of wrong and right (Gilson, 1939).

The ultimate sanction and index of moral conduct lies within one's own self. Any human being who does not wish to be harmed by others must not think of harming others. However, other interpretations can be extracted from the above verse which may indicate that no end ever justifies any means. Human moral conduct must, therefore, be a criterion of belief and reflect a close relationship with God. Although the Islamic Holy Constitution recognizes reason as the principle tool for determining the greatest good, it provides the Muslims with examples to follow and to use as models for resolving misunderstanding or disputes. Consequently, the first generation Muslim followers of Islam have emulated the prophet's behaviour as an example of human conduct. The Islamic Holy Constitution equates personal conduct with ones personal relationship with God. Therefore, any practice of the Islamic religion based on immoral behaviour will not be accepted. The realistic approach of the Islamic Holy Constitution, the practical solutions it offers to human problems and the noble objectives it sets for man, mark its sagacity and distinction. One of the major characteristics of the Islamic Holy Constitution is that it is not the static as generally believed but flexible. It is a kind of dynamic prudence that provokes the mind. In this prudence, there is stirring dynamism and there is moving force attested by historical evidence as well as by the *Quran* itself.

Another significant characteristic of the Holy Constitution is its ethical practicability. It does not indulge in wishful thinking. Nor do its teachings demand the impossible or float on rosy streams of unattainable ideals. It accepts man for what he is and exhorts him to become what he can be. It does not brand man as a helpless or hopeless creature, condemned from birth to death, but it conceives of him and portrays him as a noble, honourable and dignified being. The practicability of the Islamic Holy Constitution and its ethical teachings is established by the examples of the prophet and Muslims, and the distinctive approach of the *Quran* is that its instructions are aimed at the general welfare of man and are based on the possibilities within his reach. A third characteristic is moderation or harmony between the divine and the human, the spiritual and the material, the individual and the collective, and so on. The Islamic Holy Constitution pays due attention to all facets of life and all needs of man and deals with them in such a way as to help man to realize the noble objectives of his being.

The Islamic constitutional prudence functions in three principal dimensions: inwardly, outwardly and upwardly. Inwardly, it penetrates into the innermost recesses of the mind. It is aimed at the healthy cultivation of the individual from within. The outward function of the Islamic Holy Constitution embraces all walks of life. It covers the principles of the entire field of human affairs from the most personal matters to the complex collective relations stretching from local to global. It reaches areas beyond any system of law or code of ethics and dealing with human transaction in such a way as to give them a moral touch. In its upward function, the Islamic Holy Constitution focuses on the one supreme God. Man is merely a trustee in the vast domain of God, and the sole purpose of his creation is to worship God. This does not pre-text for seclusion or passive retirement from life. It either opens before man the new horizons of thought or guides him to exemplified ends of high morality and acquaints him with the eternal sources of peace.

It is clear, therefore, that the Islamic Holy Constitution is no enemy of reason and ethics. It does not regard them as hindrance to spiritual or material progress as it is clearly stated that even divine revelation is not to be accepted unquestioningly and uncritically. Man is exhorted from accepting anything without reflection and interpretation. He must conduct himself in the light of ethical guidance and reason. Thus, it was worth-while to consider the role that the Islamic Holy Constitution assigns to ethics and reasons both in the secular and the spiritual spheres. In the next section, the basic foundation of the Islamic social system is described in the light of the *Quran* and *Surrah* principles.

INDIVIDUAL AND SOCIETY

The social life in Islamic philosophy is based upon supreme principles that are designed to secure happiness and prosperity for the individual as well as for the society. Such notions as class conflict, social discrimination, caste system and domination of the individual over society or *vice versa* are alien to the conception of social life in Islam. Nowhere in the *Quran* or in the Islamic tradition can one find any mention of one's superiority over the other on account of class, origin or wealth. On the contrary, there are many verses of the Islamic Holy Constitution to remind mankind with vital facts which serve as principles of the social structure of the Islamic system. Among these is the fact that humanity represents one family and the unity of mankind is conceived in the light of the common origin (parentage of Adam and Eve). Thus, every human being is a member of the universal family and is entitled therefore to enjoy the common benefits as he is enjoined to share the common responsibilities. When people realize that they all belong to Adam and Eve, there will be no room for racial prejudice or social injustice or second class citizenship. In the Islamic Holy Constitution, there is a constant reminder of this important truth. The unity of humanity by nature and origin is reflected in the following verse:

> This is to eliminate racial pride and the claims to national or ethnic superiority and pave the way for genuine brotherhood (4.1.)

The relations between the individual and society are based on the essential unity of man's origin. The role of the individual and society is considered mutually complementary. The individual is responsible for the common welfare and prosperity of the society. In this way, the individual works with a sound social mindedness and a genuine feeling of inescapable responsibility. It is his role to do the utmost for his society and contribute to its common welfare. On the other hand, the society is also responsible for the welfare of the individual. Normally, when the individual is able to work, he is the contributor and society is the beneficiary. Subsequently, in old age or otherwise he is the beneficiary and society is the contributor. Thus, duties and rights correspond harmoniously, whereas responsibility and concern are mutual. There is no authority to dominate the individual and abrogate his personal identity. Likewise, there is no individual or class of individuals to exploit the society and corrupt the state. There is harmony, peace and mutual security and there is a constructive interaction between the individual, society and state. Besides the unity of humanity, mutual responsibility and concern, the social life in Islamic conception is also characterized by cooperation, goodness and piety. It is marked with full recognition of the individual and his sacred rights to life, property and honour. It is also marked with an effective role played by the individual in the domain of social morals and ethics.

In an Islamic society, the individual cannot be indifferent. He is enjoined to play an active part in the establishment of sound social morals by promoting and practising the good and combating the evil in any form with all lawful means at his disposal. In so doing, not only does he shun evil and uphold good but also helps others to do the same. The individual who feels indifferent to his society is a selfish member. His morals are in trouble and conscience is in disorder. The Islamic conception of social life is very lofty, sound and comprehensive. The substantial elements of this structure are: sincere love for one's fellow human beings, mercy for the young, respect for the elders, genuine feelings of brotherhood and social solidarity, mutual responsibility between the individual and society, and respect for the rights of other people to life, property and honour. In the *Quran* and *Surrah*, one finds numerous instructions like these which are as follows:

> ...Fulfil all obligations... and help you one another is righteousness and piety, but help you not one another is sin and rancor... (5:1-3).

Anyone who has no mercy for the young and respect for the elders is not one of us Muslims (prophetic statement). However, it has always been the aim of Islam to create such a social atmosphere which seeks to establish a social milieu in which the human personality can function freely and grow to its full stature.

AN OVERVIEW AND CONCLUSION

The main objective of this paper was to explore and examine the crucial issues of ethics, individual and society in Islamic philosophy. It was done by selecting the most significant works of eminent writers and thinkers who have contributed to revealing the texts and treatises on Islam in general and the Islamic society in particular (Al-Maududi, 1990 and Asad, 1970). However, it was found that the hermeneutic approach of inquiry into social life is the most appropriate one for such a type of study. Accordingly, the Islamic philosophy is interpreted and contemplated from the point of view of those who profess it and adhere to its ideology.

In other words, the Islamic philosophy and tradition is being looked at from an interpretative angle in order to understand correctly the original settings and its positions on ethics, individual and society. Hermeneutic approach necessitates an interpretative inquiry into the original and basic texts of collective knowledge on any subject. In case of Islam, the *Quran* and *Surrah* are found to be the richest sources of wisdom, knowledge and information. The interpretative or hermeneutic approach of inquiry into social aspects of life has emerged as a result of the failure of positivist tradition which was dominant in the field of social science research for quite a long time.

The positivist tradition claimed to be a scientific and objective method in the study of social science. The failure of positivist tradition was attributed to many causes like its negligence to the role of values, norms and tradition in society, besides its excessive stress on irrelevantly precise and unduly sophisticated methodology and narrow focus on micro aspects of life. Unlike the positivist approach, the hermeneutic approach or as popularly known as the interpretative approach insists that causal laws and generalizations are not adequate to analyze and understand social phenomena. Thus, because of the substantial difference between the natural and social phenomena, human actions, thoughts and institutions are not subject to these laws which are employed by the positivist approach and claimed their applicability to all human sciences whether natural or social.

The main tenets of Islamic philosophy, its meaning, origin and its developmental phases are discussed in the light of interpretative perspective. We have examined and described their contribution to ethical and social order as contained in Islamic philosophy which in turn is sourced from the *Quran,* i.e., the very words of the God and the *Sunnah* (utterances and deeds of the Prophet). The difference between the *Quran* and *Sunnah* lies in the fact that the former is divine in form and content, whereas the latter is divine in content alone. However, the difference in nature between both inspired the scholars and jurists of Islam to develop a system of authenticating *Sunnah's* utterances and practices in order to keep it in tact. On the other hand, the secondary sources such as *Ijma* (consensus), *Qyar* (analogical reasoning) and *Ijtihad* (elaboration) provided a wide coverage to areas of life about which the primary sources, i.e., the *Quran* and *Sunnah*, do not contain guiding rules and provisions to deal with the contemporary issues of our day.

While interpreting the Islamic Holy Constitution it was found that reason is assigned a vital role and importance. A man is warned not to accept anything uncritically even if it comes from the Holy Revelation or otherwise. Generally, it is observed that the differences and confusion arise from the conflicting relations between divine and human reasoning. It is also generally concluded that the divine laws are meant to provide the utmost benefit to mankind and therefore in case of any clash between the two, they ought to prevail over human laws which are affected by many limitations such as partisan passions, self-interest and despotism.

Ethics, on the other hand, have been discussed in order to study and comprehend human conduct and the motivation behind man's performance of that conduct. Having in mind reason as the only determining factor, the concept of the greatest good has been discussed. Thus, the ultimate sanction of man's moral conduct lies within the individual himself.

In Islam, an individual enjoys a special status as that of a vicegerent of God on earth. He is responsible for spreading good and forbidding evil in his course of vicegerency. This special status also requires him to commit to broader liberal concept such as justice, equality, freedom and tolerance of non-Muslims in the Islamic political order. The Islamic socio-political structure is erected on such holy commitment of its followers and sustained by them. It thus becomes clear that Islam was one of the first religio-philosophical systems to identify the basic structure of a society with such lofty principles and ideals to sustain the pillars of its polity and society. The functions and organization of the Islamic state are not different from any other state. In short, the Islamic state is to provide for three essential conditions to the well-being of its people, i.e., the complete security of life and prosperity, a living for those who cannot work or do not find a decent job and finally a just and equal socio-political order.

However, it must be mentioned here that the Islamic Holy Constitution does not precisely organize a fixed rigid structure, as it provides scope for periodic changes in order to cope with the contemporary requirements of the hour. So far as the individual is concerned, the Islamic Holy Constitution provides for comprehensive rights for dignified survival and development of the self. The Islamic scholars point out a special feature of these rights stating that these rights cannot be restricted, limited or abridged by any human agency as they are divinely ordained rights. Such human rights have been laid down by the Holy Constitution as basic rights for man, child and woman as a human being. It may be mentioned that the basic and sole source of these rights is the *Quran* and *Sunnah* which conceive of a just world order for all to prosper in an environment which is free from fear, oppression, domination, exploitation and deprivation.

While evaluating the utility of the hermeneutic or interpretative approach of inquiry into social and political aspects of life, it has been revealed that classical texts are viewed as a rich source of information and knowledge. Their importance lies in the fact that they provide us with a scope to understand the public affairs, experiences and aspirations of a particular society, i.e., Islam in this case. Looking at the Islamic tradition from a hermeneutic perspective was the most appropriate method for our purpose. Today, the Islamic society is encumbered with its own dogmas, lethargy and superstition. Only through the focus of hermeneutic interpretation, which calls for interpreting and explaining the old texts from the point of view of their agents, some revival and restoration of old, original glory can be achieved.

The adoption of hermeneutic approach has enabled us to have a clearer view about concepts of ethics, individual and society in Islamic philosophy. This exercise has helped us to a great extent to form a correct understanding and achieving almost a complete communicability with meanings of life experiences, ideals and expectations of Islam. It is also felt that adopting any other approach in studying such a theme would not have provided us a clearer view about the Islamic traditions and their tenets. It is only the hermeneutic or interpretative approach that helped us to peep into the divine contents of the *Quran* and *Sunnah* as well as the Islamic Holy Constitution. This was only an exploratory exercise. More in-depth inquiry must be taken up as a preparatory measures to penetrate (somewhat more closely held contemporary) Muslim social order in India for various socio-cultural interventions from social work perspectives.

[I am deeply indebted to Mohamad A. Wahab, a Nigerian Islamic scholar for generously allowing his time and material to be used for this paper. I have benefited a great deal from numerous long discussions with him. However, any error of interpretation or judgement is solely mine.]

REFERENCES

Abulala, S. Almaududi (1990), *Political System of Islam*. New Delhi: International Islamic Publishers.

Ahmad, Hassan (1976), *Early Development of Islamic Jurisprudence*. Islamabad.

Al-Marwardi, Ali M. (1977), *International Encyclopedia of Islam*, Vol. I. New Haven: Yale University Press.

Asad, Mohamed (1970), *The Dictionary of Islam*. Cairo: El Azhar El-Islamih.

Baviskar, Amita (1995), *In the Belly of the River: Tribal Conflicts Over Development in the Narmada Valley*. Delhi: OUP.

Chandra, Sudhir (1987), "Conflicted Beliefs and Men's Consciousness about Women: Widow Marriage in Later Nineteenth Century Indian Literature," *Economic and Political Weekly*, 21(51), 20 October.

Dar, Bashir Ahmed (1969), *Quranic Ethics*. Lahore: Institute of Islamic Culture.

Engineer, Asghar Ali (1981), *The Origin and Development of Islam*. Bangalore: Orient Longman.

Gadamer, Hans-Georg (1975), *Truth and Method*. London: Sheed and Ward.

Gibb, M.K. (1955), *Mohammadanism*. New York: New American Library.

Gilson, Etiene (1939), *Reason and Revelation in the Middle Ages*. New York: Wiley.

Hamidullah, Mohamad (1975), *The First Written Constitution in the World*. Lahore: Mohamad Ashraf Publications.

Held, David (1980), *Introduction to Critical Theory: Horkheimer to Habermas*. London: Pluto Press.

Hippler, Jochem and Lueg, Andrea (eds.) (1995), *The Next Threat: Western Perceptions of Islam*. London: Pluto Press.

Iqbal, Mohamad (1975), *Towards Understanding Islam*. New Delhi: Crescent Publishing Co.

Paper, Montgomer W. (1968), *The Sociologist and the Prophet: Reflection on the Origin of Islam*, Vol. 2. London: Pogson Presentations.

Rosenthal, Erwin (1962), *Islam in the Modern National State*. Cambridge: CUP.

Ryder, Dennis (1952), *The Search for Legitimacy*. London: Cadell and Cadell.

Suhrud, Tridip and Bhagat, Varsha (1994), "Patterns of Conjugality: Letters of Vidyaben Nilkanth" (in Gujarati), *Arthat*, 13 (1), January-March.

Wellhausen, Julius (1972), *The Arab Kingdom and its Fall*. Calcutta: Calcutta University Press.

Yadav, Yogendra (1986), "Political 'Science': Positivist Method and Philosophic Critiques," *Indian Journal of Political Science*, 47(4), October-December.

5

Vivekananda: Socio-Spiritual Approach to India's Social Problems

by Satya P. Agarwal

After making a comparative study of religious responses to the social challenges of the modern age in various Asian countries, Robert N. Bellah (1965) identifies four types of such responses, namely: (i) conversion to Christianity, (ii) traditionalism, (iii) reformism, and (iv) neo-traditionalism. According to him, India provides a good example of 'reformism' which has been defined by him as "a movement that re-interprets a particular religious tradition to show not only that it is compatible with modernization but also that, when truly understood, the tradition vigorously demands at least important aspects of modernity" (Bellah, 1965:215). In this paper, it is intended to describe the life and work of Vivekananda in order to show how he developed a reformist-modernist perspective and formulated a socio-spiritual approach to India's social problems by basing it on a harmonious synthesis of *karmayoga* and *Vedanta*. It took shape in form of the foundation of Ramkrishna Mission and its numerous social service activities like helping the needy in the time of distress, famines and epidemics like plague. Happily, Vivekananda's life and work is increasingly becoming more and more relevant to the challenges that the Indian society is facing towards the closing years of this century. It is assumed that the solutions to India's many social problems must be hidden and rooted in its rich religio-philosophical traditions of long standing. It is upto us as to how we source these traditions.

A BRIEF LIFE-SKETCH

Naren Prior to Meeting Sri Ramkrishna

Swami Vivekananda's pre-monkhood name was Narendra Nath Datta or Naren for short. The Dattas belonged to an aristocratic section of the *Kshatriya* (warrior) caste of Bengal, and they displayed several of the traditional characteristics of the *Kshatriyas*, including a faith in leading an ostentatious life, in general, but also producing an occasional *sannyasin* (renouncee). For example, Naren's grandfather, a rich and cultured man, had abandoned his wife and children, a high position, fortune, and society at the age of twenty-five, to retire into the forest and became a *sannyasin*, and from that day had never been seen by the family. Naren's father Visvanath Datta, a solicitor in the Calcutta High Court, was known for his varied interests and activities. Being conscious of his own superior position in the society, he exhibited a broad outlook on social and cultural matters, including a feeling of indifference to caste. Naren's mother, Bhuvaneswari Devi was a highly educated woman of regal majesty, whose heroic spirit had been nurtured on the great Hindu epics. During private conversation with his disciples in America, Vivekananda later acknowledged the deep influence of his mother and said: "It is my mother who has been the constant inspiration of my life and work" (Rolland, 1970:222).

Born in 1863, Naren exhibited in his boyhood, talents in several fields, and the rich family circumstances enabled him to cultivate as many of them as he could possibly do in the early years of his life. The type of personality which Naren developed by 1880 (that is, before he met Sri Ramkrishna for the first time) has been described by Romain Rolland in the following words:

> The possessor of physical courage and the build of an athlete, he [Naren] was a past master in all physical exercises. He could box, swim, row and had a passion for horses. He was the favourite of

> youth and the arbiter of fashion. He danced great religious dances with consummate art, and had a delightful voice, which later was to charm the ear of Ramakrishna. He studied vocal and instrumental music for four or five years under famous Hindu and Mussulman professors. He wrote tunes and published a documented Essay on the science and philosophy of Indian music. Indeed he was everywhere regarded as a musical authority.... At college he was distinguished for his brilliant intellect, embracing with equal zest the sciences, astronomy, mathematics, philosophy, and Indian and western languages. He read the English and Sanskrit poets. He devoured the historical works of Green and Gibbon. He was fired by the French Revolution and Napoleon. From his childhood up he practised, like so many Indian children, the habit of meditation. At night he used to pore over the Imitation of Jesus Christ and the *Vedanta*. He loved philosophic discussions (1970a:223-4).

A number of philosophic as well as practical questions arose in Naren's mind and he sought answers to such questions by consulting senior college students like Brajendra Nath Seal as well as the leaders of the *Brahmo Samaj* (a religious organization set up by Rammohan Roy as a part of his effort to bring about religious reforms), including Devendranath Tagore. The advice that Naren received through such consultations naturally varied, and each piece of advice seemed to provide partial help to Naren in his "search for truth". For example, Seal put forward the merits of rationalism, and he even spoke in terms of the "God of Reason". According to Rolland (1970a:226), Brajendra's viewpoint could satisfy only Naren's 'intellect' but not his 'heart' mainly because Brajendra's rationalism was of a peculiar kind as it claimed to be a mix of the pure monism of the *Vedanta*, the Hegelian dialectic of the Absolute Idea, and the Gospel of the French Revolution: Liberty, Equality and Fraternity. His belief that the principle of individualism was "the evil", and Universal Reason "the good" did not fully agree with Naren. Naren's heart and senses were looking for the living revelation, the realization of the Absolute, about which some holy *Guru* could say to him, "I have seen Him, I have touched

Him, I have been He."

In comparison to Seal's philosophy of rationalism, the *Brahmo Samaj* spirit of 'categorical reform' seemed to provide a way out of the orthodoxy and social divisiveness of the idol-worshipping Hindu. Naren joined the movement of young *Brahmos* in Bengal for the education and unity of the Indian masses without distinction of caste, race or religion. Some of them attacked orthodox Hinduism even more bitterly than did the Christian missionaries. But the *Brahmo* spirit also failed to satisfy Naren's heart as his free and living intellect found them to be narrow, fanatic, anti-Indian wisdom and bad in knowledge of west. Although Naren remained with it for some time but his heart remained restless.

As a last attempt to seek answers to the questions that made him live "in great turmoil of soul", Naren went to Devendranath Tagore and asked him: "Sir, Have you seen God?" Although Tagore recognized the depth of feeling and sincerity that prompted Naren to raise such fundamental issues, he gave no direct reply to his question and only said: "My boy, you have the eyes of a *yogi* (one who practises *yoga).* You should practise meditation" (Nikhilananda, 1975:16). Naren returned unsatisfied, and his inability to achieve the reconciliation of his mental struggles started showing up in the form of dreams, as he himself recalled in later days:

> From my youth up, every night just as I fell asleep, two dreams took shape. In one, I saw myself among the great ones of the earth, the possessor of riches, honours, power, and glory; and I felt that the capacity to attain all these was in me. But [at] the next instant I saw myself renouncing all worldly things, dressed in a simple loin-cloth, living on alms, sleeping at the foot of a tree; and I thought that I was capable also of living thus, like the *Rishis* [hermit saints] of old. Of these two pictures, the second took the upper hand and I felt that only thus could a man attain supreme bliss.... And I fell asleep in the foretaste of that bliss.... And each night it was renewed.... (Rolland, 1970a:228-9).

Such was the condition of Naren in November 1880 when a

friend of his, Surendranath Mitra, a rich gentleman converted to Christianity, asked Naren to sing a religious hymn, in the presence of Sri Ramkrishna who had by that time been widely recognized as a great spiritual leader.

Naren and Sri Ramakrishna Together

Although Naren's singing drew Sri Ramakrishna's attention, the latter had the capacity to peep into the "depth of Naren's unsatisfied soul", and he asked Naren to come and see him at Dakshineswar. At their next meeting, Naren's song moved the Master deeply, and he started the process of obtaining Naren's participation in his mission, to which Naren initially resisted. In later years, Naren recalled this occasion and described it thus:

> He [Sri Ramakrishna] said, "Ah! you have come so late. Why have you been so unkind as to make me wait so long? My ears are tired of hearing the futile words of other men. Oh! how I have longed to pour out my spirit into the breast of somebody fitted to receive my inner experiences!...." He continued thus, sobbing the while. Then standing before me with folded hands he said, "Lord, I know that you are the ancient sage *Nara*, the incarnation of *Narayana*, reborn on the earth, to take away the misery of humanity." I was amazed. "What have I come to see?" I thought. "He ought to be put in a straitjacket! Why, I am the son of Visvanath Datta. How dare he speak thus to me?"....But I remained outwardly unmoved and let him talk (Rolland, 1970a:230).

A few minutes later, when the Master and Naren joined the group of friends assembled in the larger room, Naren heard the Master say (and these words were an answer to his own nocturnal strivings): "God can be realized. One can see Him and speak to Him as I speak to and see you. But who takes the trouble to do so? People will shed tears for a wife, children, or possessions. But who weeps for the love of God? Yet, if a man weeps sincerely for Him, He will manifest Himself to him" (Rolland, 1970a:231).

Naren gradually felt that Sri Ramakrishna was "worthy of

respect", but the former also wanted to be on his guard to escape the latter's "eccentric behaviour". The type of conflict between his 'intellect' and 'heart' that Naren had earlier experienced in his relations with Brajendranath Seal, now seemed to reappear, but in a reverse form. Naren was struck by the incomprehensible power of Sri Ramakrishna. It attracted him, as a magnet attracts iron, but he himself was made of stern metal. His reason would not submit to domination. If in his recent relations with the rationalist Brajendranath Seal it had been his heart that strove against his intellect, now his intellect mistrusted his heart. He was resolved to maintain his independence, and to accept nothing from the Master except what could be rigorously controlled by his own reason. The uncritical faith of the others roused his contempt.

Although several important developments took place to bring Naren and the Master closer and closer, a special mention needs to be made of what happened after Naren's father suddenly died in early 1884, leaving the family heavily indebted and facing starvation. In spite of the B.A. degree, Naren could not get any job and was hard put to maintain his widowed mother and younger brothers. At last, unable to bear the distress of the family, and in sheer desperation, he fell at the feet of Sri Ramakrishna and requested him to approach Mother *Kali* (one of the many Goddesses, destroyer of evil) on his behalf. Sri Ramakrishna, on the contrary, asked Naren to go himself and ask the favour from the Mother *Kali*. Naren went to the temple, but as soon as he stood before *Kali*, he saw a miracle. He found the Mother Goddess in a living visible form. He forgot the worldly affairs and, prostrating himself before her, prayed that he might be endowed with true knowledge and a spirit of devotion and renunciation. When on his return he was questioned by Sri Ramakrishna, he remembered that he had forgotten to pray to the Mother to remove his misery. He was sent back, and again a third time, but with no better result.... He was assured by Sri Ramakrishna that his family would not be wanting in bare necessities of life, and so it turned out, as

Naren could secure some jobs.

Sri Ramakrishna gradually prepared Naren to be the head of the group of sincere devotees who would carry out the Mission after he himself passed away. He never concealed his feelings about Naren's future destiny. When Naren implored the Master to show him the way to *nirvikalpa samadhi*----the attainment of eternal bliss after sundering all earthly ties---he was administered a sharp rebuke. "Fie on you!" exclaimed Sri Ramakrishna, "I never thought you so mean as to be anxious for your own salvation only whereas you have powers to do much good to mankind." At his insistent request the Master one day gave him a glimpse of it and said: "Just as a treasure is locked up in a box, so the realization of the supreme bliss will be locked up and the key shall remain with me. You have work to do" (Majumdar, 1965:19-20).

Sri Ramakrishna also taught Naren that the proper way of doing good to mankind was to view it as worship to God, and that it was sheer arrogance if any feeling of superiority were to be associated with compassion. As the Master put it: "Compassion! Who are you to be compassionate? God alone can have compassion for the mortal. But service to man should be done as worship to God---*Jiva* [life] is none else than *Siva*." Naren understood what the Master had in mind, and he told his friends: "Today I have heard a new truth of great significance. In time I shall broadcast this for humanity" (Patel, 1987:1).

A mysterious incident symbolizing the transmittal of special powers from Sri Ramakrishna to Naren, as confirmed by Vivekananda himself, has been described by Majumdar (1965:20-1) very profoundly. Knowing that his end was nearing and in order to endow Naren with the spiritual wealth which he himself had acquired after years of super human efforts and unprecedented austerities, Sri Ramkrishna called him to his side only three or four days before his *mahasamadhi* (final trance). Having seated him in front and looking intently into the eyes of his dear disciple, he fell into a deep trance. Naren felt the powerful impact of a tremendous force passing into his own body and soon lost all body consciousness. When, after a while, Naren came to himself, the Master was found shedding tears. When interrogated, Sri Ramakrishna softly replied: "Oh Naren, today I have given you my all and have become a *fakir* (beggar). By the force of the power transmitted by me, great things will be done by you; only after that, will you go to whence you came."

Naren also learnt from the Master the supreme lesson that it is more "glorious to help even one man" than to be freed from the cycle of birth and death. In the pre-Ramakrishna Hindu tradition as commonly understood (or rather misunderstood), personal salvation or *mukti* was viewed as the highest attainment, and taking birth in the *sansara* (that which constantly moves), for whatever reason, was considered a symbol of imperfection. Sri Ramakrishna, by his own example, helped revive the social service-oriented Hindu view, which was close to the *Bodhisattva* ideal, viz., putting the salvation of all above one's own salvation. In the closing days of his worldly life, Sri Ramakrishna permitted visitors to seek his guidance on spiritual matters, even though doctors wanted him to take complete rest. Sri Ramakrishna also explained to Naren and to other disciples, the secret of reconciling worldly life with spiritual development, which, in the *Bhagavad Gita*, has been identified as the technique of non-attachment or renunciation of the egoistic feeling of doership. One of the parables which Sri Ramakrishna used to clarify his teaching on this subject was the following:

> As a wet-nurse in a rich family brings up the child of her master, loving the baby as if it were her own, but knows well that she has no claim upon it; so think ye also that you are but trustees and guardians of your children whose real father is the Lord God in Heaven (Majumdar, 1965:18).

Vivekananda Carrying on Sri Ramakrishna's Work

The work done by Vivekananda during the sixteen year period

(1886-1902), after the passing away of the Master, can be broadly divided into four significant stages, as under:

(i) Initial attempts in India from 1886 onward, culminating in the Kanyakumari Resolve of 1892.
(ii) First visit to the West, including speeches at the Parliament of Religions, and subsequent work (1893-1896).
(iii) Founding of the Ramakrishna Mission (1897).
(iv) Strengthening of the organization and worldwide network of activities and relationships (1898-1902), till his departure from this world in 1902.

For purposes of the present argument in this paper I would like to state that the most significant point is that Vivekananda revolutionized the traditional image of *sannyasins* by making social service an integral part of their life. Although a formal shape to his new ideas was given in 1897, all his activities from 1886 onward helped prepare the ground for introducing so radical a change. A first-hand observation of the miseries of the poor in the various parts of the country culminated in what is commonly called "The Kanyakumari Resolve of 1892", and about which Vivekananda himself wrote in a letter from America:

> At Cape Comorin, sitting in Mother Kumari's temple, sitting on the last bit of Indian rock, I hit upon a plan. We are so many *sannyasins* wandering about and teaching the people metaphysics - it is all madness. Did not our Gurudeva use to say, 'An empty stomach is no good for religion?' That these poor people are leading a life of brutes is simply due to ignorance. Suppose some disinterested *sannyasins*, bent on doing good to others, go from village to village, disseminating education and seeking in various ways to better the condition of all down to the *candala* (impoverished, poor), through oral teaching and by means of maps, cameras, globes and such other accessories—can't that bring forth good in time?.... We, as a nation, have lost our individuality, and that is the cause of all mischief in India. We have to give back to the nation its lost individuality and raise the massess.... (Sarma, 1944:265).

THE SOCIAL PROBLEMS OF INDIA

Vivekananda's assessment of the social problems of India was realistic, rather than academic, because he wandered all over the country for years, with a staff and a begging bowl in his hand. This was done prior to his journey to the West. Initially, after the passing away of his Master, he had thought of going on a pilgrimage to the holy places like Varanasi, Ayodhya, Vrindavan, and *ashramas* (hermitage) of *yogis* in the Himalayas. However, after a couple of years spent on such visits, he turned his gaze to the common people for whom the struggle for survival itself was the basic reality. Rolland has emphasized the significance of these travels which provided him with a first-hand knowledge of the poverty, ignorance, disease and misery of the masses:

> He wandered, free from plan, caste, home, constantly alone with God. And there was no single hour of his life when he was not brought into contact with the sorrows, the desires, the abuses, the misery, and the feverishness of living men, rich and poor, in town and field; he became one with their lives; the great Book of Life revealed to him what all the books in the libraries could not have done (for after all they are only collections), which even Ramkrishna's ardent love had only been able to see dimly as in a dream—the tragic face of the present day, the God struggling in humanity, the cry of the peoples of India (1970b:21).

What bothered Vivekananda even more than the poverty itself was the gulf between the rich and the poor, between the strong and the weak, and further, the ugly sight of the strong dealing a death-blow to those who are comparatively weak, without any standard of morality. Is this a country or hell, he asked, a country where millions of people live on the flower of the *mohua* (used in making liquor as well as food) plant, and a million or two of *sadhus* (wandering renouncees), and a hundred million or so of Brahmins suck the blood of these poor people, without even the least effort for their amelioration? This is our native land, he bemoaned, where huts and palaces existed side-by-side.

With such a wide gulf between the rich and poor, asked Vivekananda, how can we have unity and fellow-feeling which are the secrets of national greatness? Born, as it were, a disunited mob, we cannot combine. All these dissensions pained Vivekananda.

Oppression of the masses, according to Vivekananda, was a big factor leading to the downfall of the country. Another equally significant factor was tyranny over women. The way they were kept under conditions of servile dependence on men made them so weak as to be "good only to weep at the slightest approach of a mishap or danger" (Majumdar, 1965:132). Evil customs were particularly injurious to girl-child marriage, big gap in the ages of husbands and wives, ill-treatment of widows, and so on. What pained Vivekananda was that such evil customs were being adhered to in the name of religion. Vivekananda lamented that in contrast to the death-defying message of the Hindu scriptures—fearlessness and strength—the modern Indian society lived in a perpetual sense of fear. Lack of self-confidence and moral strength, according to him, could be partly traced back to physical weakness, which was identified by Vivekananda as "the cause of at least one-third of our miseries":

> In spite of the greatness of the *Upanisads* [religious book], in spite of the boasted ancestry of sages, compared to many other races, I must tell you that we are weak, very weak. First of all is our physical weakness. That physical weakness is the cause of at least one-third of our miseries. We are lazy, we cannot work.... What we want is vigour in the blood, strength in the nerves, iron muscles and nerves of steel, not softening namby-pamby ideas (Majumdar, 1965:115).

Tracing the Roots of the Social Problems

Of the many angles from which the social problems of India such as economic, political, sociological, historical, cultural, religious and spiritual could be analyzed, Vivekananda placed the greatest emphasis on the religious and spiritual problems. He based this on his interpretation of what has been the 'nerve-centre' of India's life from time immemorial. According to him, each nation, like each individual, has one theme in this life, which is its centre, the principal note round which every other note comes to form the harmony. In India, religious life forms the centre, the keynote of the whole music of national life.... Social reform in India has to be preached by showing how much more spiritual a life the new system will bring; and politics has to be preached by showing how much it will improve the one thing that the nation wants—its spirituality (Vivekananda, Vol. III, 1972:220-2).

One of the commonest ways of expressing the state of degradation is by summarizing it in philosophical terminology as *tamas,* which is one of the three *gunas* (traits/characteristics/qualities) of *prakriti* (nature), the other two *gunas* being *rajas* and *sattva. Tamas* denotes ignorance, inertia; *rajas* denotes incomplete knowledge, intense activity; and *sattva* denotes right knowledge, peace. While introducing the "Problems of Modern India" to the readers of the *Udbodhana* (the Bengali journal of the Ramakrishna Order, 14 January, 1899), Vivekananda used the expressions "drowned in utter *tamas*", "under the cloak of austerity", and "taking the plea of *sattva*".

The linkage between religion and social conditions has to be understood as explaining both the positive and the negative aspects, in the sense that, while social progress in the past rested on religious maturity, a deterioration in the social situation at present could be traced back to religious perversion. Vivekananda linked India's doom to ritual-centred priestcraft, orthodoxy, fanaticism, superstitions, and religious intolerance. "Having forgotten the true spirit of religion", said Vivekananda, "the priestly class made fools of common people by pushing them blindly from one ritual to another, from one evil custom to another. Caste distinctions became more and more rigid, and religious orthodoxy took pride in laying down hard and fast rules as to who can marry whom and who can dine with whom. People discussed for years such meaningless questions as whether to take food with the right hand or the left. If such a country does not go to ruin what else will?" asked Vivekananda (Seminar, 1964:109). Religious perversion also appeared in the ugly forms of exclusiveness and touch-me-not-ism. Vivekananda asked the perpetrators of such a tyranny as well as the sufferers to come out of their narrow holes. He made them aware about the futility of discussing for ages what food or which caste is touchable or untouchable. He advised them to kick out the priests who are always against progress (Vivekananda, Vol. V, 1972:10).

While the priestly class demanded blind adherence to evil practices in the name of tradition, a section of the city-dwellers took pride in aping the West and in denouncing India's past. No serious attempt was made to understand the good points in the spiritual tradition of the society. Vivekananda did not spare this westernized class either. They think copying West in daily life is progress. But little do they know that this kind of imitation never makes for progress. It is also wrong to laugh at the ancient sages, ridicule the entire tradition of Hindu thought and view the Hindu religion as the superstition of fools. It is a sign of aweful degradation of man. When a man begins to hate himself and is ashamed of his ancestors, it is the sign of his end.

But how did we create these two degrading extremes----the superstitious priest and the city-dweller imitating the West? Vivekananda identified the root cause as the lack of proper education. By education, he does not mean the amount of information put in the brain that lies there undigested all through the life. Alternatively, what he wanted was life-building, man-making, character-making assimilation of ideas. Vivekananda lamented that this was not possible because we have no hold on the education of the nation, neither secular nor spiritual. In his view, the education imparted was entirely negative. A negative education or any training that is based on negation is worse than death. The first thing the child learns in school is that his father is a fool; secondly, his grandfather is lunatic; thirdly, all teachers are hypocrites; and lastly, all sacred books are lies. He leaves school as a bundle of negation, lifeless and boneless confused mass. This education in fifty years has not produced one original worthy man in the three Presidencies.

While Vivekananda lamented the lack of 'man-making' education in general, he felt even more strongly that the women of India were neglected by denying to them, any kind of education, status and opportunities of development. The evil of sex-discrimination, according to Vivekananda, represented a negation of the *Vedantic* doctrine of the divinity of all human beings----men and women alike. Viewing women as the emblem of Divine Mother, he cried in agony: "The emblem of the Divine Mother has been reduced to a slave to bear children. Why is it that our country is the weakest and the most backward of all countries? Because *Shakti* (women symbolized as strength) is held in dishonour here. There is no chance for the welfare of India unless the condition of women is improved. It is not possible for a bird to fly on one wing only" (Majumdar, 1965:132). In fact, Vivekananda's British disciple, Sister Nivedita, who was an educationist in England, was assigned the important task of opening a girls' school in Calcutta, where 'real' education could be given.

Non-adherence to moral and social values, by large sections of the Indian society, was partly due to a wrong interpretation of the Hindu scriptures, and in particular of the *karma* (deeds) doctrine. Vivekananda had a chance to point this out when in February 1897 an enthusiastic preacher belonging to the society for the protection of cows came to Calcutta for an interview with him. Bengal was at that time in the grip of a famine, and hundreds of thousands of people were falling into the jaws of death. So Vivekananda suggested to the preacher that, since their society had plenty of resources, they could provide food to the starving people. The preacher argued that the starving people cannot be helped as famine itself is a result of their *karma*. To this Vivekananda reacted that if we accept the rationale of *karma*, then it is useless to try or struggle for anything in this world. Cows too are slaughtered by the butchers because of their *karma*. To his claimed that *Shastras* have declared cow as our mother, Swami made a poignant ridicule that "who else could give birth to such accomplished children?" Swami was greatly distressed to see such abuse of *karma* theory of Hinduism (Vivekananda, Vol. VI, 1972:450-2).

PLAN OF ACTION BASED ON PRACTICAL *VEDANTA*

By January 1897 when Vivekananda returned from the West to India, he had made up his mind to initiate a plan of action based on harmonization of spirituality and social service. The underlying views of Vivekananda can, in the terminology of the *Gita*, be also called "the *karmayoga*-based socio-spiritual approach to India's problems". He unfolded his plan of idea and action in a speech in Madras as follows:

> My plan is to follow the ideas of the great ancient Masters. They were the great originators of society.... Circumstances have become a little different, and in consequence the lines of action have to be changed....
>
> The first work that demands our attention is that the most wonderful truths confined in our *Upanisads* must be brought out from the monasteries and be scattered [and] broadcast all over the land...
>
> One word more. This national ship, my countrymen, has been ferrying millions and millions of souls across the waters of life. But today, perhaps through our own fault, this boat has become a little damaged, has sprung a leak. If there are holes in this national ship [viz., society of ours], we [as] its children, let us go and stop the holes. Say not one harsh word against this society. I love it for its past greatness.... I do not dare to put myself in the position of God and dictate to our society, "This way thou shouldst move and not that. Ours is only to work, as the *Gita* says, without looking for results" (Vivekananda, Vol. III, 1972:213-27).

By making special mention of the *Upanisads* and the *Gita*, Vivekananda made it clear that his plan represented the harmonization of *Vedanta* and *karmayoga*, or 'practical *Vedanta*' as he called it. He also called it 'real worship', as he explained in his address at Rameswaram temple: "It is in love that religion exists and not in ceremony, in the pure and sincere love in the heart. External worship is only a symbol of internal worship; but internal worship and purity are the real things.... This is the gist of all worship----to be pure and to do good to others" (Vivekananda, Vol. VII, 1972:163 and Vol. III, 1972:141).

One of the ways in which Vivekananda brought out the distinction between the 'monastery-based *Vedanta*' and 'practical *Vedanta*' was how he identified the root cause of misery. Whereas in the former (i.e., monastery-based *Vedanta*) the root cause of misery is only 'ignorance', Vivekananda (explaining practical *Vedanta*) specified 'ignorance' as well as 'wickedness' as being equally responsible for human bondage and suffering. He emphasized that helping needy with all your power is a good *karma*. Such noble acts purify (*chitta-suddhi*) the hearts. It is this internal purity which manifests the God *Siva* who resides in every heart. He declared ignorance and wickedness as the dirt and dust that are on the mirror of our hearts that must be wiped out (Vivekananda, Vol. III, 1972:142-3).

Vivekananda's intention in putting as much emphasis on wickedness as on ignorance was to say that a true knowledge of *Vedanta* must be reflected in compassionate behaviour. He knew that many of the orthodox scholars who knew *Vedantic* scriptures by heart were as much guilty of unkind treatment towards the low caste, poor countrymen as also other high caste Hindus who were not scholars. Practical *Vedanta*, according to Vivekananda, meant theoretical as well as practical knowledge. Vivekananda points out the futility of glorifying the philosophical and spiritual message of *Vedanta* on one hand and ignoring the humanity which is simply fed on the talks of *Vedanta*. The same ocean of humanity is hated, condemned and held responsible for its own ignorance and starvation. But none tries to convert the theoretical message of *Vedanta* into a practical strategy to help the needy and free them from their hopeless conditions. Swami makes an appeal that a true *Vedantic* should go all out to help the needy sinking millions of India, even if need be at the cost of one's own salvation.

On other occasions, Vivekananda gave the same message (viz., help the poor to the extent of giving up your own salvation) under the title of 'unselfishness'. There is an obvious parallel to the *Bodhisattva* ideal of *Mahayana* Buddhism which refers to "one who treads the path not for his own salvation alone but for the salvation of all" (Prem, 1958:217). As Vivekananda explained his concept of sharing with others. Vivekananda argues that enjoying any goodness all by yourself does not give as much pleasure as by sharing the same with others. By the means of realizing *Advaita* (non-dualism, a branch of *Vedantic* philosophy propounded by Shankaracharya), what you achieve is your own salvation of liberation. The important point is how does your own personal liberation help the rest of the world which also is keenly awaiting liberation. The true greatness lies in liberating the whole universe before finally leaving the body. The bliss so received will be eternal, matchless and infinite. Your presence will be everywhere in the world of soul at matter. The entire sentient and insentient world would become as your own self. This is precisely the practical *Vedanta* (Vivekananda, vol. VII, 1972:163).

Vivekananda characterized 'unselfishness' as the test of religion. According to him, the philosopher, the worker and the devotee all meet at one point, that one point being 'self-abnegation'. Conveying the same idea from another angle, he characterized 'selfishness' as the chief sin. He gave a very simple explanation of selfishness and a selfish man. A selfish man is he who only thinks of himself first. Primacy of self in every respect is selfishness. Such a man is strangely preoccupied with self in the matters of worldly materialistic possessions as well as in getting *mukti* from it. He wants everything first. Whereas a selfless man puts himself last in all matters. Selflessness is the real test of a good religion. Such a man is indeed spiritual and closer to *Siva* whether ignorant or learned (Vivekananda, Vol. III, 1972:143).

Vivekananda uses another terminological variation to convey the same message by coining the famous phrase '*Daridra Narayana*" which means the service of the poor is the service of God. To *Siva*-worshippers he said, "*Jiva* is *Siva*", and explained further that *Siva* is not to be searched in images and temples alone. *Siva* is also to be discovered in the suffering poor, weak, diseased and helpless. One who helps a needy poor man without any distinction of caste, creed or race, pleases the *Siva* more than one who worships Him only in temples.

According to Vivekananda, thinking of the poor man as God minimizes the risk of arrogance that may be run in the process of helping a man. By having faith in God, one gives up the fruits of work unto the Lord, and worshipping Him thus, one does not expect any reward from mankind for the work one does. Expecting no reward for the work done, as taught by the *Gita*, is a relatively easier way of giving up attachment to the fruits of work. Not that the work will not bear fruit; in fact, the law of *karma* says that any action done cannot be destroyed until it has borne its fruit. A *karmayogin* does take into account what effect his actions will have on others, but he does not hanker after deriving selfish gains therefrom.

A favourite idea of Vivekananda was that we do good deeds in the world, apparently to help the world, but really to help ourselves. The main effect of work done for others is to purify ourselves; this forgetfulness of self is the one great lesson we have to learn in life. Every act of charity, every thought of sympathy, every action of help, every good deed, is taking so much of self-importance away from our little selves and making us think of ourselves as the lowest and the least; and therefore it is all good. Here we find that *jnana*, *bhakti*, and *karma*----all come to one point. The highest ideal is eternal and entire self-abnegation, where there is no "I", but all is "Thou", and whether he is conscious or unconscious of it, *karmayoga* leads man to that end (Vivekananda, 1984:83).

Within the range of deeds that can be done to help others, Vivekananda included a wide variety, providing material benefits as well as giving knowledge, both secular and spiritual. He recognized the changing needs of the society with the passage of time. Speaking in terms of the Hindu terminology of the four *yugas* or time-periods, he interpreted Vyasa's words as: "What is needed in this *Kaliyuga* (time-period of sinners, evil-doers) is giving, helping others, the highest of gifts is the giving of spiritual knowledge, the next is the giving of secular knowledge, next to that is the saving of life, and the last is giving food and drink" (Vivekananda, Vol. III, 1972:133). However, leaving aside Vyasa's order of priorities, Vivekananda made a plea on another occasion for "first bread and then religion". What we want is not so much spirituality but bringing down of the *Advaita* into the material world. It is incorrect to stuff them too much with religion, when the poor fellows have been starving (Vivekananda, Vol. III, 1972:432).

To pay attention to both the secular and the spiritual needs of the society is a special feature of practical *Vedanta*. Similarly, it seeks to harmonize science and religion. In a lecture delivered in England, Vivekananda declared that science and religion will meet and shake hands. When the science teacher asserts that all things are the manifestation of one force, it actually reminds us of the God of whom we hear in the *Upanisads*. Vivekananda advised those desirous of helping others to do their utmost but with greatest humility. While helping they should put themselves in place of the receivers of their services. Vivekananda also advises the receivers of help to first try to self-help and have self-confidence. Because it is a tremendous error to feel helpless. One should avoid to seek help from anyone. We are capable of our own help. If we cannot help ourselves, there is none to help us. The *Gita* says: "Thou thyself art thy only friend, thou thyself thy only enemy. There is no other enemy but this self of mine, no other friend but myself" (verse VI 5). This is the last and the greatest lesson.

'Self-confidence' was given so much importance by

Vivekananda that, in practical *Vedanta*, it plays the same role as "faith in God". For achieving success in his plan of action, Vivekananda's main requirement was "men who believe in themselves". In fact, the essence of practical *Vedanta* was viewed by him to be a "man-making religion":

> What we want is muscles of iron and nerves of steel. We have wept long enough. No more weeping, but stand on your feet and be men. It is a man-making religion that we want. It is the man-making theories that we want. It is man-making education all round that we want.

Men, men, these are wanted: everything else will be ready, but strong, vigorous, believing young men, sincere to the backbone, are wanted. A hundred such [men] and the world becomes revolutionized. The will is stronger than anything else. Everything must go down before the will, for that comes from God and God Himself; a pure and strong will is omnipotent (Vivekananda, Vol. III, 1972:223-4).

INSTITUTIONAL COMMITMENT TO SOCIAL SERVICE

A Novelty Achieved After Fraternal Resistance

Hindu tradition speaks of *bhaktas* and saints loving all creatures and helping the needy. But these were generally individual efforts without much organizational support. Also, many of these *bhaktas* felt as if they were being pulled in two directions, one represented by worship of God's image, reading of scriptures, meditation and preaching to devotees, and the other represented by rendering service to the sick, the poor and the neglected. With the worsening economic and social conditions in India, the importance of rendering service was recognized by reform movements like *Brahmo Samaj*, but some of its leaders gave the impression that the inspiration for rendering service came mainly from western influences including Christian missionaries. Therefore, such movements could not arouse mass support all over the country on a long-term basis.

Ramakrishna Mission founded by Vivekananda in 1897 distinguishes itself as a religious organization in modern India which adopted social service as one of its main goals and which drew the inspiration for this mainly from the Indian tradition. In fact, six sources of inspiration have been mentioned, namely, the Master Sri Ramakrishna, other *bhaktas*, wandering monks, the *Upanisads*, the *Bhagavad Gita*, and the Buddha. Although Vivekananda gave a concrete shape to the social service programme of the Ramakrishna Mission, he said he was only carrying out the teaching of his Master, Sri Ramakrishna. The strong emphasis of *karmayoga* in the entire approach of the Ramakrishna Mission is a clear indicator of the impact of the *Bhagavad Gita*. While Vivekananda based the doctrine of *karmayoga* mainly on the *Gita*, he often referred to the Buddha as an 'ideal *karmayogi*'.

Sri Ramakrishna was characterized by Vivekananda as one who saw God in every being, whose heart wept for the poor, for the weak, for the downtrodden. But Sri Ramakrishna did not thrust such ideas on his disciples. When the problem of awakening spirituality in the hearts of the common people was raised with the Master, he had said: "Religion is not for empty bellies" (Rolland, 1970b:286). Sri Ramakrishna had also declared: "The day when Naren comes in contact with suffering and misery, the pride of his character will melt into a mood of infinite compassion" (Rolland, 1970b:10).

In 1886, when Sri Ramakrishna had fallen seriously ill, his intimate disciples (twelve in number) organized themselves under the leadership of Naren to serve the Master with utmost care, love and veneration. This whole-hearted love of God and devotion to the Master and his ideas led to the formation of the brotherhood, which soon after the Master's departure from this world developed into a *Matha* (monastery of the Ramakrishna Order). However, its members were often on move with no coordinated and systematic plan of work and it took Naren several years of wandering throughout India and of sharing the misery and privations of the oppressed classes before he was able to assert in 1892 that, to care for the poor and to raise them is the first duty of every religion. Subsequently, Vivekananda's coining of the phrase *Daridra Narayana* elevated the service of the poor to be equal in importance and value to the service of God. Furthermore, Vivekananda constantly reminded his brother-disciples (who wanted to carry out the teachings of the Master) that the only way to help the poor was through the spirit of *niskama karma* (an act without desire of reward) of the *Gita*:

> Why should we expect anything in return for what we do? Be grateful to the man you help, think of him as God. Is it not a great privilege to be allowed to worship God by helping our fellowmen? If we were really unattached, we should escape all this pain of vain expectation, and could cheerfully do good work in the world (Vivekananda, 1984:72).

Following the successful visit to the West, and after witnessing the keen interest that the people in South India expressed in his plan of action, Vivekananda arrived in Calcutta in February 1897. At that time the central idea in his mind was to put into practice what he had so long preached, by making the monks devote themselves to an active life of service for the masses and thus to make the monastic organization a potent instrument for social and spiritual regeneration. His vision of utilizing the energies of the monks for spreading education among the illiterates, helping them fight against poverty and disease, removing social evils and inequities, and raising them to a higher level of morality, meant an innovation in the monastic practices as commonly understood in those days. It was not surprising, therefore, that there were voices of dissent among his brother-disciples. Nikhilananda explains what lay behind this fraternal resistance to Vivekananda's plan of action:

> The dissenting monks were individualists, eager for their personal salvation. They wanted to practise austerities and penances, enjoy peaceful meditation, and lead a quiet life of detachment from the world. To them God was first, and the world came next. At least

> that was the way they had understood Sri Ramakrishna's teaching. These young monks thought that for one who had taken the monastic vows, the world was *maya* [illusionary attachments]; therefore all activities, including the charitable and philanthropic, ultimately entangled one in worldly life (Nikhilananda, 1975:236).

Vivekananda knew that the narrow vision of the young monks, focusing on an exclusive search for *mukti*, could only be widened by giving clearer instructions and sincere assurances. Therefore, he repeatedly pointed out to his brother-disciples that to worry about personal liberation was unworthy of those who called themselves disciples of Sri Ramakrishna. *Karmayoga* activities carried out with a sense of dedication to the Almighty was as efficacious a means of salvation as meditation and austerities. With so much of misery and ignorance prevailing in the society, the duty of Sri Ramakrishna's disciples, as Vivekananda explained to his colleagues, was to serve the needy as the visible manifestations of God. He also told them that he wanted to create a new brand of monks, who would take not only the traditional vow of personal salvation, but also a new vow of service to humanity.

After a good deal of clarification, Vivekananda's views prevailed, and he proceeded to give institutional shape of his plan of action. He explained his ideas at a representative meeting of the monks and lay devotees held at Calcutta on 1 May, 1897. He was convinced, he said, that lack of organization was a serious defect in the Hindu society. He also cited the example of the Buddhist organization which spread that religion in large areas of the world. He therefore asked for the cooperation of all in order to organize the educational, philanthropic and religious activities which had hitherto been carried out in an unsystematic way. The meeting unanimously approved of Vivekananda's proposal, and in a subsequent meeting on 5 May, 1897, the Ramakrishna Mission with the following aims and methods of action was formally established (Majumdar, 1965:69-70):

1. The aim of the Mission is to preach those truths which Sri Ramakrishna has, for the good of humanity, preached and demonstrated by practical application in his own life, and to help others to put these truths into practice in their lives for their temporal, mental and spiritual advancement.
2. The duty of the Mission is to conduct in the right spirit the activities of the movement inaugurated by Sri Ramakrishna for the establishment of fellowship among the followers of different religions, knowing them all to be so many forms only of one undying eternal religion.
3. The activities of the Mission should be directed to the establishment of *mathas* and *asramas* in different parts of India for the training of *sannyasins* and such of the householders as may be willing to devote their lives to educate others, and to the finding of the means by which they would be enabled to educate the people, by going about from one province to another.
4. Foreign Department will be responsible to send trained members to the countries outside India to bring about a closer relation and better understanding between India and foreign countries.
5. The aims and ideals of the Mission being purely spiritual and humanitarian, it shall have no connection with politics.

These goals are to be attained by the following methods of action:

(a) to train men so as to make them competent to teach such knowledge or sciences as are conducive to the material and spiritual welfare of the masses;
(b) to provide and encourage arts and industries; and
(c) to introduce and spread among the people in general *Vedantic* and other religious ideas in the way in which they were elucidated in the life of Sri Ramakrishna.

Side by side, with the setting up of the Ramakrishna Mission, Vivekananda also wanted to systematize the working of the *Matha*. Although the *Matha* had nominally come into existence in 1886, it had to be shifted from one location to another and its functioning was guided largely by unwritten rules based on an implicit understanding of Vivekananda's wishes. In December 1898, when the *Matha* shifted to Belur on a permanent basis, Vivekananda strengthened its organization by putting down in writing an elaborate set of rules. The *Matha* being a purely monastic institution, the rules provided for disciplined life and spiritual practices, and emphasize the needs of strength of character, self-reliance and faith in the Master. The training to be imparted to the new monks in the *Matha* clearly reflected the wider vision of Vivekananda, as the following two rules show:

> This *Matha* is established to work out one's own liberation, and to train oneself to do good to the world in every way, along the lines laid down by *Bhagavan* Sri Ramakrishna. For the women too there will be started a similar *Matha.*
>
> The root of all misery in India is the wide gulf between the lower and upper classes. Unless this difference is made up, there is no hope of any well-being for the people. Therefore, we must send preachers to all places to give the masses education and religious teaching (Majumdar, 1965:71).

Although all the monks appeared to be satisfied with the way Vivekananda explained to them his new concept of religion, namely, the worship of God through the service of the needy, a lingering doubt was still bothering some of them whether the real formulator of this concept was Vivekananda or Sri Ramakrishna. They had heard Sri Ramakrishna speak time and again against preaching, excessive study of the scriptures, and charitable activities, and exhort aspirants to intensify their love of God through prayer and meditation in solitude. Therefore, they regarded Vivekananda's activities as out of harmony with the Master's teachings.

But things came to a climax one day at Balaram's house in Calcutta, when Jogananda, a brother-disciple whom Sri Ramakrishna had pointed out as belonging to his 'inner circle' of devotees, said that the Master had emphasized *bhakti* alone for spiritual seekers and that philanthropic activities, organizations, homes of service for the public good, and patriotic work were Vivekananda's own peculiar ideas, the result of his western education and travel in Europe and America.

Vivekananda at first replied to it in good humour. But he suddenly flared up. "You think you have understood Sri Ramakrishna better than myself !.... Your *bhakti* is sentimental nonsense which makes one impotent. Hands off ! Who cares for your Ramakrishna? Who cares for your *bhakti* and *mukti*? Who cares what the scriptures say? I will go into a thousand hells cheerfully, if I can rouse my countrymen, immersed in *tamas*, to stand on their own feet and be men inspired with the spirit of *karmayoga*. I am not a follower of Ramakrishna or anyone, I am a follower of him only who carries out my plans ! I am not a follower of Ramakrishna or anyone, but him only who serves and helps others, without caring for his own *bhakti* and *mukti*" (Nikhilananda, 1975:246). This incident of dissent to his plan created a tremendous impact on both the sides. Vivekananda offered convincing explanations to the dissenting brother-disciples and it was over for ever. So profound and convincing was the impression created by this dissenting incident that no protest was afterwards made against Vivekananda's plans and methods of work. The *karmayoga*-based socio-spiritual approach to India's problems formulated by Vivekananda was thus fully adopted by Ramakrishna Mission.

Although the right technique rendering *seva* (service) is given by *karmayoga*, an ultimate answer to the question: "Why should we render *seva* to the poor?" is provided by *jnanayoga* or *bhaktiyoga*. A common argument put forward by *bhaktas* in India is that although a knowledge of the identity of *atman* in all beings does provide an intellectual base for *seva*, this by itself is not enough because *seva* also calls for a feeling of compassion. The *bhaktas*, therefore, feel that the rendering of *seva* with compassion is achieved more easily in the path of devotion, as compared to the path of knowledge. The Indian tradition seems to provide general support to this. Moreover, although monks of the Ramakrishna Mission combined *Advaita Vedanta* with *seva*, they too have an element of *bhakti*. In fact, Vivekananda believed in a harmonious development of *karma, bhakti* and *jnana*, and in his final message to the disciples, he clearly gave priority to *seva* over other aspects of these paths when he said: "Let the reading of the *Vedanta* and the practising of meditation and the like be left to be done in the next life ! Let this body go in the service of others" (Rolland, 1970b:166).

As we mentioned, the Ramakrishna Mission, under Vivekananda's guidance, kept itself aloof from politics. Whatever might have been the reasons underlying this policy, it averted a likely threat of dissolution of the Mission by the British government in 1916. Rolland gives a graphic account of what happened after Vivekananda's death and how the revolutionary political agitators (who tried to use the *Gita* as a proof of their alleged link with the Ramakrishna Mission) placed the Mission on a collision course with the British government. In 1905, the year of the division of the province of Bengal, marked the beginning of the *Swadeshi* movement and political unrest. The (Ramakrishna) Mission refused to take part in them as it was not their main objective. In 1908, it was obliged to make a rule not to receive strangers at night in its establishment as it was found that their hospitality was feared to have been abused for political goals of revolutionaries. It transpired from the answers of political prisoners that more than one, disguised under the robe of a *sannyasin*, had cloaked their designs under the Mission's name, work and religion. Copies of the *Gita* and Vivekananda's writings were found with several of them when arrested. In 1916, the Governor of Bengal announced that the revolutionaries were joining the Ramakrishna Mission in order to achieve their ends. The Mission was spared as its friends in high places intervened and the danger of dissolution of the Mission was averted.

Exemplary Dedication and Widening Coverage of Service Activities

Practical *Vedanta* was the foundation on which the whole structure of the new organization was sought to be built by Vivekananda from May 1897 onwards. Reference has already been made earlier to the opposition of some of the brother-disciples to this new mode of salvation propounded by Vivekananda. He, however, not only stuck to his guns, but even went to the other extreme of denouncing every other form of salvation. His retort to his critics that he would follow this path even if it went against the teachings of Ramakrishna indicates the depth of his convictions, commitment and feeling in the matter. The same spirit of dedication was expressed by him in letters written to his friends. For example, in a letter to Mary Hale in July 1897, he expressed a feeling of satisfaction:

> Only one idea was burning in my brain—to start the Mission for elevating the Indian masses, and that I have succeeded in doing [so] to a certain extent. It would have made your heart glad to see how my boys are working in the midst of famine and disease and misery-nursing by the mat-bed of the cholera-stricken *pariah* [lowly placed, downtrodden] and feeding the starving *candala* [impoverished, poor] and the Lord sends help to me, to them, to all (Majumdar, 1965:111).

However, difficult tests of the organization's capability to fulfil its mission against heavy odds were still to come. In April 1898, when Vivekananda was in Darjeeling to recoup his health, news reached him of the outbreak of plague in Calcutta. On 3 May, 1898, Vivekananda reached Calcutta, although his health was not good. He thought he might be of help to his people. They were terror-stricken by the plague and dismayed by the plague regulations. It was as if a storm were about to burst over Calcutta. People were fleeing in panic. Troops were called to quell riots. Vivekananda grasped the gravity of the situation at once. On the day of his arrival at the *Matha* he drafted a plague manifesto both in Bengali and Hindi. He wanted to start relief operations immediately to help the afflicted. When a brother-monk asked him, "Swamiji, where will the funds come from?", he replied with a sudden fierceness of decision: "Why, we shall sell the newly-bought *Matha* grounds, if necessary ! We are *sannyasins*; we must be ready to sleep under the trees and live on daily *bhiksa* (alms) as we did before. What ! Should we care for *Matha* and possessions when by disposing of them we could relieve thousands suffering before our eyes !" Fortunately, this extreme step was not necessary, for Vivekananda soon received promises of ample funds for his immediate work.

When plague again broke out in 1899, the Ramakrishna Mission undertook relief work under the leadership of Sadananda, assisted by Sister Nivedita and others. About Sister Nivedita's part in the work, we have it on the authority of the historian, Sir Jadunath Sarkar, an eyewitness, "that when the sweepers had fled away, he chanced upon a white woman one day clearing the streets with broom and basket in hand. This was none other than Nivedita, whose courage and sense of civic duty spurred the local youths to take up the cleansing of the lanes and streets, following her example, and make their quarters free from the threat of the pestilence" (Majumdar, 1965:72).

Sadananda himself similarly set an unprecedented example. If the stench of garbage accumulated in a narrow lane repelled even the practised sweepers, he would non-chalantly snatch the basket and spade from one of them and set about removing the decomposed heap till the sweepers too would step forward to help him. At the end, he would congratulate them and embrace them warmly, regardless of their social distance and dirty bodies. Or if there was an uncared-for patient, he would hug him and nurse him to recovery. These incidents bring out in bold relief the ideal of service enunciated by Vivekananda and the exemplary spirit of his close associates, which showed the steadily growing strength of the new organization.

More than ninety years have elapsed since the Ramakrishna Mission faced the initial challenges of rendering service to the needy under the most difficult circumstances. The fact that this institution not only maintained the spirit of dedication but also widened the coverage of service activities is a tribute to Vivekananda and his followers. Although a detailed account of such developments is beyond the scope of this paper, it is of interest to note that the social work activities of the Ramakrishna Mission now cover as many as six broad areas, namely: (i) educational work; (ii) health; (iii) cultural activities; (iv) rural uplift; (v) tribal welfare; and (vi) youth movement.

Indira Patel, after describing the work being done by the Ramakrishna Mission in each field, singles out "the inculcation of the right attitude" as a special feature of the Mission's training which is described as follows:

> One point which should be made clear is that the Mission's centers enlist youths or disciples and train them as social workers, the only difference between the academic training and the training imparted in the *Matha* lies in the initial emphasis on discipline, both mental and physical, with a view to inculcating the right attitude over and above generating a sensitivity, so essential in all social work (1987:92).

Emergence of the Monks as Pillars of the Mission

Renunciation and service, according to Vivekananda, are the two-fold national ideals of modern India. The work of Ramakrishna Mission can be described as: "To practise and preach these ideals." Organizationally, the principal workers of the Mission are monks or *sannyasins*. In a speech to newly initiated monks in Calcutta towards the end of April 1897 (that is, just a couple of days before the establishment of Ramakrishna Mission), Vivekananda spoke of the glory of renunciation: "The real aim of *sannyasa* is "*atmano moksartham jagaddhitaya ca*", that is, to attain one's highest freedom and the good of the world" (Vol. VI, 1972:504). This famous Sanskrit phrase was coined by Vivekananda to summarize the *karmayoga*-based socio-spiritual approach to India's problems. Without having *sannayasa*, none can really be a knower of *Brahman* as proclaimed in the *Vedas* and the *Vedanta*. It is not possible to live the worldly life and also be knowers of *Brahman*. That is the flattering self-consolation in which the seekers of crypto-pleasure flourish. He who has the slightest desire for worldly pleasures, even a shred of some such craving, will feel frightened at the thought of the path you are going to tread; so, to give himself some consolation he goes about preaching that impossible creed of harmonizing *bhoga* (enjoyment) and *tyaga* (renunciation). There cannot be true freedom without renunciation. Highest love for God can never be achieved without renunciation. "*Nanyah panthah vidyate ayanaya*", that is, there is no way other than this. Even the *Gita* says: "*Kamyanam karmanam nyasam samnyasam kavayo viduh*", that is, the sages know *sannyasa* to be the giving up of all work that has desire for its end" (Vivekananda, Vol. VI, 1972:504-5).

In a speech in California in January 1900, on the subject of "My Life and Mission", Vivekananda explained that the Indian concept of *sannyasa* is as old as the *Vedas*. Gradually, a regulation was established that every man and woman towards the end of their lives, must get out of social life altogether and think of nothing except God and their own salvation. This was to get ready for the great event—death. So, old people used to become *sannyasins* in those early days. Vivekananda pointed out how a big change in the functioning of *sannyasa* was brought about by Buddha. He (Buddha) being a young *sannyasin* did not sit and think of death, he went about preaching and helping people.

In the latter part of the same California speech, Vivekananda admitted that monastic systems in modern India have merits as well as defects. What he wanted as a balance between the monastics and the householders. Specially for purposes of preaching, he said, the monks are more suitable because of the long tradition:

> The whole national soul in India is upon monasticism. You go to India and preach any religion as a householder: the Hindu people will turn back and go out. However, if you have given up the world, they say: "He is good, he has given up the world. He is a sincere man, he wants to do what he preaches." What I mean to say is that monasticism represents a tremendous power.... The monk in India is greater than the prince. There is no reigning sovereign in India who dares to sit down when the yellow 'robe' is

there. He gives up his seat and stands. Now, that is bad, so much power, even in the hands of good men—although these monastics have been the bulwark of the people. They are the centres of knowledge and reform. But better methods need to be worked out.... What we can do is just to transform the monastic system, give it another form. This tremendous power in the hands of the *sannyasins* of India has got to be transformed, and it will raise the masses up (Vol. VIII, 1972:89).

Monasticism transformed to serve the Indian masses—this is how Vivekananda conceived of the Ramakrishna Mission. It is only because the monastic institution exists in the country, said Vivekananda, that great men like Sri Ramakrishna are born here. He raised a question: "Why is it that in spite of its faults, this noble institution stands yet supreme over all the other institutions of life?" And he also provided an answer: "It is because the true *sannyasins* forgo even their own liberation and live simply for doing good to the world." Emphasizing this to the newly initiated *sannyasins* at Calcutta, Vivekananda concluded his address:

> For the good of the many, for the happiness of the many is the *sannyasin* born. His life is all vain, indeed, who, embracing *sannyasa*, forgets this ideal. The *sannyasin*, verily, is born into this world to lay down his life for others, to stop the bitter cries of men, to wipe the tears of the widow, to bring peace to the soul of the bereaved mother, to equip the ignorant masses for the struggle for existence, to accomplish the secular and spiritual well-being of all through the diffusion of spiritual teachings and to arouse the sleeping lion of *Brahman* in all by throwing in the light of knowledge.... So achieve the consummation of human life before you pass off. *Arise, awake, and stop not till the goal is reached* (Vol. VI, 1972:511-12) [emphasis added by the editor].

ROLE OF *BHAGAVAD GITA*

The *Bhagavad Gita* had a very significant role in the life and work of Vivekananda. Although he did not write a verse-by-verse commentary covering the *Gita* as a whole, he quoted and explained selected verses from it. In fact, in his short opening address at the Parliament of Religions in Chicago in September 1893, he quoted a verse from the fourth chapter of the *Gita*. Majumdar highlights the special relevance of what Vivekananda quoted from the *Gita* to the broad objective of the Parliament of Religions itself. Vivekananda regarded the Parliament as a vindication, a declaration to the world, of the wonderful doctrine preached in the *Gita*, and quoted the following verse: "Whosoever comes to Me, through whatsoever form, I reach him; all men are struggling through paths which in the end lead to Me" (1965:41).

The most significant elements from the teachings of the *Gita*, which Vivekananda explained to his followers, listeners and readers, and himself utilized in his work, are contained in the 1896 publication entitled *Karmayoga* which has proved to be the most popular written work of his (1984). Various aspects of *karma*, including "The secret of work", "What is duty?", "We help ourselves, not the world", and so on, are discussed by Vivekananda, not only from a theoretical angle but also in relation to life in modern times. One of the main messages which he wants to convey is the supreme importance of being "ready to sacrifice himself for others", "expecting no personal gain in return":

> However much the various systems of philosophy and religion may differ, all mankind stands in reverence and awe before the man who is ready to sacrifice himself for others... When you give something to a man and expect nothing—do not even expect the man to be grateful—his ingratitude will not tell upon you, because you never expected anything, never thought you had any right to anything in the way of a return (Vol. I, 1972:86-90).

Vivekananda spoke about Sri Krishna and the *Gita* again in the course of four lectures delivered in April-May 1900. He described Sri Krishna as "the most rounded man" he knew of, wonderfully developed equally in brain and heart and hand (Vol. I, 1972:457). Every moment of Sri Krishna, said Vivekananda, was alive with activity, either as a gentleman, as a scholar, as a poet. This all-rounded and wonderful activity and combination of brain and heart, Vivekananda saw in the *Gita*—"and nothing can approach it anywhere", as he declared emphatically.

Vivekananda recognized Sri Krishna as "the first man, way before Buddha, to open the door of religion to every caste". Thereafter, Vivekananda compared these two great personalities: "Buddha's activity was on one plane, the plane of teaching. He could not keep his wife and child and become a teacher at the same time. Krishna preached in the midst of the battlefield.... It means nothing to this man---the flying of missiles about him. Calm and sedate he goes on discussing the problems of life and death. He practised what he preached in the *Gita*: He who in the midst of intense activity finds himself in the greatest calmness, and in the greatest peace finds intense activity, that is the greatest *yogi* as well as the wisest man" (Vol. I, 1972:457).

The *Gita* verses which Vivekananda explained in the course of the above mentioned lectures occur mostly in the first six chapters. The ideas that he emphasized were essentially the main elements of *karmayoga*, but in some cases he introduced additional details. For example, he said, with reference to the opening statement of Sri Krishna in the second chapter: "The *Gita* opens with this very significant verse: Arise, O Prince, give up this faint-heartedness, this weakness. Stand up and fight.... Not one step back, that is the idea.... Fight it out, whatever comes. Let the stars move from the sphere. Let the whole world stand against us.... Arise, awake, stand up and fight. Die if you must...." (Vol. I, 1972:459-61).

Analyzing the initial arguments of Arjuna in the *Gita*, Vivekananda sensed in them an attempt "to cover this weakness with the flowery names of love and higher moral ideas". This is a common human weakness, said Vivekananda:

> Many a time comes when we want to interpret our weakness and cowardice as forgiveness and renunciation. There is no merit in the renunciation of a beggar. If a person who can give a blow forbears, there is merit in that. If a person who has, gives up, there is

merit in that. We know how often in our lives through laziness and cowardice we give up the battle and try to hypnotize our minds into the belief that we are brave.... Appropriately, the *Gita* opens with a strong call to Arjuna to give up faint-heartedness, to give up weakness (Vol. I, 1972:459-60).

Another section of the *Gita* highlighted by Vivekananda was the one containing the *Lokasamgraha*-verses of the third chapter (III, 20-26). He translated *Lokasamgraha* as "working for the good of others", and citing the example of Sri Krishna Himself, Vivekananda asked men of knowledge to help the ignorant and gradually bring them up:

> Even if you have known the secret that you have no duty, that you are free, says Sri Krishna, still you have to work for the good of others. Because whatever a great man does, ordinary people will do also. If a great man who has attained peace of mind and freedom, ceases to work, then all the rest without that knowledge and peace will try to imitate him and then confusion would arise. Behold, Arjuna, says Sri Krishna, there is nothing that I do not possess and nothing that I want to acquire. And yet I continue to work. If I stopped work for a moment, the whole universe would be destroyed. That which the ignorant do with desire for results and gain, let the wise do without any attachment and without any desire for results and gain (Vol. I, 1972:467-8).

Vivekananda characterized this as "a very powerful idea which has become the ideal in India" (Vol. I, 1972:468). Undoubtedly, one of the powerful forces that had inspired him when he started the Ramakrishna Mission in 1897. It is sufficiently highlighted in this paper that Vivekananda formulated a socio-spiritual approach to India's problems based on a harmonious synthesis of *karmayoga* and *Vedanta*. He called it 'practical *Vedanta*'. Thus, although the immediate source of inspiration for the founding of the Ramakrishna Mission was the life and teachings of Sri Ramkrishna, the ultimate sources, belonging to the long Indian tradition, also included the *Upanishads*, the *Gita*, the Buddha and the wandering monks, for whom rendering selfless service to the needy was a spontaneous act.

REFERENCES

Bellah, Robert N. (1965), "Epilogue" in Robert N. Bellah (ed.), *Religion and Progress in Modern Asia*. New York: Free Press.

Majumdar, R.C. (1965), *Swami Vivekananda: A Historical Review*. Calcutta: General Printers.

Patel, Indira (1987), *Vivekananda's Approach to Social Work*. Madras: Sri Ramakrishna Math.

Prem, Sri Krishna (1958), *The Yoga of the Bhagawad Gita*. Baltimore: Penguin Books.

Rolland, Romain (1970a), *The Life of Ramakrishna*. Calcutta: Advaita Ashram.

---- (1970b), *The Life of Vivekananda and the Universal Gospel*. Calcutta: Advaita Ashram.

Sarma, D.S. (1944), *The Renaissance of Hinduism*. Banaras: Banaras Hindu University.

Seminar on (1964), *Swami Vivekananda's Teaching*. Coimbatore: Sri Ramakrishna Vidyalaya.

Swami, Nikhilananda (1975), *Vivekananda: A Biography*. Mayavati: Advaita Ashram.

Swami, Vivekananda (1972), *Complete Works* (Eight Volumes). Calcutta: Advaita Ashram.

Swami Vivekananda (1984), *Karmayoga*. Calcutta: Advaita Ashram.

PART II
NGO Sector and Disciplinary Concerns

6

The NGO Sector in India: Historical Context and Current Discourse

by D.L. Sheth and Harsh Sethi

The last two decades have witnessed a veritable mushrooming of NGOs in India. What, however, is inadequately appreciated is that the conversion of voluntarism into primarily a favoured instrumentality for developmental intervention has changed what was once an organic part of civil society into merely a sector---an appendage of the developmental apparatus of the state. Further, this process of instrumental appropriation has resulted in these agencies of self-activity losing both their autonomy and political-transformative edge. What is required, therefore, is to reorientate voluntarism from a framework of subserving the needs of delivery to one promoting self-governance in the widest sense.

The relative inability of both the official planning system and the market economy to create a significant dent in India's poverty and inequality indices has given rise over the years to deep skepticism about the ability of the institutional structure of democracy---legislatures, parties, unions, *panchayats*---to politically process the problems and needs of the poor into a structure of effective policies.

It is in this context of a search for an alternative, efficacious instrument to foster developmental change that we need to locate the increasing interest in what have been described as non-governmental organizations (NGOs). Though the label 'NGO' does not fully reflect all the phenomena of citizens' participation, involvement and political innovation, we shall for the moment continue to employ the term, with the proviso that our reference is to the much wider area of social action.

Notwithstanding the phenomenal growth of the NGO sector in recent years, it has received surprisingly scanty attention from academic researchers and social analysts. Within social science literature, the phenomenon continues to be approached from the narrow standpoint of respective disciplines, ignoring its overall structural location and transformative potential; more important, however, is that the phenomenon itself has changed, expanded and diversified considerably in the last decade: not only may the label NGO be problematic today but the very conceptual apparatus developed by these disciplines is inadequate for grasping the radically changed reality.

In India, the term 'NGO' itself is of fairly recent coinage. Earlier, the common term was voluntary organizations or agencies, referring essentially to organizations registered under the Societies Registration Act of 1860 and equivalent legislation. The literature now abounds with diverse terminology, often used interchangeably.

The purpose of this essay is first to sketch the historical context of NGO development in India. We will then focus on different thematic clusters of the present social science and political discourse, both to draw out emerging issues and to work towards a future research agenda.

THE HISTORICAL CONTEXT

Pre-Independence Phase

While entities called NGOs may appear to be a new phenomenon in India, several of their roles, activities and functions were performed in the past by a variety of local organizations. History bears a continuous testimony to non-state efforts and initiatives towards building structures of socio-economic security by the people for themselves. The state did not constitute a frame of reference for these activities; the traditional mode of organizing self-help and philanthropy was essentially societal and not statist in nature. It is only with the growing centrality of the modern state that terms such as 'voluntary' and 'non-governmental' sectors came into prominence to describe those few welfare and developmental activities which originate outside the state structure and within society.

A clearly identifiable shift in this mode of organizing societal activities occurred during the colonial encounter. On the one hand, the para-state organizations, mainly of the Christian churches, started intervening in the social and religious life of the indigenous population through education, health, social welfare and reform. These activities often received the protection and patronage of the colonial state.

On the other hand, as part of anti-colonial resistance, the nineteenth and the early twentieth century saw the emergence of numerous indigenous organizations devoted to social and religious reform. As part of this process, several castes adopted the new function of dispensing welfare to their members. They set up associations for the specific purpose of catering to the educational, health and other welfare needs of their members.

It was with a view to regulating and monitoring activities of such new organizations, that the colonial Indian state enacted the Registration of Societies Act, 1860 initially for the Bombay Presidency. Self-help and philanthropy in India originated with the emergence of voluntary organizations during the colonial period. As they were linked with social reform activities, which in turn were associated with movements of anti-colonial resistance, they also acquired a political dimensions: the colonial state became a frame of reference for defining their scope of activities and their legal identity. The idea of voluntary work began to be understood as non-state or non-governmental activities. Major religious and social reform movements directed their activities to make demands on the state for enacting new social legislation for implementing reforms they sought to propagate.

Raja Ram Mohan Roy (1772-1833) and his *Brahmo Samaj*

opposed child marriage, the *sati* system and propagated widow marriage. Ishwar Chandra Vidyasagar (1820-1891) started a campaign in favour of widow marriage and education of girls. K. C. Sen (1838-1884) advocated inter-caste marriage, widow marriage and the removal of the purdah system. Swami Dayanand Saraswati, founder of the *Arya Samaj*, opposed child marriage, idol worship and caste discrimination. Mahatma Phule (1827-1888) fought for the removal of untouchability and for the welfare of the depressed classes, known today as the Scheduled Castes. Maharishi Karve (1858-1962) devoted his entire life to the education and rehabilitation of widows. These religious and social reform movements transformed the old parallelism between the state and society into a direct interaction between the two.

The second major shift in the nineteenth century paradigm of organizing voluntary work occurred at the turn of the century when Gandhiji entered the Indian political scene. Gandhiji sought to recapture the constructive spirit within society which drew upon the innate resources of the people. Rather than treating the indigenous population as raw material of reform, which in essence meant at best westernization and at worst collaborating with the colonial regime, the Gandhian movement focused on reorganizing people's own resources for goals of material and spiritual well-being which they were enabled to set for themselves. Over a period of time, a network of organizations was formed as part of this movement, covering such diverse field as *khadi* and village industries, education, health, agriculture, dairying and animal husbandry, often in opposition to state policies. Several organizations for women, Harijans and tribals and generally for the rural poor came into existence, their activities informed by an approach which did not separate politics from social work or issues of material well-being from spiritual concerns of human beings. In the process it drew the hitherto excluded sections of society into the national movement for Independence, but more particularly into the growing voluntary sector which was now described in terms of social service and constructive work.

It was during this phase that social action acquired a pronounced political content and politics a firm base in society. This fusion of social action and politics resulted in viewing the colonial state not so much as facilitator, but as a road-block to the process of social transformation. It emphasized social and cultural regeneration of the entire society in place of the late--nineteenth century accent on issue-based reform activities. Instead of making demands on the state for extending its protection and patronage to voluntary or social reform action, it emphasized people's own empowerment through constructive work.

The third trend emerged from the new realities created by the growing hegemony of the Congress party during the Independence movement. Its roots lie not in the world of social action but in politics, which then spilled over into the world of social action. Beginning with the ideological splits in the Independence movement, this trend got consolidated in the early decades after Independence. It owes its origin to the mobilization and organization activities of the Communist and Socialist parties. Several groups of activists working either in their front organizations, or later independently, began to take up issues ignored by the groups belonging to 'social reform'; or 'the Gandhian' genre. For them the central issue was the conflict of interests and the resulting exploitation of the poor. Social and economic justice, rights of the people, land reforms, tenancy rights, minimum wages for landless labour, removal of bondage and slavery, tribal rights over forest produce and rights of slum dwellers and destitutes became the agenda for these groups. As they proceeded to work on these issues, their distance from the parent political parties increased, since many of these were not considered important political issues by the parties wedded to an electoral calculus.

The Current Phase

The early years of Independence, almost until the end of the

1960s, saw a decline of the once vibrant sector of Gandhian organizations. While the more religiously inclined bodies (both Christian and non-Christian) continued their activities, periodically winning plaudits for their educational and health activities and relief of famine and distress, the Gandhian sector lagged in this regard. Many of its leading figures moved to the more lucrative sector of Congress party politics and governance. Their organizations moved closer and closer to the State, and their reliance on government funds increased, such that gradually little difference could be seen between their work and the government programmes of social welfare. With the government launching ambitious programmes of Community Development and *Panchayati Raj*, most organizations became involved in implementing official programmes, and began at best to be seen as local, more community-based agencies to ensure people's involvement in planned development.

The institutional framework of representative democracy mainly the *panchayats* and the development blocks paralleled these developments. Studies of these experiments tended to be laudatory and hagiographic with respect to either the personalities involved or American-style ideology of private initiative of helping to maintain the autonomy of individuals and of communities from the government. Nevertheless, the government assistance and collaboration constituted the very basis of such an idea of autonomy.

Between the late 1960s and the early 1980s, a spate of famines, inflation, devaluation, unemployment, the breakdown of the hegemony of the Congress party, and the rise of militant movements----all created not only political and social instability but also impelled fresh thinking and action on the twin grids of development and politics. From the Maoist upsurge in the late 1960s to the clamping down of the Emergency (1975-1977)---the period was one of intense disillusionment with the conventional institutions of planning, politics and development. It was at the same time a period of excitement over new issues and movements coming to the fore. Thousands of young people, outside the framework of formal party politics and the government, initiated groups and activities relating to the rural and urban poor. To the earlier concerns of poverty, inequality and removal of social injustice were now added issues of gender, environment, human rights and peace. Struggles and movements for organizing the poor, conscientization and people's empowerment became key words for social activists. Politics once again became central to social activism.

Expectedly, the commentaries and the debates of this period began to acquire political overtones, quite different from the more staid period of the 1950s and 1960s. The focus on empowerment necessitated a different framework of description and analysis. The language of governance and of welfare began to be replaced by the language of rights and struggles. The non-governmental sector now began to be assessed in terms of its efficacy in promoting new issues, helping organize the poor and contributing towards a new framework of rights and entitlements.

Even as this new spurt of activities and writings began to make its impact, most academic research still remained confined to the study of community development and *Panchayati Raj* oriented organizations: the youth clubs, the *Mahila Mandals*, to name a few. The conventional developmental concern for "harnessing the energies of the young," through programmes like the National Service Scheme and the Nehru Yuvak Kendras continued to exercise its grip over the academic imagination.

Beginning with the *Janata* rule (1977-1979), the discourse on non-governmental efforts and organizations has undergone a change. At one end of the spectrum is a tendency that identifies itself with both the national movement phase and the struggles of the 1970s, culminating in the anti-Emergency struggles. Intensely political, it is articulated around issues and organization of the oppressed. Whether under the broader rubric of human rights, gender, ecology and identity or around more defined issues like child labour, minimum wages, bondage and slavery, displacement of populations by big development projects, occupational health hazards, banning of harmful drugs and processes, bride burning, and so on—this concern is reflected in both the radicalized middle class and subaltern organizations. At the other end of the spectrum is a tendency which reflects a revised formulation of the 1950s and 1960s, namely, one of viewing non-governmental organizations as links between government and people in the process of planning and development. It emphasizes instrumental efficacy and professionalization of NGOs. The focus here is on cost-efficiency, greater ability to involve people in development projects, innovation in programme and planning processes, and strengthening delivery systems. Alongside is a relatively recent tendency of middle class professional-support organizations involved in serving other organizations, rather than direct communities—through documentation, research, training (both management and skills), networking and publications. Their preferred activities include public interest litigation and media exposure concerning issues being fought by smaller organizations on the ground. This new sector of agencies is fairly independent from the traditional governmental, business, political and religious influences.

The multiple and conflicting tendencies of that period, the inter-meshing of different activities and concepts, has led to a proliferation of partisan writings; not reasoned argument but polemical tracts. More importantly, as we shall trace later, it has led to serious differences in the overall appreciation of the meaning and significance of NGOs and their work.

NGOs IN INDIA: A LITERATURE REVIEW

For the purpose of this survey, keeping in mind the definitional complexities, we have clustered the available literature under the following categories: morphological studies; intra-organizational studies; efficacy studies; relationship studies of organizations—with the government, with political parties, with donor agencies, with client/base groups; and assessment/impact studies.

Morphological Studies

Information on such aspects of NGOs as numbers of organizations, their classification by function and activity, size, location and spatial spread of work, funding, number of personnel, and profiles of members is at best available partially. To get a comprehensive listing of even the registered organizations, one would need to look at the records of the government agencies set up for this task. And even here, one would get no idea of the numbers that have become moribund, have shifted in activity-mix or location and so on. The few directories available, other than being very partial and outdated in their coverage, only give data about names of the key persons, dates of registration, activity-mix, areas of operation and number of employees. Rarely is even a brief profile/assessment of the organization and programmes added. Probably the most comprehensive listing available today is with the Ministry of Home Affairs, charged with implementing the Foreign Contribution Regulation Act. Their data, unfortunately locked into their computers, refer to about 14,000 organizations, obviously only those that have a foreign-funding linkage.

With even these basic data unavailable, questions such as who joins these organizations, for how long they stay, working conditions, further breakdown of these numbers by activity, ideology and size are difficult, if not impossible, to answer. Nevertheless, we have a few attempts at an overview of these phenomena (Verghese, 1977; Kothari, 1984a; Sheth, 1984; Sethi, 1984, 1986; Dhanagare, 1988). The studies suggest that while a majority of the organizations are still involved with welfare, relief, charity and developmental activities (health, education, appropriate technology, local level planning and so on), from the mid-1970s onwards there has been a significant increase both in issue-based groups (both sectoral like women, law, ecology, and single issue such as bonded labour, child labour and so on) and in groups involved primarily in helping the poor organize to fight for their legal rights. More recently, there has been a proliferation, if not in numbers then definitely in media coverage, of groups involved in activities supportive of other locally-rooted NGOs, through activities like documentation, use of audio-visual aids, training including management training, theatre, printing journals, advocacy and the like.

The studies also suggest a change in the profile of those who join NGOs. Unlike during the earlier phases when those involved in relief, charity and welfare activities were mostly retired persons, now more younger people (both men and women) look towards the NGOs as career option. The setting up of agencies like Foundation to Aid Industrial Recovery (FAIR) and PRADAN, or of the Institute of Rural Management at Anand, is indicative of the heightened interest of middle class professionals in NGOs. Equally significant is the banding together of young people locally under an NGO banner to attract funds for local/community advancement (Bhatt, 1988).

Macro data on funding too are difficult to obtain. For instance, while there are rough estimates of the extent to which the government supports NGOs (between Rs. 250 and Rs. 300 crores over the Seventh Five Year Plan period, with talk of scaling this up to Rs. 100-150 crores/year in the Eighth Plan), and of the extent of foreign-funding (averaging Rs. 250-300 crores/year during the 1980s), we have no estimates of indigenous, private philanthropy (in spite of the setting up of a Centre for Corporate Philanthropy in 1986), or the extent of support offered to NGOs from beneficiary groups or sympathizers. Even less do we have an indication, particularly with respect to foreign-funding, as to the regions, activities and groups towards which this funding is directed.

There is an urgent need for further studies which map out this area, otherwise not just our understanding but also policies will continue to be formulated on inferences based on policy statements of funding agencies and political parties.

Intra-Organizational Studies

Closely pertaining to the broader morphological concerns, are issues pertaining to the internal structure and functioning of NGOs. There is a common stereotype held by many observers and policy planners that an NGO is small, convivial, participative and innovative, demonstrates a high leadership quality, is cost-conscious and austere, locally-rooted and responsive, and thus a worthwhile instrument for welfare, developmental and mobilization organization programmes.

Some of these commonly held assumptions can easily be challenged. It is obvious that organizations involved with different types of activities are likely to be very different. A local development or action group, a group involved in a specialized activity either in the local area or as a support group, a network or umbrella organization, attract different types of volunteer activists and display different salary and working conditions, leadership styles and levels of organizational democracy.

Though one periodically encounters very large groups sometimes employing nearly 1,000 people and with annual budgets of Rs.3-5 crores, the typical NGO still remains small, financially insecure, with the salary and working conditions often more severe than in comparable academic, business or governmental jobs. Partly this is due to a strong sense of idealism still surviving among several non-funded groups and the influence of the older Gandhian or religious base organizations which lay a great emphasize on austerity. The more modern corporate NGOs are but a recent phenomenon, and with many of them operating in an insecure financial market, their viability lies in being able to work with lower salaries and perks.

Case studies provide a much better basis for understanding these questions, though it must be admitted that the few that have been published are quite dated. Shah and Chaturvedi's study (1983) of the VIAS group, on behalf of a funding agency NOVIB, points out that even for a large and complex organization salaries are low and lifestyle austere. Decision-making, though concentrated in the small groups of founders, is essentially informal and involves all *karyakartas* (workers/members). Recruitment is not based on formal qualifications, in fact emphasis is given to experience. Other such evaluative studies of SWRC Tilonia (Sethi *et.al.*, 1989), UNNAYAN (Sethi *et.al.*, 1988) and Kishore Bharti (Sethi, 1977) bear out the emphasis NGOs place on evolving participative structures (both formal and informal) of decision-making, and low inequalities in salary.

An earlier study by George and Srivastava (1977) of the Bhartiya Agro Industries Foundation, a pioneer in cattle breeding and dairying programmes, reflects a different picture. It does appear that as the pendulum of activities swings more towards formal skills, the number of middle class professionals increase, the salaries and working conditions become better and the hierarchy more formal.

Bhatt's study (1988) of small action groups in the tribal belt of Gujarat presents a radically different picture, with most groups composed totally of local people who work on a purely voluntary basis. Debates about life-style and decision-making continue to dog the sector, caught as it is between the conflicting demands of being converted into a formal sector with increasing need for professional and managerial skills and older, deeply internalized values of austerity and service (Sundar, 1986).

The growing number of training institutes and programmes indicates that most NGOs suffer from a lack of desired skills. While many of the groups are adept at local communication and organizational tasks, their familiarity with modern technologies and techniques is low. This absence becomes more marked in the new environment of greater formality and funding intensity, where the demands now being placed on the NGO sector are different.

More important are questions related to internal democracy, participation in decision-making—and the degree of institutionalization that NGOs display. While recognizing that the operational style of many of the organizations is indeed informal and collective/participative, a degree of substitutionism continues to exist between the leaders and activists and between the activists and the people (Sethi, 1984). Many of the organizations, including the more modern and professional ones, revolve round the founding, often charismatic, personalities. Rarely are they able to transcend them, either in developing a second tier leadership or in producing new leaders after the original set had departed. This high degree of transience has serious implications, not just for institutionalization (Gupta, 1986), but also for formulating long-term programmes.

Efficacy Studies

We now turn to studies which attempt to examine the popular perception of NGOs as effective development and political instruments. The issues addressed here include NGO efficiency, cost-effectiveness, ensuring better participation of client communities, flexibilities and an innovativeness to conform to, adapt and partly mould the changing environment.

While most studies available refer to a single agency, there are a few efforts which examine a spectrum of agencies to draw more general conclusions. A recent review of NGOs supported by the Ford Foundation in the areas of rural resources and poverty, social justice and human rights and women points out that "the different reviews validate the popular perception of NGOs playing a useful intermediary role between the state and the community. This is as true of the social action as of the development groups" (Sundar, 1986).

The review also confirms the flexibility, creativity, innovativeness and commitment of the NGOs while simultaneously highlighting their weaknesses and limitations. The latter stem essentially from their small size, fragmentation and powerlessness, in short a fundamental incapacity to act institutionally over a long time (Sethi, 1984, 1986). Gupta (1986) also confirms this failing, highlighting the "PVO lack of understanding of the process of institution-building or rather the dynamics of the process of growth of an organization". He further argues that while this lack of institutional sense may not harm NGOs involved with routine maintenance functions, it can cripple organizations concerned with change on structural situations.

Similarly, Oakley and Dillon (1985), in a major study of NGOs in India, Bangladesh, Brazil and Ghana, point out that while the NGOs were relatively successful in fostering participation of client groups, their ability to institutionalize these processes was weak. This weakness seems most marked in groups engaged in income generation activities. Collective spirit, it appears, gets progressively eroded as the activity starts generating profits.

Subramanium (1982), in a critical review, points out that the success of individual voluntary agencies can be traced to: (a) the halo: a great cause favoured by the founders that binds the voluntary agency's personnel; (b) the hero: charismatic leadership of a social entrepreneur; and (c) funds: disproportionate inputs of resources due to easy access to donors. He argues that since these conditions are not easily replicable, the voluntary agencies' innovations remain 'backyard glories' with little hope of being extended to other parts of the country. The gap between the project and the programme often remains unbridgeable.

While it seems generally true that projects which are successful are so because of a fairly unique constellation of circumstances, that their cost effectiveness is often due to inputs by volunteers who put in long hours on low wages/salaries, that comparing them to large government programmes is methodologically fallacious, there are nevertheless many small lessons from these experiences which can contribute to improvement in larger programmes. The entire strategy of relying on locally trained *dais* (mid wives) in rural medicare programmes was evolved from the experience of Dr. Arole and his team in Jamkhed (Coombe, 1980), the lesson being that instead of trying to scale up successful project, the strategy should be incorporating replicable lessons in larger programmes.

More than as instrumentalities to implement larger, mainly official programmes, NGOs have been far more successful in raising issues (dowry death, rape), in resisting harmful legislations (the proposed forest policy legislation of 1983), in activating the public interest litigation system, in highlighting atrocities, and in working with deprived strata and communities. To put it more sharply, greater success is achieved in non-core economic areas and in regions and with strata least enmeshed in the modern capitalist process. Thus, *Chipko* (Bandopadhyaya and Shiva, 1987) and similar efforts, resisting ecologically degrading policies and programmes have enjoyed greater success than efforts after the Bhopal disaster to curb polluting and dangerous industry; rural medicare efforts such as those initiated by Arole, seem to fare better than those aimed at reforming modern urban hospitals.

Does this then imply that the essential role of NGOs is to help transform society from a pre-capitalist state to a capitalist one, notwithstanding their self-perception as struggling for a socialist transformation? Omvedt (1980) explores this question as does Tornquist (1984). While we will touch upon these themes in a later section, such writings, though based more on exploring theoretical/ideological presuppositions, indicate potential areas of success for NGO action.

At the end, we still remain unclear as to the reasons behind the current excitement with NGOs. In the absence of detailed empirical research, it is difficult to substantiate whether the 'favoured' status of the NGOs in the development and political discourse is due more to disappointments with the traditional organizations (bureaucracy, parties) which were expected to usher in social change or whether the NGO sector is inherently endowed with the needed qualities. While we have many examples of successful, even innovative and exciting work by NGOs in many sectors, their ability to either go to scale or to successfully transplant their lessons and experiences into larger organizations or programmes remains in doubt. For this we now turn to the relationships that NGOs have managed to establish with other organizations.

Relationship Studies

The most important relationship for the NGO sector is with

the government. Since both the government and the NGOs represent a diverse and confused universe, there is no fixity to their relationship—which is marked both by admiration as also suspicion and hostility. As we have tried to indicate in the background sections, this conflicting relationship has itself gone through different phases, occasioned both by shift in the environment and in official policy and perception. It is not just the government but also the NGOs who react to any move that they perceive to be detrimental to their own interest.

In a fascinating debate around proposals to set up a National Council of Rural Voluntary Agencies (NCRVA), each of these different tendencies came to the surface. The Adviser, NGOs in the Planning Commission, purportedly the prime mover behind this effort, argued strongly for both a code of conduct for NGOs and the establishment of a national council akin to the Press Council of India or the Bar Council of India. He was strongly attacked and blamed for wanting to officialize the sector. His spirited reply (Roy, 1986) and the further responses (Baxi, 1986) raise serious issues, both for the sector and for independent scholars, particularly of discipline, accountability and legitimacy. Though the government often complains that NGOs neither meet their targets nor submit accounts, the current trend is for this relationship to widen and deepen. Even the latest programme of National Technology Missions envisions NGOs taking a lead role in the adult education, immunization and drinking water programmes.

The NGOs, while obviously relishing their newly instituted status and importance, including the increased availability of funding, are still very critical of the operationalization of this relationship. Procedures for securing government grants are extremely trying, and the levels of corruption and kickbacks disturbing. What equally galls the NGOs are efforts at external monitoring and evaluation, seen essentially as incursions into their autonomy. The limitations of the current contributions stem essentially from an assumption of two well-defined sectors---government and its antonym, non-government, as also a focusing on instrumental concerns. More studies are needed to trace this relationship over time and focus more on the shifting implications of collaboration and contention.

Most NGOs are in the domains of relief, welfare, charity and development. The general assumption is that, unlike political parties or groups, NGOs are local rather than national and concerned more with reform in civil society rather than its transformation through the capture and subsequent deployment of state power. The relationship between NGOs and politics seems functionally limited to either providing space for retired and non-active politicians or at best preparing a social consciousness base for political parties to make use of as they see best. Some would grant them the role of non-political articulators of interest groups.

However, from the *Sarvodaya* and constructive work organizations in the nationalist phase to social action groups attempting to conscientize, mobilize and organize the poor, both in a framework of struggling for juridical rights—even expanding the notion of rights—the political tendency among NGOs has operated differently: it assumed that power interpenetrates and breaks out of the confines of power concentrated exclusively in the institutions of the state. Jayprakash Narain's notion of *Lok Satta* (people's power) as distinguished from *Raj Satta* (state power), the notions of countervailing power and non-party political process (Kothari, 1984b) are all attempts to capture this tendency.

Political parties seem sensitive to the political possibilities encoded in the voluntary sector. Be it the sharp reaction from the left parties (Karat, 1984) of accusing social action groups, particularly those with a foreign-funding linkage, of operating on "behest of their imperialist masters to undermine the influence of the revolutionary forces", or more favourable statements by other parties which incorporate issues raised by NGOs into their political manifestoes, it is clear that political parties view the growing importance of this sector with interest and concern.

In addition to more detailed studies of the actual relationship of different types of NGOs with parties of different persuasion in different contexts (for instance, most opposition parties and NGOs collaborated against the Congress party in the anti-Emergency struggles and in the 1977 elections), what is needed is an understanding of how grass-roots issues can be made viable for electoral politics. Otherwise, the relationship is likely to be an instrumentalist one----the political parties try to make use of the moral legitimacy and material resources base of NGOs; NGOs seek help from political parties in their conflict with the government.

The relationship with donor agencies, too, is not without its complications. Here, the reference primarily is to foreign donor agencies, since the involvement of non-government indigenous co-financing agencies in the sector is low.

While a majority of the studies seem to hover around the operationalization of the donor-recipient relationship, the availability of funds and the degree of interference, there has been interest in the wider implications of the spread and deepening of this relationship. In a major article, Karat (1984), a Central Committee member of the CPI(M), charged that the growth in this phenomenon was the result of a conscious strategy of western imperialist powers, who through funds, ideological support and recognition were fostering anti-national and anti-left forces in the country. The debate that followed (Karat, 1985; Pattanayak, 1985; Sethi, 1985) unfortunately remained at the level of polemics, with those related to the organizations named in Karat's article reacting to clear their name.

In the absence of firm data about foreign donor agencies----their background, sources of funds, modes of selecting partners, and so on----it becomes difficult to comment upon this issue. With philanthropy becoming a big business, donor agencies scout around for markets in potential recipients. And with the quantum becoming large, as for instance in neighbouring Bangladesh, co-financing agencies can often subvert or distort national priorities and policies. The decision of the donor consortium to give aid *only* through NGOs in the instance of the recent cyclone in that country is a pointer in this direction.

Efforts have also been made to trace the influence of foreign donors in promoting certain issues and in highlighting only certain aspects of a country's development. While we are not aware of any study along these lines, autonomous women's groups, ecology groups, groups struggling around issues of cultural identity, anti-nuclear groups, and so on are often accused of being foreign inspired.

An equally crucial issue is the impact of relatively easily available large sums of money on the NGO sector. There are, for instance, charges commonly made that the agencies cause rifts in existing NGOs and help dissenting factions to form their own organizations in an effort to widen their market. A proliferation of easy money can also alter the operating style, the cost calculus, even the basic motivations and ideological underpinning of the sector. The phrase commonly heard, "while government-funding is ideologically preferable, foreign-funding is much more convenient" is disturbing, because the availability of easy money may be altering the basic relationship between the agency and the community. Sharma (1987), in an incisive analysis of social movements like *Chipko* and *Swadhyaya*, traces their strength to their internalization in the community. These efforts, unlike the normal NGOs, neither need nor seek external assistance, nor do they need to look elsewhere for validation.

On the other side, various commentators have remarked about the globalization of issues made possible through the donor agency mediation. The relationship, they argue, is not one merely of cash transfers in a framework of philanthropy, but one of globally linking up like-minded groups struggling on similar issues. Thus, work in India gets enriched by experiences elsewhere and *vice versa*.

What is needed is not only more detailed empirical examination of foreign-funding and donor agencies and their impact on the thought and working processes of different NGOs, but reflections on the larger political and ethical implications of constantly relying on grants to engage in social interventionist activity. Pattanayak (1985) and Sharma (1987) have attempted to raise questions about the basic nature of voluntarism. We feel that more such contributions are required.

The real success of an NGO lies in the relationship that it is able to forge with the base group/communities with which it is directly involved. Are the NGOs in actual operation any different from either the local bureaucracy that ordinary people have to deal with, the local political-electoral bodies, or the political parties? What is the nature of participation that they are able to engender? To what extent are people satisfied with the services offered? Have the more organizationally inclined NGOs managed to ensure the emergence of base organizations, which can then look after the task of relating to the outside world? The self-description of NGOs as catalysts, their preoccupation with becoming dispensable, of not creating dependencies, are all reflective of these concerns.

As elsewhere, research-based studies on these questions are rare. Most evaluative studies of single NGOs focus more on the intra-organizational dimension, the relationship with base groups being difficult to assess. Broadly speaking, the relief, welfare and charity groups are seen as more efficient and less corrupt dispensers of goods and services. This partly explains why at times of calamities, donor organizations in most cases prefer to work through NGOs, rather than the officialdom. Developmental groups not involved in income generation programmes, but engaged in activities such as running health and education programmes, creches and distress homes for women, are seen as more efficient, concerned and less corrupt. Nevertheless, the relationship between the agency and the people is one of structural inequality, with NGOs operating essentially as 'middlemen', albeit without the power to tax or repress.

The real test of this relationship lies in the index of organizational development. The key questions relate not only to the quantum or extent of organizational success, but to the modes of ensuring this objective. For instance, it is now commonly recognized amongst most NGOs that economic or service programmes are not very conducive towards developing organizations of the poor. Equally, it is realized that it is easier to create organizations around real and perceived grievances which can be converted into demands on the state. To help set up organizations which will garner local resources for collective development has, by and large, been a difficult objective to fulfil.

In addition to working out the organizational possibilities encoded in different activities, NGOs need to be seen as 'steadfast allies' who will stand by the people in case of trouble for a genuine organization of the poor to emerge. Studies on SEWA, the Working Women's Forum, *Bhoomi Sena*---all cases of relatively successful organizing---indicate that what breaks the barriers of suspicion between the NGO and the people is the ability to communicate genuine risk-sharing rather than real or perceived success.

The political social action groups, while successful in their initial organizational work, continue to face problems generated by their own internal weaknesses, fragmentation and the lack of control over the political climate. Particularly in regions which have seen repeated agitations and repression, people are not keen to come under an organizational banner, since that may attract more hostile attention.

In any final instance, only if the NGO is seen as existing not for its own good can a meaningful relationship of trust and confidence develop with the people. Their fear, particularly in today's climate, as more official programmes now involve NGOs, is that a blurring would take place between local government functionaries and them. As NGOs start chasing targets, and become more accountable to the government or donor agencies, their internal criteria for validation is likely to shift, converting them into just another instrumentality, which unfortunately is not accountable even in the sense that politicians or administrators are accountable.

Assessment/Impact Studies

For a sector whose basic definition and contours are so little systematically studied, the commentary on the overall impact of the phenomena is surprisingly freely available. What may be less obvious is that these assessments are strongly influenced by the structural location of the commentators.

Most commentators today accept that the NGO phenomenon is a major one, though whether it qualifies to be a 'fifth estate' is debatable. It is also accepted that the sector incorporates within itself a wide variety of organizations and activities, each with its own working methods and ideology. This variety and complexity is growing and consequently all attempts at assessment are at best partial.

To what extent have NGOs fulfilled the expectations or the promise that they have generated? Have they successfully contributed to a deepening of equitable development or a shift in policy, to the raising of new issues, or to an increase in public awareness and in empowering the people? What have been the implications of NGO activity for the nature of institutional democracy in the country?

As we argued, both the reality and its representation present a mixed picture. Leading voluntary activists and donor agencies expectedly present a rather positive picture (Verghese, 1977; Pant, 1986). So does the literature emanating from UN bodies and the World Bank (Quereshi, 1988). All these studies have contributed to the image of the NGO as a locally rooted, responsive, flexible, innovative, creative and effective developmental agency. It is not that they do not recognize the limitations of size, fragmentation, localism or transience but they find the development of the NGO sector a welcome and encouraging phenomenon.

The political parties, particularly those of the left, view this development with apprehension. Karat (1984) is perhaps the most vocal of those who are unfavourably disposed to the phenomenon in question, which is perceived as detracting from politics wedded to transforming the basic structural parameters of the society. An increasing penetration of and reliance on foreign-funding only exacerbates this apprehension. The government sector, as we have seen, has a mixed view, in which they would like to involve NGOs as mediators and as delivery mechanisms, with partial recognition of the organizational role, but would like the activities kept 'within limits' (Planning Commission, 1985). Additionally, since increasing official funding is now being made available for this sector, there is a desire, through efforts like the NCRVA and a code of conduct to work out the modes of accountability.

Within the academic community the response has been mixed, with different scholars disagreeing on the importance they would give to this phenomenon. Kothari (1984a), Sheth (1984) and Sethi (1984, 1986) see in this a major grass-roots political movement and a hope for a deepening and a redefinition of politics in the country. The phenomena of activist groups and grass-roots formations have, in their view, contributed not only to an articulation of new issues and styles of relating and working, a heightened consciousness and organization of sections of the oppressed and exploited hitherto relatively untouched by the political parties, but also to major shifts in the consciousness and working of other sectors of society. While not arguing that the voluntary, non-party tendency can by itself take on the task of transforming state and society, they attribute to it a major catalyzing role. Bose (1985) and Dhanagare (1988) are far more cautious in their assessments, focusing more on the fragmentation of the sector. In either case, most assessments, even though tentative, share the view that the NGO phenomenon bears close watching.

What the literature clearly lack is empirical studies with a bearing on the larger implications for governance. Is a proliferation of groups healthy for the future of institutional democracy? Do these groups and their activities help vitalize the more mainstream structures of government and local electoral bodies? Is the future tendency likely to be similar to the one in Bangladesh, where NGOs have emerged as a major power bloc, controlling millions of dollars and many people? What does all this do to the more ingrained societal ethos of self-help, autonomy and cooperation?

IMPLICATIONS FOR FUTURE RESEARCH

As we have argued, the major interest in the NGO phenomenon has been displayed by practitioners of development rather than the research community. The interest of government, development co-financing agencies, international bodies like the World Bank and the United Nations not unexpectedly generated literature on issues such as training, management skills, cost-effectiveness of NGO operations, ability to induce participation in target communities---what we have classified as efficacy studies. An overwhelmingly instrumentalist bias not only diverts attention from macro-societal concerns but also introduces an atheoretical tendency in the various contributions. It is this distortion that needs to be corrected for a proper appreciation of the induced activity and self-activity in society sought to be captured under the NGO rubric.

This overall interventionist ethos should not be deprecated, because issues of action and intervention can neither be understood nor facilitated by a detached/objective outlook. More importantly, such an approach helps bring to the surface another reality, often hidden in the policy-oriented writing. In the process, it not only helps us to understand the NGO phenomenon from the viewpoints of the subjects of inquiry but facilitates an alternative reading of the conventional texts of politics and governance.

Nevertheless, the overwhelming focus on issues of practice, and that too within a framework of efficient delivery of pre-decided packages, has meant that questions ranging from basic issues of definition and classification to those tracing the implications of the growth of the NGO sector on agencies of state and society have been ignored. Does, for instance, the growing support to NGOs imply a dilution of the welfare functions of the state? Does it imply a growth of private enterprise in the country? What does a proliferation of activist groups do to political parties and the political process? Does increasing funding, both governmental and foreign, lead to a decline in self-reliance and community orientation? Is the growth of the NGO sector reflective of a decentralized mode of increasing state control over society? All such questions are crucial, and need to be explored, both through more detailed and rigorous empirical studies as also through redefining the questions such that they do not remain confined to mere practical concerns.

The NGO phenomenon is, in our view, simultaneously a reflection of organizational innovation to respond to shifting market trends, and an assertion of the irreducible autonomy of individuals and communities against an increasing encroachment by the state in daily life. This contradictory impulse needs to be captured to make the concept of governance more amenable to the assertions of people's rights such that the state functions not above but brought within the parameters of civil society.

REFERENCES

Bandopadhyaya, J. and Shiva, V. (1987), *The Chipko Movement*. Seminar paper, February.

Baxi, Upendra (1986), "Two Threats to Democratic Social Action", *Mainstream*, 2 August.

Bhatt, Anil (1988), *Development and Social Justice*. Delhi: Sage Publications.

Bose, Pradeep (1984), "The State and Ideology of Social Action", paper presented to Seventeenth All India Sociological Conference.

Coombe, Simon (1987), "The Indigenous Voluntary Agency Sector and Rural Change in India: Towards a Definition", unpublished paper, Department of Town and Country Planning, University of Sydney.

Dhanagare, D.N. (1988), "Action Groups and Social Transformation in India", *Lokayan Bulletin*, 6(5), 37-59.

George, P.K. and Srivastava, U.K. (1977), *Rural Development in Action*. Bombay: Somaiya.

Gupta, Ranjit (1986), *Institution-Building Support to Non-government Rural Development Organizations*. Ahmedabad: IIM.

Karat, Prakash (1984), "Action Groups/Voluntary Agencies: A Factor in Imperialist Strategy", *The Marxist*, 2(2).

— (1985), "Justification for Imperialist Financed Activities", *Economic and Political Weekly*, 20(18), 4 May.

Kothari, Rajni (1984a), "Grass-roots", *Seminar*, January.

— (1984b), "The Non-Party Political Process", *Economic and Political Weekly*, 19(5), 4 February.

Oakley, Peter and Dillon, B. (1985), "Strengthening People's Participation in Rural Development", unpublished paper, University of Reading, April.

Omvedt, Gail (1980), "New Strategies of the Bourgeois", *Frontier*, 5 January.

Pant, Niranjan (1986), *PVOs/NGOs: Evolution, Opportunities and Constraints*. Mimeo, US AID, March.

Pattanayak, K. (1985), "Non-Party Groups and their Dependence on Foreign Money", *Economic and Political Weekly*, 20(39), 28 September.

Planning Commission (1985), *The Seventh Five Year Plan 1985-90*. Delhi: Planning Commission.

Quereshi, Moeen, A. (1988), "The World Bank and NGOs: New Approaches", *Lokayan Bulletin*, 6(4).

Roy, Sanjit Bunker (1986), "Discipline and Accountability", *Mainstream*, 20 September.

Sethi, H. (1984), "Groups in a New Politics of Transformation", *Economic and Political Weekly*, 19(7), 18 February.

— (1985), "The Immoral 'Other': Debate Between Party and Non-Party Groups", *Economic and Political Weekly*, 20(8), 2 March.

— (1986), *NGOs in India: A Troubled Future*. Delhi: NORAD.

Sethi, H., Das, P.K. and Fernandez, O. (1988), *UCP-2: An Interim Evaluation*. Den Haag: UNNYAN/NOVIB.

Sethi, H., Sharma, J. and Rosenberg, R. (1989), *Evaluating SWRC Tilonia*. Den Haag: HIVOS.

Shah, A.M. (1987), "Untouchability, Untouchables and Social Change in Gujarat", in Paul Hockings (ed.), *Dimensions of Experience: Essays in Honour of David G. Maudelbaum*. Berlin: Moulton.

Shah, Ghanshyam and Chaturvedi, H.R. (1983), *Gandhian Approach to Rural Development*. Delhi: Ajanta Publications.

Sharma, Suresh (1987), "Voluntary Efforts and Institutional Funding", *Lokayan Bulletin*, 5(2).

Sheth, D.L. (1984), "Grass-roots Initiatives in India", *Economic and Political Weekly*, 19(6), 11 February.

Subramanium, Ashok (1982), "The Small Step and the Great Leap", IIM Working Paper 439, Ahmedabad.

Sundar, Pushpa (1986), *Private Voluntary Agencies in India's Development: The Ford Foundation Experience*. Delhi.

Tornquist, Olle (1984), "Problems of Radical Political Strategy Under the Rise of New Capitalism", *AKUT 28*, Stockholm.

Verghese, B.G. (1977), "Voluntary Action: A New Mission for New Missionaries", *Voluntary Action*, 19(2), January-October.

7

Social Work in the Changing Scenario

by C.P. Goyal

We are caught in the midst of constantly changing times. The phenomenon of change is all-pervasive. Its impact on individuals, collectivities, institutions and processes in the society is inescapable. Wisdom lies in perceiving the process of change adequately and correctly so that the socio-political institutions can be sufficiently geared to retain their relevance and utility in such moments of flux, drift or shift (Heller, 1986). Social institutions must have resilience to adjust to new situations. In this paper, an attempt is made to examine the prospects and potential of profession and discipline of social work in India with regard to such new challenges of changing times. In the first section, general threads of social transformation and its impact on practice of social work are examined. It reviews relevance of major issues and their impact on social workers. In the second section, limitations and scope of governmental socio-political policies *vis-a-vis* the needy groups of workers are examined. It also hints at changes at perception level in social workers. The third section seeks to re-establish the relevance of social work profession and pleads for tapping the growing scope of its role in changing scenario. The final section looks into the question of growing role of professional associations by recapitulating its genesis in social work and suggesting measures for acquiring efficacy.

I
SOCIAL TRANSFORMATION AND SOCIAL WORK

Change is the law of nature but the human history has not witnessed changes in social systems and structures during the last two thousand years as extensively as during the last about two hundred years. Mass production, tremendous scientific and technological advances, the great ideological divides, shifting and novel forms of habitats, social relations and social institutions have undergone a complete metamorphosis during this period. The pace of change and progress is so breath taking that it has posted a question mark to the very survival and existence of human species (Meadows *et.al.*, 1978). The material progress of man has come to threaten the very life on earth in all forms. Industrialization has already began to wipe out numerous species of flora and fauna. Social relations and institutions are under greater stress and strain today than ever before. However, human efforts to rescue the mankind from these threats have not lagged behind and socio-political interventions in the life of man and system of society have progressively tried to meet the new challenges (Toffler, 1970:18-19). Specifically speaking social work is one such possible and substantive intervention. As a science and art of social intervention, it has progressively evolved and in the process it has produced a band of professionals trying to intervene into numerous issues of human existence starting with limited efforts of distributing charity and social assistance to shaping a new social order in collaboration with other social science disciplines.

In recent times, there have been many changes in society and they in turn have affected the academic discipline of social work in many ways. In view of this process of hectic and abrupt changes, the professional social workers are called upon continually to update their awareness of the ways in which changes affect individuals, groups whom they work with and also how they (Jacob, 1994:1-2; Ramchandran, 1990:12) affect themselves. Change is often evolutionary and it is quite difficult to pinpoint the actual moment when change has occurred. Attitudes towards so many traditional values have changed. For instance, just look at one area of social concern, viz., the practice of adoption. Today, it is acceptable for adopted children to search for information regarding their origins. It was not so eight to ten years ago. Sometimes change is forced upon us and sometimes it just seems to evolve and envelop us (Gore, 1985).

Let us examine major issues of our times which affect social workers and their clients today. The issue is the imbalance between economic goals and human goals or needs. The dominant motive of capitalist society is that of profit (Rand, 1967). But that is not the case with the concerns of social work. We, the social workers and professionals, therefore, insist on production as the means to fulfil human needs. Human beings providing their labour are regarded as resources or commodities, and wages as costs of production. The capitalist logic views labour as one of the factors of production like other innate factors as land and capital itself (Haq, 1976). The capitalist society discards those who are not productive, and calls them *lumpen*-unemployed and unemployable strata of society. Welfare programmes are used as a capitalist strategy to compensate for some of its failures, shocks and tensions, born of this logic and arrangement and we need to understand social work in this light (Leo, 1976).

In India, we see that powerful national and multinational corporations (MNCs) through absorption of smaller corporations are becoming all-powerful and rabid profiteers. As Stopford and Strange (1991) argue, some of these MNCs, in due time, will become more powerful than the popularly elected government and will not be accountable to the host as well as home governments. Look at the way they have increased our national balance of payment deficit. As a result, the welfare programmes are not designed to interface with the capitalist system of production but they are expected to compensate for the deficiencies and failures of the (capitalist) system and that too, strictly operating within the limits of its overarching framework.

The political parties in India, except the leftist ones, are developing along the capitalist lines to serve the interests of dominant economic groups such as industry, organized labour and the large as well as rich agriculturists. It is difficult under this system for any political party to represent the interests of all and in particular of those excluded from the production process. It seems scarcely possible for any government, even the one professing and claiming to be a socialist government, to represent the interests of the poor and the *lumpen*. The traditional antagonism of corporate rulers and wealthy millionaires towards trade unionism of the labour is almost vanishing under the new system of administration. Organized workers are today financially far better off and secure than ever before. In fact, the number of millionaires is also concomitantly on the rise. There is a distinct evidence of accumulation of wealth within fewer and fewer hands in society. At the same time, the process of pauperization is also on rise.

The governments, however, are elected to power on the strength of traditional political views, promises made to the electorate and their ability to muster support of the people by employing one or the other narrow denominator of caste, religion, region or language. Of course, this is not so simplistic, as there are other issues which influence public opinion and affect the outcomes of election campaigns. We have a socialistic government tilting towards market economy. Congress has been in office for over 40 years during the last fifty years. And yet, what has happened to the promise of eradicating poverty, unemployment, illiteracy, ill-health through nine Five Year Plans and input of millions of rupees? What has happened to our promises of literacy and education for all, work to all eligible hands, to those unemployed, particularly the youth of this country? A universal health care system for all citizens to provide basic health care is still a distant dream. What about the improved chances of severely disabled people across the country to receive the medical and rehabilitation services they need? What about the care of the destitutes and aged of our society? The real problem in India is that the social policies are losing out, with the current (almost exclusive) focus on economic policies. The primacy of economic goals is playing havoc with the agenda of social urgencies. Cuts in the budgetary provisions on health and welfare are to be expected plan after plan if one accepts that money spent on those rejected by the labour market is seen as a cost or loss, and not as an investment in future. The proportion of households living in poverty has increased if not remained static.

II
LIMITS OF VARIOUS INTERVENTIONS

The government is attempting to address to some of these problems. The tension between economic and social policies can be seen in a different perspective also. Passive income support through numerous state-run welfare measures for those people who are able to work but could not get jobs is now being changed. It is increasingly viewed as a type of support which will allow such people (currently outside the labour market) to enter or re-enter the work force by achieving certain degree of skill and thereby employability. While, on the one hand, the policy-makers are attempting to improve options for the 'non-productive' but potential work-force, certain sections of the society continue to blame the victims of the system. Terms such as 'social parasites', 'social liabilities' or 'social burden' are the evidences of that kind of thinking. This is typical thinking of the entrenched classes in the society.

The state now expects people to take more responsibility for themselves. This is most obvious in the health area where the sick are sick because they smoke and drink, do not do enough exercises, eat the wrong foods and so on. Those who meet accidents, and are at fault must take the consequences. Once again the victim is blamed. Social workers, working in such an unkind, unsympathetic and inhumanitarian conditions, find themselves dealing with a greater degree of guilt, depression and lowered self-esteem amongst their clients. A situation is now emerging in our society where the unemployed and therefore non-productive workers are blamed and viewed as a cost on society, unworthy of any investing in, a social burden and an economic loss. However, some attempts are being made to change the situation for workers outside the regular workforce. There are still others who are seriously disadvantaged in this scenario, such as the old people, children, minorities, the *dalits*, the disabled, the unemployed and the women. These are the people who constitute the major bulk of social work clientele. Consider, how difficult it is to put forward and sustain the claim that the money spent on the children of disadvantaged families is an investment in the future of this country. An exercise in human resource development must be taken up to see as to what type of people are potentially more able to be productive even in the capitalist sense.

Part of the consequence of rejection of the non-productive worker is on account of the shift in national policy since 1989, i.e., pushing the country towards privatization. While standards of health care in our public hospitals are not perfect, they are good by world criteria. With fiscal cuts in the health budget, there is an alarming move to greater privatization. With more private hospitals and nursing homes coming up to provide better health facilities to the patients is a proof of this trend. I shudder to think of the effect of this move on our public health system. I see doctors and nurses succumbing to the temptation of receiving higher salaries, better facilities and availability of technologically advanced equipments. An exodus to move into the private sectors may occur which may in turn further downgrade the public hospital system. What will it mean for us as social workers in the so altered hospital system? We need to place our views, our values, before the committees who are making decisions on these issues----right now, both at the policy and planning stages.

The professional social worker has to accept that privatization is occurring on account of governmental initiative and that social workers should be participating in decisions about which services should remain in the public sector and which can be satisfactorily performed by private practitioners. And then get in there and claim some territory which is uniquely ours. In doing this, the social workers must safeguard themselves from unknowingly serving the interests of just one sector to the disadvantage of the others. We must not be used to pursue the interests of the powerful, and neglect those of the powerless. Social work is vulnerable to accommodating the more powerful and dominant interests as we have found aligning with the establishment more convenient.

Looking at the financial constraint of our clients, it is clear that the social workers need to know the system and goals which make up the way the society is organized, structured and changed. This is very important indeed. Social work traditionally had a commitment to enhancing the value of and respect for human dignity. We need to re-commit ourselves to narrowing, if not abolishing completely, the disparities between the productive and non-productive members of the society. We must address ourselves to the disastrous effects of poverty in a country which is so rich in resources, including its people. The citizens should have basic human rights to food, shelter, work and education as instructed in the Directive Principles of State Policy vide the Constitution of India. We must continue to actively address to this issue, with a sound background and up-to-date knowledge of what is preventing the elimination of existing injustices and structural inequalities.

How do we achieve this goal as individuals? How do we make our student aware and educate him to do it? And how do we as an association of social work profession strive for it? We need to be clear about our role as academic, professional and practising social workers today. Our values and skills need to be directed at empowering people to take control of their lives; to get back into the work force, if they are unemployed; to gain their position in the mainstream society as equal citizens with equal access to economic and political power; to activate change in neighbourhoods and communities in which they live; and to make decisions about their various inter-institutional relationships and families.

The issue of power and powerlessness is one which has concerned social workers for a long time. I hope that social workers have begun to realize that identifying themselves with powerless clients in a powerless situation gets them nowhere. Very soon it leaves them feeling depressed, angry and useless, saps their energy, confuses the issues and removes any possibility of taking control of the situation and activating a change, both for themselves and their clients (Freire, 1977). Individual social workers believe that the situation is impossible and isolate themselves from the mainstream. They leave the field feeling guilty and angrier than ever before. Some social workers identify themselves with those in power along the veritable hierarchy of politicians, police, bureaucracy and industrialist and symbolically keep close to the clients while actually distance themselves from the client group. Powerlessness is frustrating and absolute powerlessness frustrates absolutely. Besides feeling of absolute powerlessness is a dangerous and self-destroying emotion. We cannot afford to see ourselves as powerless, as in such a condition we achieve nothing for ourselves or our clients. A positive frame of mind is indispensable to the practice of social work that is aiming at empowering a particular clientele.

It has been observed that too much of the social work education component is based on client-orientation, and too little emphasis is placed on the ways of managing systems, colleagues and effecting changes at work places. After all, only about half or one-third of social worker's time is spent with the clients. The social workers are caught in the maelstrom of increasing demands, diminishing resources and bureaucratic lack of appreciation of the dilemmas they face. It is time to look upon ourselves as having limited resources and once our capacity is full, we should close the door. What about the training for this sort of understanding and skill required by social workers? We encourage our clients to gain control in seemingly uncontrollable situations but seem less capable of doing it for ourselves. Social workers, by and large, are frightened of the organizations they work for, often justifiably. Haven't you heard social workers say, "Oh, I don't want to rock the boat. After all, I have to work with these people." Social workers need to be more comfortable and confident in themselves to effect changes for themselves and their clients.

III
GROWING SCOPE AND RELEVANCE OF SOCIAL WORK

Social work is both a practical and intellectual profession. The students, therefore, must be offered an opportunity for critical thought, inquiry, discussion and dialogue. The content of curriculum must be relevant to our religio-philosophical tradition and historical, social, cultural and political context. Social workers should also acquire political skills. We seem to go on, year by year, saying these things without really implementing them. As I said in the beginning, society around us continues to change. If educators are not producing graduates skilled in using existing resources, then the practitioners should soon be knocking at the doors of our schools and telling us what is wrong with the courses. The educators must listen to when practitioners share their observations and make comments on various aspects of our profession. Without this well-grounded feedback, it is difficult for social workers to adapt to changing needs. Social work students should, therefore, be able to question the nature and character of society, and not allow important principles to be sacrificed for political, economic or personal expediency. Social change can be effected by social workers with flair, imagination and creativity, provided they have learned to use an array of skills with boldness and in an intelligent manner.

Field work placements should be offered where practitioners can demonstrate success in achieving improvements for client groups. Along with this, attention must be paid to such aspects of learning as to social advocacy, record-keeping, statistical analysis, research, writing and submission of assignments, the use of lobbying, searching out and making use of those who are on positions of influence and power. Education should encourage the development of articulative and assertive skills and learning how to use the methods which are understood by those whom we are seeking to influence. The appropriate use of anger, of mass media, of outrage at injustice, the use of verbal and non-verbal and written skills, and presentations must form part of the social work training and education. We need to learn how to form coalitions, find our allies in common cause and combine forces. Social workers are traditionally enablers, facilitators and change agents and the methods we use must change as the time changes.

Though activating the clientele for social change has been a part of the broader social work task, it calls for a higher level of sophistication today as we live in very complex modern society comprising numerous sensitivities of sorts. There are members of this profession throughout India who have been very successful and who have been able to expose injustices in a manner which has received attention of those who are in positions of decision-making today. Social workers are employed at all levels within the profession. They have discovered that nothing succeeds like success to build confidence and to achieve success. Let others learn from you.

As social workers we should make sure that the people we serve are involved in the decision-making. Why should the handicapped, the elderly, relatives and caretakers not be involved in decisions on allocation of welfare and other resources? Is it because they are the consuming and non-productive costs to society? It is erroneous to view them as clients. They should be viewed and treated as rightful and legitimate claimants. They have a right to obtain our services and help. The community can and must be more involved in decisions pertaining to its priorities of various issues. Groups must be given the opportunity to discuss and possibly forge collective demands in the interests of the entire collectivity. We may not get all we want, resources will remain scarce and limited (Meadows *et.al.*,1978), but power and control will be in the hands of the beneficiaries and not just with the bureaucrats.

Social workers, employed in all areas of social work practice, have a responsibility to see that their clients get the best possible attention, care, have access to all possible and relevant information and are involved in making decisions affecting their lives. This is true whether the client or a patient in the community is suffering from schizophrenia, or is a destitute family dependent upon public assistance, or with children as a sole parent, or is an ex-convict just emerging from prison sentence to take up the life 'outside' again.

The social workers must learn necessary skills and strategies for achieving such goals while on the job. Students cannot learn enough about the problems of individual situations before starting to work. New graduates must ask for, and demand supervision in their first jobs. Skilled practitioners must offer supervision and give legitimate time to less experienced colleagues to have opportunities for discussion and learning on the job. Continuing professional education is thus needed.

The development of a clear professional knowledge of self is crucial for all social workers. Of what possible use can we be, if we do not know what we are, what special skills we have, what contributions as social workers we can make to our clients—communities, groups, individuals, our colleagues and the work place. Just to be "a member of the team" or committee set up or constituted by governmental or non-governmental organization is not enough. We should be proud and confident enough to know that as social workers we have something very special to offer. This is particularly important today when other professionals are developing skills in areas which have traditionally been the prerogatives of social workers. We practise social work in a number of different environments; e.g., within community organizations, large bureaucracies and small agencies; in the country side and in cities; and in the government and non-government organizations. We work with groups and individuals.

Social work has existed, pretty much and long as we know it, for over fifty years. That is a sufficient length of time for us to have acquired a body of knowledge and a commitment to the standards of practice. We have recently come to accept that social workers must be accountable for their work in a structured and measurable way. Quality assurance is a reality in the work place, and not just a term to be merely talked about. In analyzing the work we do, social workers have demonstrated that they are capable of creativity. There is plenty of opportunities to work within the goals of the employing agencies, and still maintain integrity and good client care. Continuous updating and improvement is a challenge which must be met both intellectually and practically. Continuing education, therefore, is essential to move realistically forward.

Social workers in India started organizing themselves with the dawn of independence way back in 1947. It began with setting up an umbrella organization of social workers. It comprised of voluntary and professional educators, organizations and institutions in the field of social welfare. Even the government departments concerned with social work joined in this effort. It was initially then called the Indian Conference of Social Work and later re-christened as the Indian Council of Social Welfare (ICSW). It was to the credit of this then newly founded body that it aroused interest in professionalization of social work, provided a national platform for discussion of social welfare issues, made petitions and presented charters of demands to relevant bodies and brought in its fold hundreds of individuals and scores of institutions. It also set up its state branches, some of which were actively crusading for the cause of social welfare.

IV
ROLE OF PROFESSIONAL ASSOCIATIONS

To focus on issues of professional interest and to emphasize professional perspectives, the professional social workers also established a National Association of Trained Social Workers called the Indian Association of Trained Social Workers, with its chapters in most states and metropolitan towns. Efforts for its establishment had begun in 1952 but it became a reality in 1962 at the Delhi Meet of the ICSW when it was formally registered as a society. Efforts for organizing the institutions of social work education were on way and in 1960 resulted in the birth of Association of Schools of Social Work in India (ASSWI).

Till 1975, these associations were very active. But the first two have become almost non-existent after the Emergency. The former became defunct because of the infiltration of political elements and the latter because of the poor interest of the professional social workers themselves, as they became more interested in issues of their immediate and personal career-advancing and benefits. The only professional association that has survived all these years is the Association of Schools of Social Work in India. However, its credibility was eroded during the intermittent years because of the mushroom growth of social work training institutions and power-patronage yearnings of its official members. Thanks to the efforts of rescue made at Bombay in 1993, the Association has started, not running, but at least moving on tracks.

The ASSWI has been demanding the setting up of a Council of Social Work Education by law and in 1994, we saw a ray of hope of fulfilment of this aspiration. Unfortunately, due to its criticism by some of the members of its own professional fraternity, it has been shelved for the time being. There has been a sense of distrust between the educators and the bureaucrats. It was hoped that the establishment of the Council will also strengthen the schools' and professional workers' associations. But it has remained as an unrealized dream.

I believe that more social workers have now come to realize that the professional association must be strong. It must resource as well as represent them. It will meet their all legitimate and pressing needs. Such an association will function with vigour at local, national and international levels. Belonging to professional bodies is not only worthwhile but highly desirable. Those social workers who do not belong to such associations are actually denying to themselves the manifold opportunities for professional growth, cohesion and support. They are also denying to themselves the opportunity and importance of joining and staying together in order to form a power base which is inevitable for organizational survival and growth in a plural, open and diverse democratic polity like ours (Weiner, 1991). Social workers should be prepared to be the conscience-keepers of the entire society (Stein, 1976). They must speak on behalf of the inarticulate and disadvantaged. They must render voice to the voiceless by not only all the time speaking for themselves but also by enabling them to speak. A strong association with wide representation of social workers can and must do this. Democratically representative governments respond to the legitimate calls of professional associations and they, in turn, expect them to respond to their calls.

Finally, social work is one of the few professions which offers its members the opportunity for continued growth, understanding and development of the self as well as the entire society. A definition of social work which guided me professionally and shaped my commitments is as follows: "Social work is the conscious, purposeful, disciplined use of the self" in understanding ourselves and others. Social work as an occupation is quite ideologically-oriented and capable of being a prime mover of socio-economic change in society.

REFERENCES

Freire, Paulo (1977), *Cultural Action for Freedom*. New York: Penguin Books.

Gordan, Childe (n.d.), *Man Makes Himself*. 3rd Edition, London.

Gore, M. S. (1976), *Social Aspects of Development*. Jaipur: Rawat Publications.

Haq, Mahbub Ul (1976), *The Poverty Curtain: Choices for the Third World*. New Delhi: Oxford University Press.

Heller, Frank (1986), *The Use and Abuse of Social Science*. London: Sage Publications.

Jacob, K. K. (ed.) (1994), *Social Work Education in India*. Delhi: Himanshu Publication.

Leo, Huberman (1976), *Man's Worldly Goods*. New Delhi: People's Publishing House.

Meadows, Donella, Meadows, Dennis, *et.al.* (1978), *The Limits to Growth*. London: A Potomac Associates Books, Pan Books.

Ramchandran, P. (1990), *Issues in Social Work Research in India: A Collection of Papers*. Bombay: TISS.

Rand, Ayn (1967), *Capitalism: The Unknown Ideal*. New York: New American Library.

Stein, H. D. (1976), "Social Work Developments and Changing Functions," *Social Services Review*, March Issue.

Stopford, John M. and Strange, Susan (1991), *Rival States, Rival Firms: Competition for World Market Shares*. New York: Cambridge University Press.

Toffler, Alvin (1970), *Future Shock*. London: Pan Books.

Weiner, Myron (1991), *The Indian Paradox: Essays in Indian Politics*. New Delhi: Sage.

8

Field Training for Social Development

by Sandhya Joshi

According to the *Human Development Report* (1994), published by the United Nations Development Programme, India ranked 135 amongst 173 nations of the world. Human Development Index (HDI) is a composite expression of three basic ingredients of development, viz., longevity measured by life expectancy; knowledge measured by adult literacy (two-thirds weightage) and mean years of schooling (one-third weightage); and standard of living measured by purchasing power, based on real Gross National Product per capita adjusted by purchasing power parity. In statistical terms, India has the largest number of people in absolute poverty estimated at 350 million in 1992; the largest number of illiterate adults, i.e., 272 million, especially illiterate females (169 million); and the highest numbers of under-five mortality per year at 3.5 million.

The ominous scenario underscores the ongoing concern amongst social work educators of imparting a relevant and social reality-based training to development professionals. In 1986, the University Grants Commission had invited proposals for undertaking action research "Experiments in Field Training for Social Development" and in 1988 one such project was launched at the Faculty of Social Work, M.S. University of Baroda. This paper is based on the experience and insight gained from the project undertaken for three and a half years in the slums of Baroda city. The project area comprised a homogeneous population of 49 Harijan (on the bottom rung of the caste ladder) families. The core objectives of the project were:

(a) to evaluate the training needs of MSW students working for social development of the urban poor and impart appropriate field training; and
(b) construct relevant social work intervention models to produce indigenous literature.

This paper is divided into four major sections viz., (i) development constraints and limit-situation of urban poor; (ii) development perspective in social work education; (iii) specialized skills training package; and (iv) conclusion.

I
DEVELOPMENT CONSTRAINTS AND LIMIT-SITUATION OF URBAN POOR

Project families, much like the urban poor elsewhere in India, were afflicted by several developmental constraints or 'blocks' inherent in their social situation. The term 'limit-situation' was borrowed by Paulo Freire (1977:71) himself from other Brazilian authors such as Alvaro Vieira Pinto to simply mean a set of factors which hold people back from attaining a decent standard of living, i.e., which "prevents them from moving from where they are to where they want to be or could be". Our observations on the limit-situation of target people can be classified under three heads as follows: (1) self-imposed limits; (2) psycho-social oppression; and (3) lack of information and low competencies.

Self-Imposed Limits

One of the most debilitating handicaps in the situation of the target families was the limits imposed by these Harijan respondents upon themselves. Their immediate environment and relatives "back in the village" have much to do with the tendency to underestimate their own strengths and capacities on one hand and low aspirations on the other. They seem patently powerless to break free from the shackles of their own caste norms. For instance, the practice of child marriages (boys are married by 15 to 16 years and girls between 12 and 14 years) which are consummated within one year of the ceremony is one such shackle. They trap the incumbents further in a vicious circle of incomplete education (even for boys as they must look for 'paid jobs' upon marriage); early parenthood leading to economic dependence on parents and grand-parents which makes it impossible for younger generation to defy their elders; and adopt more forward-looking or progressive ways. Extended one-to-one discussions, role plays, skit completion exercises, etc., were used by the project functionaries to lighten the cultural strangleholds and reduce the barriers to development.

Then there were some individuals who were intrinsically unaware of their own worth and potentials—a kind of human failing which is independent of the caste factor. With such people, the project team consciously encouraged self-expression, habit of multifarious thinking and develop confidence to solve their own problems.

In the third category, we came across individuals who firmly believed that "government must solve all their problems" and they carried no responsibility of their own. Even when faced with problems of grave import but which were at the same time amenable to simple solutions, they would sit back endlessly waiting for government intervention. For instance, when the one and only handpump in the locality would go out of order and spell terrible hardships for all, these individuals would not allow recourse to a simple solution like each family paying up an odd rupee or so to pay for a hired mechanic to do the repairs. And this kind of over dependence on local self-government administration was carried forward by them in all matters small or big. The project people worked to make such people understand the principle of "more for less", i.e., how small efforts by individuals could collectively help solve problems more efficiently, i.e., increase productivity in general terms.

Psycho-Social Oppression

Limiting factors arising from the centuries-old phenomenon of dehumanization of the Harijans and other lower castes by the upper caste sections of the Indian society are well known. Interventions by the government and voluntary welfare organizations in the form of constitutional protections, legal provisions, social education and vigilance, etc., have improved the situation to a great extent since independence. Yet, no one can deny the existence of psycho-social oppression of the low caste groups even today; whether it occurs in a subtle form or in more blatant and repulsive ways. What is more disturbing, however, is the fact that a large majority of the lower castes have 'resigned themselves to' or 'accepted' the discriminatory and humiliating treatment meted out to them by 'those above'. Perhaps, because the latter enjoy the sanctions of the religious scriptures and cultural traditions of the society.

In order to treat the above mentioned social malady, the project director and the project associate resolved to carry out assertiveness training of the target beneficiaries at individual level whenever possible and guide the student workers accordingly. But what is assertiveness? According to Hepworth and Larsen (1990), "assertiveness embodies specific components of behaviour that enable individuals to express their opinions, feelings, wants and preferences in a manner that respects the rights and feelings of others even when such expressions risk aversive consequences such as criticism, disapproval or punishment."

Bucell (1970), in an empirically derived self-report inventory for the assessment of assertive behaviour, identified the following relatively different types of assertive behaviours or response classes: (i) refuse requests; (ii) express unpopular opinions; (iii) admit personal shortcomings; (iv) accept compliments; (v) express positive feelings; (vi) make requests for changes in behaviour; and (vii) initiate and maintain conversations.

The basic message that is conveyed by persons who are assertive is that they 'count' and that their ideas, perceptions and opinions are important. By contrast, persons who relate non-assertively attempt to appease others and to avoid conflict, they convey through their behaviour that their needs, wants and opinions are not important and that others are superior to them. To illustrate patterns of psycho-social oppression experienced by target families and their resultant withdrawn, passive or non-assertive behaviour, we present here a few episodes that took place during the project work.

One of the student workers was assigned to work with a group of either school dropouts or out-of-school adolescent boys to assess whether they were interested in resuming formal schooling, or alternately undertake some vocational training and then do the needful for gaining some employment. The worker identified eleven adolescent boys who had dropped out from school not more than two years ago and since then had either worked on temporary jobs or remained in a futile search of one. The worker presented to the group different options available to them and held systematic discussions to highlight the pros and cons of those options. Two out of the eleven boys showed inclination to resume their studies and the remaining nine wanted to take up some skill training jointly. Accordingly, the worker advocated on their behalf and while two candidates returned to formal schooling, the other nine were enrolled for a two-week training programme at an institute located not too far from their residence.

By the time, the vocational training course started, our students had discontinued field work due to term end vacations. However, on the first day of the training course, the worker did visit the institute to wish the boys "best of luck". That day eight of the nine candidates had turned up and they looked very enthusiastic and happy for having been selected at the course. Little did we know at that time that all of them would be forced to quit *en masse* the very next day, due to the discriminatory and humiliating treatment meted out to them. It was only much later that we learnt that on the second day the group of Harijan boys was singled out by the institute officials to sweep the compound and clean the toilets. Our clients left in protest. If we take a narrow view of the situation it seems as if the boys apparently asserted themselves against the unjust demands made upon them. But, unfortunately, they asserted themselves only to a limited extent and not all the way. Wouldn't it have been much better if they had refused to carry out the unreasonable orders and yet gone ahead to complete the training? Many issues arising out of this episode could be discussed here but the main point of psycho-social oppression is already made.

In another incident, a youth from the target community was being helped by a student worker to secure his Scheduled Caste certificate from the concerned government department to equip the former to avail benefits of special assistance programmes for Harijans. Our student worker oriented his client about the location of the concerned office, contact person, timings, etc., and further advised him to carry a pen with him as he would be required to fill up a form. Accordingly, our client reached the relevant department on his own as directed and asked for the requisite form. He got the form alright but the concerned clerk asked him to pay rupees three and offered to fill it up on behalf of the former. Although our client was educated upto ninth standard and could have very well filled up the form himself (which was in vernacular and was also free of cost) yet he quietly paid rupees three for the patently unnecessary service. When our student worker later asked the client why the latter did not speak up that he could fill up the form on his own and thereby saved the 'fee', he (the student worker) was told that in that case "the clerk would have been annoyed and he [clerk] might hold it against me and not attend to my work properly when I approach him next time."

The cluster families were being collectively helped by us in securing electricity connections. The assignment involved several component tasks like: contacting the local Municipal Corporator, filling up requisite application forms along with some fee, and follow up the progress with the local ward office, and also with some officials of Gujarat Electricity Board, etc.

The student workers were duly instructed to only initially accompany the members of the working committee to the various offices so that on one hand the student himself/herself could learn the process involved and on the other hand people got training to manage solving of their problems themselves. Accordingly, the student workers gradually discontinued the follow-up visits to the concerned offices along with people's representatives. The working committee members, however, maintained a direct contact with the project director or project associate who continued to monitor the process. The people's representatives were found to be working quite enthusiastically till one day when they disclosed to the project associate that "the officers don't give us a proper response in absence of student workers". Their reported experience was inadvertently confirmed by one senior official whom the project director happened to meet at a public function. The project director was asked "why don't your students come along with those community leaders any more?... so difficult to understand what they rattle... they waste so much time!" That's the attitude of our so-called public servants whose job is to attend to the legitimate needs of all citizens under their jurisdiction including the less educated, unsophisticated, poor people.

Lack of Information and Low Competencies

It is believed that information is power. Conversely, lack of information creates a condition of powerlessness. Several research studies have shown that Harijans and backward classes suffer from an all-pervasive limit-factor of lack of information of various developmental programmes and services aimed at elevating their standards of living. Similar observations were made about the project families. During 1990, when all educational institutions in the city were indefinitely closed down and there were frequent incidents of violence due to Mandal reservation issue, the project team carried out a spot survey of level of awareness and opinion on job reservations amongst the youth and men in the target cluster. Hardly 30 per cent respondents were found to possess satisfactory level of knowledge and the rest could only say that "some reservation problem" is there. Those who were aware of the provisions were also satisfied with it but they did not seem to think that the provisions could bring about any significant change in their community.

During normal times, it was found that the knowledge of the procedures for securing caste certificates and social security benefits like old age pension, widowhood pension, disability pension, etc., was rather limited. Awareness of economic welfare programmes like loans and subsidies for various purposes was somewhat better. Awareness and utilization of health facilities like mother and child health care including immunization and family planning which were available literally 'across the road' was low. Knowledge about women's rights, marital counselling services, institutional care services for battered women, etc., amongst women were almost non-existent. In the sector of small savings again, utilization of available bank and postal schemes was also initially nil. Knowledge of procedures for securing civic amenities like electricity, an approach road, handpump, etc., was slightly better.

In order to upgrade people's knowledge, productivity skills and teaching new skills, demonstrations of various skill training courses were organized periodically at the cluster site with the help of local Shramik Vidyapeeth. Some experts from women's organizations were invited to deliver talks on women's issues. A visit to Vikas Jyot, particularly to familiarize women with marital counselling services, was arranged. Health professionals, bankers, leadership training experts, local Municipal Corporator, etc., were some of the other personnel invited to help bridge the knowledge gap in various fields. Film shows on social themes, one or two day leadership training camps for women and men, orientation visits to vocational training institutes by unemployed youths, cookery competitions of nutritious foods like soya bean flour, green vegetables and sprouted cereals, etc., comprised other important inputs.

II
DEVELOPMENT PERSPECTIVE IN SOCIAL WORK EDUCATION

At a Faculty Development Workshop on Field Work at University of Delhi (held in March 1981 in which the author also participated), the concept of developmental social work was discussed threadbare by the social work professionals and the following aspects emerged:

> Developmental approach was need-oriented rather than problem-oriented; it was holistic; had a broader, national, macro and long term perspective; had anticipatory and preventive aspects; it laid emphasis on class in preference to case; it was promotional; and it encompassed social action and social change components.

After some discussion, it was also agreed that it was not the question of developmental versus traditional but of traditional and developmental. The latter had a perspective; it worked for planned change and it was goal-oriented. It stressed equality and discouraged inequality in all forms. It focused on the weaker and the weakest sections and helped them to get a rightful share of resources and services. It called for a redistribution of incomes, status and decision-making power. In developmental approach oppositional practice cannot be overlooked. To a query by a member, "whether development approach was applicable to advanced countries", the consensus was that it was so in so far as the approach stressed reducing and removing inequalities in all forms. A few examples of developmental approach in field work were cited as follows.

It was said that in a hospital or any health service delivery system there were class, ethnic and linguistic biases in the provision of services. The student could take up assignments of correcting these situations. Similarly, a school social worker who went beyond his commonly accepted role and function and initiated a programme of non-formal education of slum children by the school children was also classified as a social worker with a developmental perspective. Singh (1985) makes an additional point that developmental approach can be used for normal population groups as well as in so far as human resource development is one of the perspective concerns of the said approach.

The specialized knowledge required for developmental approach would include a sensitive and close appreciation of the immediate clientele situation, surrounding exploitative elements in environment, oppressive structures, vested interests and political processes. Here political action component of social work discipline does not mean direct participation in politics but implies that the practitioner seeks to properly inform the concerned groups about how their problems could be solved through the available political instruments or by changing the existing machinery. It also helps people to organize themselves for a dialogue with the power lobbies and seek justice for themselves. However, failure of such correct procedures would leave no other option with the people but a recourse to an oppositional or confrontational stance. The developmental social work approach would endorse the same.

Package of Training Inputs

Having summarized the basic premises and perspectives in developmental social work in the previous sections, we now present the actual training inputs. It can be seen here that while some of the inputs were commonplace supervisory training inputs, some additional modalities were also incorporated to meet the project goals. The training inputs are as follows:

a. Supervisory Conferences
b. Talks by Experts
c. Circulation of Reading Material
d. On the Spot Guidance
e. Specialized Skills Training for Development of Urban Poor
f. Sensitivity Training
g. Presentation of Notes for Discussion by Students
h. Training in Preparation and Use of a Check List
i. Study Visits to Collateral Agencies

III
SPECIALIZED SKILLS TRAINING PACKAGE

In recognition of the far-reaching consequences of poverty upon the psyche and general characteristics of the urban poor, it was mandatory for us to identify and apply some specialized skills while working with the target group. Based on our cumulative experience under the project, the following specialized skills were found to be most essential for a comprehensive package of field training of development workers:

Assessing Developmental Needs

For an authentic assessment of developmental needs of the poor, it would be a mistake to rely on the findings of a social survey alone. One of the major reasons is that what people sometimes describe as 'needs' may actually be 'wants' and at times, they may simply remain silent on these questions or say "don't know". This did happen in the present project and we supplemented the base-line survey data by seeking information from other sources as under:

(i) *Key Informants*, viz., community leaders for legal status of the slum cluster; services provided as well as services denied by the Municipal Corporation; potential of people to contribute in development activities; e.g., a youth who was employed at a nearby health centre of the Corporation was utilized by us to regularize weekly anti-malarial measures like fumigation and distribution of preventive tablets on a permanent basis in the cluster location.

(ii) *Service Providers* like the local *balwadi* (pre-nursery) teacher, *anganwadi* worker, a community volunteer who provided remedial coaching to children when contacted by our students could give us some exclusive information about the developmental needs of children particularly in the area of health and education.

(iii) *Sub-Population Group* like *bhajan mandal* of men and women, unemployed youth (boys) group, adolescent girls' group were contacted by the students to gain insight of their specific needs, wants and priorities.

(iv) *Check Lists* as a rapid appraisal tool were used every six months for project monitoring.

Mature and Empathetic Responding of Typical Negative Behaviour Patterns of Clients

Based on our earlier experience of work with slum communities, we were aware of some typical negative behaviour patterns in this social class. As a result, the students under the project were especially trained to analyze the clientele behaviour, reflect upon their own spontaneous reactions to client's behaviour and make deliberate efforts to respond maturely and empathetically. The students were guided not to expect changes in clientele behaviour too soon but also not give up their own efforts because of which "seeds of change" were bound to be sown. Following is a list of some undesirable behaviours of slum-dwellers:

1. Tendency to show helplessness and over dependence on student workers.
2. Manipulative behaviour, e.g., telling student workers that their predecessors "did this or that" and indirectly goading the latter into "doing something directly for them".
3. Always needing to be called for pre-planned activities despite the students having clearly arranged the time as per their convenience.
4. Passive non-compliant behaviour, viz., the clients sometimes accept a responsibility but have to be reminded several times before executing it, e.g., a mother may have agreed to take her infant for immunization to the nearby health centre after receiving proper orientation from the student worker but still tends to procrastinate.
5. Certain undesirable mannerisms especially in children, e.g., often children in these communities display a compulsive behaviour pattern like, touch and cling to the newly placed student workers (as a proof of acceptance of the former by

the latter). The children use abusive language without feeling the least bashful.

There could be undesirable mannerisms in individual adult clients too and the students are guided about handling the situation professionally.

Resolving Ambivalence

Most clients of whatever social class, experience some ambivalence and tend to hold back from involving themselves fully in the helping process. In the case of urban poor the task of resolving their ambivalence is rendered more difficult because the former rarely express their skepticism, misgivings or fear and thereby fail to facilitate a frank and open discussion/dialogue between the client and worker. The students were taught to see that ambivalence of clients could be emanating from:

1. Fear of the unknown, i.e., the clients are not convinced that the proposed change would be beneficial to them.
2. Reluctance to spend money. Although several types of services are free, the clients still need to spend on transportation and other incidental expenses.
3. Differences in socio-economic and cultural backgrounds of workers and clients.
4. Pressure from husband or in-laws in case of women makes the latter ambivalent.
5. Earlier unsavory experience with social workers or other welfare personnel.
6. Fear of appearing foolish or incompetent refrains them from divulging full facts or own thoughts etc.

Once the students can understand the underlying causes of ambivalent client behaviours, the task of resolving it becomes easier.

Increasing Accessibility of Services

At times poor utilization of existing services by the urban poor can be attributed to their ambivalence due to various reasons as described in previous sub-section. Many a time, clients shy away from using a service due to barriers posed by the service delivery system itself. How often have we known clients to spend on medical care from a private practitioner even though free medical services are available in the neighbourhood? This happens because for getting free services, the patient has to wait for long hours during which home, children or work-place gets neglected. Similarly, the clients in other social agencies are spoken to in an offensive language or in a demeaning way. The procedures of filling-up various forms are complex and frightening to the client. The service agency repeatedly calls the clients for issuing a certificate, say of caste status or school leaving certificate (in case of school). The client's dignity is hurt by blatant partisan behaviour of agency personnel who often conduct themselves ineffectively and inefficiently. The students were trained to examine the underlying causes of non-utilization of services and do the needful either by taking up the matter with the agency concerned or making alternative arrangements at client's work place or home. For instance, the student workers working with a multiple handicapped person for his artificial limbs had to intervene to make the agency set aside its long-drawn procedures as the client faced lot of hardship shunting between the hospital, welfare agency financing him and his duties at home (since wife was working).

Promoting Assertiveness

Non-assertiveness is a common trait amongst the poor classes all over the world. In India, caste-based division of the society has further eroded the self-confidence of the lower castes to a level where the poor have themselves come to believe that their obligations to the upper castes far outweigh their own wants or rights. Lange and Jakubowski (1976:9) have described, "non-assertive behaviour as the one which involves the violation of one's own rights by failing to express honest feelings, thoughts and beliefs and consequently permitting others to violate oneself, or expressing one's thoughts and feelings in such an apologetic, diffident and self-effacing manner that others can easily disregard them."

Often during our work of guiding self-help efforts of people for getting electricity connections, approach road or some other facility of loan, pension or subsidy, we found that slum-dwellers do possess required knowledge of resources and procedures to an extent but what they grossly lack is the necessary self-confidence to engage themselves in self-help processes on a sustained basis. They would often want student workers to accompany them or their representatives to the various government offices and other resource agencies to present their case. The student workers also observed unequal treatment extended to the poor. Under the project, the students were trained to gradually instil greater self-confidence in their clients by constantly giving them positive feedback on one hand and removing their fears on the other. In numerous small ways, the student workers endeavoured to appreciate the talents and abilities of their clients in order to harness their latent potential. The focus was on changing the self-image of clients as individuals who 'count' and their ideas, perceptions and opinions are important.

Case and Class Advocacy

Here case advocacy implies working with and/or on behalf of individual clients or families to assure that they receive benefits and services to which they are entitled and that the services are provided in ways that do not offend their dignity. Class advocacy is a better known technique which involves acting to affect changes in policy, practice or laws that affect a particular social class or group.

During the project, at mezzo level some such issues which called for class advocacy were taken up but none at the macro level due to various constraints. The examples of class advocacy at mezzo level were: our students were instrumental in starting a weekly satellite health care centre of KGP Children Hospital at the slum location; supplementary nutrition provided to children through Municipal Corporation; electricity connections obtained for individual families (neighbourhood slum families on their own could not get these); additional standpoints of water supply; and approval of proposal for an approach road.

The students were guided to undertake advocacy in the following situations:

1. When an agency refuses to deliver services to a client or offers the service in a dehumanizing manner.
2. When gaps in services and clientele-need cause hardship or distress.
3. When clients individually or in groups are unable to effectively solve their own problems.
4. When numerous people have commonly felt an urgent need.
5. When procedures or facilities of organizations adversely affect clients.
6. Crisis situation, e.g., flood-relief work. In September 1990, the project area was heavily flooded leaving many hutments broken.

Indeed class advocacy is much broader in scope and can culminate into social action. But as a matter of policy under the project we withheld the same and refrained from it. However, we did train our students in the art of organizing client groups.

Organizing Client Groups

This basic technique involves forming action groups for social change that consist of consumers who have a mutual problem. The student workers were trained to initiate formation of the group around a common felt-need and then stimulate the group for self-help action. However, the student workers would always be available to the group as consultants for gaining information; access selected government officials and Municipal Councillors; and help solve whatever other difficulty the self-help group encountered in its course of action. This technique is especially appropriate for empowering the vulnerable sections in the society, who often find themselves marginalized from the gains of development.

IV
CONCLUSION

The National Policy of Education, 1968, sought the cultivation of moral and social values and ethos that would produce young men and women of character and ability, committed to national service and development. In the case of student social workers, placed in an open community setting, importance of deliberate inputs for an all-round development can hardly be overstated. Regarding their challenging work environment, briefly, it can be said that open community placements not only entail physical hardships but also some morally and ideologically taxing conditions which in extreme cases, could lead to a student 'burn-out'. The mandate for social work educators engaged in Field Training for Social Development is awesome indeed !

REFERENCES

Abrahamson, A. C. (1959), *Group Methods in Supervision and Staff Development*. New York: Harper and Bros. Publishers.

Bucell, M. (1979), *An Empirically Derived Self-Report Inventory for the Assessment of Assertive Behaviour*. Unpublished doctoral dissertation, Kent: Kent State University, OH.

Freire, Paulo (1977), *Pedagogy of the Oppressed*. New York: Penguin.

Hepworth, D. H. and Larsen, J.A. (1990), *Direct Social Work Practice: Theory and Skills*. Belmont: Wadsworth Publishing Co.

Joshi, S. (1991), *Field Training for Social Development: Action Research Report*. Delhi: University Grants Commission, India.

Lange A. and Jakubowski, P. (1976), *Responsible Assertive Behaviour*. Champaign IL: Research Press.

Singh, R. R. (1985), *Field Work in Social Work Education*. New Delhi: Concept Publishing Co.

United Nations Development Programme (1994), *Human Development Report*. London: OUP.

Zastrow, C. (1990), *Introduction to Social Welfare*. Belmont: Wadsworth Publishing Co.

PART III

Sites of Social Work Practice

9

Gandhi Through Five Generations: A Personal Account of Rural Social Work

by K.D. Gangrade

Loss of character has been the most important 'gift' to India in the post-independence era, especially since mid-sixties. This has been further compounded by all-round corruption prevailing in the society. Politics no longer arouses hope. It is now more seen as means of capturing and using power for personal and partisan ends. Periodic and multi-level elections to various representative bodies constitute the mechanism through which this process realizes itself. On their part, the people use politics and such electoral occasions to get as big a share of the development cake for themselves, their localities, regions, castes and communities as possible (Karlekar,1993).

These days political parties carry very little conviction with the people when they talk of ending corruption. Congress party has not been able to provide clean and efficient government. Virtually all its leaders or their relatives including those of the Prime Ministers' are not free from the charges of corruption. On the other hand, the Bhartiya Janata Party which has worked as an opposition party at the Centre, has many leaders with sticky fingers (Karlekar,1993). While the guardians of the social system did provide for penal provision against corruption, what is missing is the enthusiasm and commitment on their part to prosecute the offenders seriously.

Gandhi had rightly exhorted us: "End does not justify the means" or "means must be as pure as the end". Character and pure means require leaders of sterling qualities who can be emulated by coming generations. Today's child has neither his parents, nor teachers nor political or religious leaders who can inspire or serve as an ideal model. Individual morality is very important as it cannot be kept separate from unscrupulous policies or ideologies of the state in spite of the best efforts of an able statesman, for ordinary men have natural tendency to follow the examples of their masters. "*Yad yad acarati sresthas, tat tat ev' etaro janah, sa yat pramanam kurute lokas tad anuvartate,*" i.e., what a great man does, is followed by others. People go by the example he sets, as it has been very aptly stated in the *Bhagawad Gita* (111-21). Ultimately, this may lead to the utter destruction of the state, government and the ruler as well (Nayak, 1993:86).

We need trust worthy leaders possessing qualities of Gandhi and Jaya Prakash Narayan to transform India. Contemporary India may call Gandhi the "Father of the Nation," but very soon the world will remember him as the "Prophet of Truth and Non-violence". Romain Rolland, a French Nobel Laureate, in his short biography of the Mahatma wrote: "Gandhi obviously placed truth and non-violence first and Indian independence next." Nagarjuna, either in the first quarter of the second century or the last quarter of the first century, had eloquently propounded his philosophy that: "Life in the world when lived in the light of the highest truth, is itself *nirvana*" (Venkata Ramanan, 1978:32). We have chosen "*Satyameva Jayate*" (Truth Alone Triumphs) as the motto of free India. Let us imbibe this motto in our private as well as public life. The seeker of the truth, according to Gandhi, should be humbler than the dust. The world crushes the dust under its feet, but the seeker of the truth should be so humble himself that even the dust could crush him. Only then, and not till then, will he have a glimpse of the truth. The dialogue between Vasistha and Vishvamitra makes this abundantly clear. Christianity and Islam also amply bear this out (Gandhi, 1992:XII).

This paper is a critical assessment of downfall in our value system in post-independent India with special reference to case studies of two villages. I have drawn material mostly from my own field work, diaries and knowledgeable informants. A recourse has also been taken to some autobiographical account. I have tried my best to maintain academic objectivity in presenting and analyzing the data. I have not allowed my personal biases to influence my perceptions, impressions, work or writings. I have visited these two villages frequently for my field work—sometimes regularly and often at a gap of long intervals.

This paper has been divided into eight sections. The first section contains a discussion on Gandhi's influence on me through my family and school—the two most important social institutions of society. I have particularly narrated the experiences of a person who enters a new environment and the problems he faces in handling the situation. My admission to the school was not a smooth process as I had failed to answer the questions asked by the teacher. The grandfather's influences on me have been vividly described. The second section deals with the ideal of *bhaichara* (brotherhood or fraternity) or communitarian/collective life of the village with reference to the first generation. The collective leadership of the village trio—*Patel* (*Lambardar* or village police), *Patwari* (land record-keeper) and *Pansari* (moneylender, grocer or popularly known as *Gaon Seth*) has been graphically captured and analyzed. The first generation had upheld very high moral values and did not pay a mere lip-service. Self-protection and self-aggrandizement were not the motto of the leaders (Nayak, 1993:386). This section includes case of second generation in which the *Patwari* demonstrates how he could extract money from people by cheating them and the resultant deterioration in collective/corporate life of the village is also focused.

The third section pertains to my participation in the Quit India Movement and contains an account of having to go underground to avoid arrest. The fourth section is devoted to my studies in college and to the work done in a village along with one of my college friends as per the call of Gandhi. In this section, I have described, to some extent, the process of work beginning from adult education to all-round development of the village. The fifth section critically examines the arrival of independence and rejection of Gandhi and his values by most of the leaders and the people of India. The sixth section gives a profile of systematic work launched in the village at the instance of the headmaster of the local school and myself. This section also discusses the collapse of the whole work and complete erosion of the values that occurred with the arrival of Community Development Projects in collusion with the village *Lambardar*. The seventh section discusses the impact of mass media, western culture and unprincipled life of political leaders and political parties. The final section has specifically posed a challenge to the professional social workers to come out from their narrow shells and appeals to address themselves to larger issues confronting the country.

I
INFLUENCE OF FAMILY AND SCHOOL

I was four years old when Gandhi launched the salt *satyagraha*[1] in April 1930 (Acharya, 1990:102-124 and Bandyopadhyay, 1984:141-45). This event got so deeply ingrained in my unconscious mind that it became part of me as I went on hearing the stories about Gandhi's message and plans to free India from the British rule. The second source of my childhood memories is my own family. I was very much attached to my grandfather as he was very fond of me. Being the only male child in the family at that time, I received total attention. He used to tell me interesting stories and tales before going to bed. I still cherish fond memories of those stories as he had narrated them to me in a most remarkable and beautiful way. He was able to paint the picture of the verbal description of the stories. I now realize that my attraction to Gandhi and his works was perhaps rooted in me from my early childhood. My grandfather and the other members of the family were very active Congress workers. They had also participated as volunteers for breaking the salt laws. I was told that I had also accompanied them to the nearby tank to offer *satyagraha.* They informed me that I was greatly thrilled to witness the event and enjoyed the journey.

I began going to the village school on attaining the age of five or six. I proved to be a 'good student' as my grandfather guided me regularly. I had a shock of my life when my grandfather died of some stomach pain. He had perhaps premonition of his end as he requested his three sons to summon their youngest brother who was studying at Jabalpur. He came immediately and remained with my grandfather who breathed his last within a period of two or three days. The members of the family found it extremely difficult to cope with the loss. The grief of my grandmother became extremely uncontrollable. My elder sister, cousin brother and myself were asked by our uncles and aunts to remain with the grandmother to divert her attention and perhaps to provide, as social workers would call "emotional support." I was specially attached to the grandmother as my mother had died when I was hardly two-three years old. She gradually began to overcome shock of death of her husband. After passing away of my grandfather, the eldest son then became the head of the family. He asked the youngest brother to go to college and complete his studies. The financial support for his studies continued as before. He completed his studies within a year and could not pursue them any further as the economic conditions of the family had deteriorated and he did not want to be a burden. He took up a teacher's job in the city of Indore and enrolled himself in the evening college for studying law. As he was unmarried, he took his mother with him. A change of place was also welcome from grandmother's point of view. Besides, I too was grown up as I had passed my second standard and the village school did not have higher level. Continuing of my studies required a change of place. So I moved to Indore as the entire family endorsed the idea.

I had to be enrolled in one of the neighbourhood schools of our new rented house. Even in those days, school admissions were not given without a test and interview, although the pressure on parents and children was much less. The transfer certificate from the village school did not prove much useful. The syllabus of the schools in the then Holkar State of which Indore was the capital was much different than the schools of Central Province and Berar sub-region in which my village was located. The teacher asked me first question on rivers of Indore. I did not know the answer as I had never been to Indore before and did not move in the city to get acquainted myself with the important places. The second question was about who the Holkars were. I did not know. The third question was about the discoverer of India. I was feeling ashamed of my inability to answer these questions. In desperation, I shot back and questioned the teacher: "Does this mean there was no India?" The teacher did not like it. I was rejected and not admitted to the school. My uncle had also felt extremely bad for my inability to answer the questions. According to him, all the questions asked were simple. The cousin brother did not face any difficulty as he too was to be admitted to the 1st or 2nd standard.

My uncle brought a number of books for me to read and during holidays took us to important places to get acquainted with the history and topography of the city. In the meantime, I had an attack of typhoid which kept me down for two months. This confinement gave me an opportunity to read books in Hindi on history, geography and autobiographies of great leaders brought to me by my uncle. I read them so attentively and the memory was so sharp that I could recall a point along with the page numbers of the books that I read. In the meanwhile, my uncle had changed the house to be nearer his school to cut the time spent in commuting on bicycle. I appeared in one more test to enter school and passed it with flying colours. In this school also I was asked: "Who discovered India?" I gave a correct answer, i.e., Vasco-da-Gama in 1498 A.D. via new sea-route to India along the Cape of Good Hope of Africa. Subsequently, to my utter surprise, I had found that such questions were listed beneath the lessons in the textbooks. The teachers would only lift the questions and ask them to students.

I would like to mention that my uncle and couple of his

friends who were close to him and often visited us had an extraordinary reverence for Jawaharlal Nehru. Any criticism of Nehru was not tolerated as they were blind followers of Nehru. One of them gave me his biography to read. He also gave Gandhi's autobiography not only to read but also to digest. He wanted me and my cousin brother to develop a tough character like Gandhi so that we were not tempted to fall prey to undesirable things or habits in life. The impact of the book was so powerful that my cousin brother and myself had not touched tea or coffee. In the village, nobody in our family took tea in those days.

It would be clear from the above discussion that my family, the schools, village and the books that I read had greatly influenced me about Gandhi and his thoughts. By the time I reached Class VII, reading of almost all the novels by Munshi Premchand provided me with an insight about the plight of rural poor and their exploitation by the *zamindars* and the rural rich. One more major change came about in our routine. My uncle got married and in order to get permanent footing in the teaching job, he was required to obtain a degree of Bachelor of Education (B.Ed.). He got admission in a college in Ajmer. He kept his wife and children with one of his wife's close relatives. The house was small to accommodate us and therefore we rented a room near our school and thus began to live independently. Both of us were not a financial burden to either of our parents or uncle as I was getting a scholarship of Rs.6 per month and my cousin brother of Rs. 4. Ten rupees per month were sufficient for us to manage our lodging and boarding. The food packed in our tiffin box was so much in surplus that an additional guest had no difficulty to partake of food with us everyday. In fact, we had asked the hotel to give us unlimited quantity of food so that we could feed more people when need arose. The hotel manager was very kind to accept our request to adjust the quantity of fixed quota to suit our needs.

The teachers of the schools in which I had studied, were mostly of Gandhian orientation and thought. A good number of them had also taken to spinning the wheel daily. It would not be wrong to say that the whole country had come under the influence of the magnetic personality of Gandhi. His determination to get India its independence through the technique of non-violence was ringing all over. The period between 1921 and 1941 saw important developments in Indian politics. The Congress party organization was remodelled on a hierarchical basis with the branches in remote villages and franchise extended to all adults of Indian nationality. Its programmes involved all sections of the people. The boycott of foreign cloth was to be pursued by the rich and poor alike, *hartals* (strikes) involved industrialists as well as small shop-keepers, the seller and the customer, Hindus and Muslims, Bengalis and Marwaris. A working class population had emerged out of the slow but steady process of industrialization and trade union activities started operating among them. The Muslims had grown conscious of their position as holding the "balance of power" between the Congress and the Raj, and utilize the situation in full. Within the old framework of an old socio-economic order where new political developments were taking place, Gandhi sought to lead the heterogeneous interest under one discipline (Bandyopadhyay, 1984:IX).

The advice given to me, specially by my uncle (while he was proceeding for his studies to Ajmer), was not to leave my studies to join the Gandhian movement. He and some well-wishers did believe that the country needed highest sacrifices from the young. They were of the opinion that strategically some should go underground to avoid arrest and do work as assigned. The students were best suited to do this kind of job as they will not be easily suspected by the British Police.

II

BHAICHARA OR COMMUNITARIAN LIFE IN THE VILLAGE

The Village Profile: The First Generation Trio

Though there is a caste hierarchy in the village and social relationships are mostly based on the superordination and subordinate status of each caste, interdependence on each other usually forced them to live in harmony and peace. They mutually support each other in social, economic and political fields. The patron-client relationship is very strong in the village. The village has earned a very good name for its treatment to the oppressed and the depressed castes. The village also extends help and assistance to the other neighbouring villages in their needs.

If a villager, belonging to the neighbouring village while passing by this village, has a breakdown of his bullockcart, he is rendered immediate help. In case, he would want a night halt, the temple or the *dharamshala* (an inn) of the village would be opened for him. He will be given the food and his bullocks, water and the fodder. The village was progressing well under the leadership of the trio---the *Lambardar, Patwari* and *Pansari*. The trio was providing a collective leadership to the village. The decision-making was collective and the disputes were resolved amicably. The *nazarana* (*bakshish* or service rental or commission) was divided equally among them. The *Gaon Seth* would not accept his share of the booty but allow them to appropriate his share too. They had excellent cordial relationship among themselves and behaved like brothers while dealing with themselves as well as others. The line of communication among all the three was open and no deal was struck in the absence of the other as reported by the senior informants of the village.

The dominant caste of the village was of *Goras*`or farmers or *kisans* or *Patels*. They were called *Goras* because of their fair complexion. The other appellations were because of their occupation in the field of agriculture. They constituted 60 per cent of the total population. Next came Bhils with 20 per cent and the rest, i.e., Brahmins, Banias, blacksmiths, goldsmiths, tailors, barbers, Muslims, Chamars (tanners) and Bhangis (scavengers) formed remaining 20 per cent. In fact, there were 15 households of Brahmins, three of Banias, two each of blacksmiths, goldsmiths, tailors and barbers. The Chamars and Bhangis had one household each. The women of the village were respected and no untoward incident had happened during the time of the first generation. The trio would also participate in marriage and other ceremonies of the lower caste. The sons-in-law of these castes were treated at par with the other high castes. They were given the same respect as was due to upper caste members. This had raised the status of the lower caste members of the village. This had also raised the status of the lower castes in the eyes of other villages. They were willing to wed their marriageable wards with the prospective wards of this village. The trio also maintained excellent relationship with the district officials as they were looked after well by the *Gaon Seth* whenever they visited the village. The Congressmen of the area also found in them reliable and dependable support. The trio almost served as a power base to the Indian National Congress at the village level. All the three were active members of the Congress.

Second Generation of the Trio

Unfortunately, all three of them died within a span of six months before the call of Quit India Movement in 1942 by Gandhi. The leadership passed into the hands of their respective sons. The elder son of the *Gaon Seth* had to come from the city to take charge of the ancestral property, business and leadership of the village. He was not very much in know of village people and the dynamics of village life. The *Lambardar's* only son was a novice and a bit immature. He was whimsical and had no experience of public life. He was told by his dying father that their forefathers had amassed a fortune which was lying underground in the vessels. His father had warned him not to dig out the vessels as there was enough money over-ground to take care of the family. The son of the *Patwari* was very clever and cunning. His eye was set on the said wealth of the *Lambardar*. He wanted to use old parental ties to continue intimate relationship with the young man to enjoy life with him on his cost. He also wanted *Gaon Seth's* son to join him in exploiting the fortunes of *Lambardar's* son. The *Gaon Seth's* son refused as his father had brotherly relations with the *Lambardar*. He would like to uphold the friendship faithfully rather than dodge the young

Lambardar. The young *Lambardar* often used to take advice and guidance in village affairs from the *Gaon Seth's* city-returned son who was more informed and knowledgeable in laws and procedures. Despite such variations of personal moral codes, all three were the second generation leaders of the village who could not become an excellent team as their parents had done. The new trio was also sympathizers of the Congress. The young *Lambardar* and *Gaon Seth* became its full-fledged members. The latter was elected as the President of the Village Congress Committee.

The *bhaichara* atmosphere of the village began to receive set-backs now. The importance of the ceremonies and rituals began to decline. Their participation in the marriage and other ceremonies of the village also decreased. They offended the lower castes by not treating their guests and sons-in-law as before. The land reforms and gradual advent of market/money economy disturbed the age-old patron-client relationship. Some of the tillers of the land became the owners of the land under new legislation. The theory of 'inter dependence' was replaced by 'independence'. The services of labourers could be hired as they were no longer tied to any individual family or a group. The land owners were free to choose their labourers and *vice versa*. The village disputes, specially concerning the land, were now taken to courts rather than being amicably settled in the village as before. The villagers lost faith in *Patwari*. They felt that he had manipulated the land records to benefit some of his close relatives and friends.

The villagers had a very positive attitude towards us as we used to bring new ideas and information whenever we visited the village during the summer vacations. The villagers were keen on treating us as guests and having mango party with them. The mango season used to coincide with our visits. The villagers were also very kind to us, if need be, in offering bullock cart transport to reach railway station and catch train to Indore. The roads were *kachcha* (unmetalled) and sometimes muddy, requiring two pairs of bullocks to pull the cart through.

Thus, the second generation was not able to maintain cordial and fraternal relationship in the village that was developed by their parents. The village also lost its reputation in the surrounding villages of being helpful to them in their need.

A Case of Earning Money through Wrong Means

I would like to narrate two success stories of the young *Patwari* in which he had succeeded in his designs. He was not favourable to our studying in city. He perceived our education as a threat to his misdeeds and power. He was afraid that there will be a resistance from us to his hoodwinking the ignorant villagers. During one of our visits to village, he became very friendly to me. He would try to detract me from studies by saying that to earn money, education is not necessary. To our parents, he would say that educated people rarely returned to their village and generally settle in one of the urban towns. Higher the education, higher were the chances of not returning to the villages. It is loss to the family as well as to the village. The ladies of the family very much appreciated these arguments. The ladies of the household chalked out a strategy of getting us married at the age of 15 and 16 and thereby keep us rooted to family occupation of farming and business. Fortunately, the male-folk of the family was not convinced of the argument. They were with us and were ready to support our studies for as long a period as we wanted. Our uncle was a model for them. They had also learnt from our sources that education was key to prosperity and progress.

Once the young *Patwari* wanted to tell us how he was earning the money. He used to say that even walls would give the money provided we know how to tap them. He told us a story how he planted a poor young girl into the household of a rich farmer having only his widowed mother and himself. He was unmarried. The young *Patwari* was envious of the riches of the farmer. He wanted to appropriate one of the good orchards of the farmer. He was ready to pay a reasonable price. But the owners did not want to sell at any price as it was very profiting orchard. Besides, their status may decline and may not get a good match for the son. So young *Patwari* waited for right opportunity to come by. Once the widowed mother went out to see the girl for her son. The young *Patwari* succeeded in managing to prepare one Bhil girl for his plot. According to the hatched plot, the Bhil girl was to go to the farmer's house with the load of cow-dung cakes. She was told not to unload it till the young farmer comes out to help her unload. Further, she was to cry, scream and shout for help as soon as he touches the basket on her head, alleging that he was making advances towards her. The hidden *Patwari* would rush to the spot along with the other villagers to her rescue. The Bhil girl was of loose character and her father would send her to anybody who gave him money. The young *Patwari's* plot was successfully executed. Having caught them 'red-handed', the young *Patwari* called girl's father, *Lambardar*, the *Gaon Seth* and others who mattered, to look into the Bhil girl's complaint. A meeting was held in *Chaupal* (a common meeting place) of the village. The trial was held, respective complaints were heard and judgement was unanimously passed holding the farmer guilty. The young *Patwari* played a crucial role in influencing the judgement. He suggested parting with the lucrative orchard by the farmer and giving it to the girl to compensate her for atrocities committed on her. The suggestion was accepted by all including the farmer.

After some time it dawned on the farmer that the whole episode was fabricated. He threatened them with the legal action. The young *Patwari* panicked and came up with a compromising formula that the girl be paid Rs. 500 as courts will take long time to decide and the whole process would incur expenses of lawyers, travels, etc. The villagers did not want the dispute of the village to cross its borders. Finally, an amount of Rs. 400 was settled as a penalty which was duly paid. From this amount, Rs. 100 each was given to the *Lambardar* and girl's father and the remainder was pocketed by the *Patwari*. The *Patwari* told me that he could cite hundreds of such cases from which he extracted money from the ignorant Bhil people.

Patwari's Elopement with a Bhil Girl

The young *Patwari* told me one more scandalous incident. During harvest times he would go to his friend's fields. A large number of young girls and women were employed to harvest the ripe crops. In one such season, he spotted an extremely beautiful, young married Bhil girl in one of his fields. She was jolly and playful. He took the advantage of her nature and seduced her into having regular sexual relations. One day he eloped with her to the city where he had official work. He rented a room and began to live with her. The Bhils lodged a complaint with the village *Panchayat* against the *Patwari*.

The village *Panchayat* summoned the *Patwari* and the girl to appear before them. The *Patwari* informed the *Panchayat* that the girl was working as a domestic servant in the city on her own accord. The girl confessed that she willingly went without informing her in-laws and husband as they were beating her and harassing her for not bearing children since two years of married life. The husband was also to marry again and keep her as a servant and the wage-earner. After her stay with *Patwari*, the girl was not accepted by her parents-in-law and the husband and the *Patwari* also left her to become a prostitute as his family-members opposed him. The *Patwari* went scot-free despite everyone's knowing of his crime of ruining an innocent married girl's life. The villagers were too afraid to do anything against the *patwari*. *Patwari's* power of position and knowledge of law outclassed the collective village social power. He could not be taken to court, tried and punished as villagers were mortified to think of its individual consequences on them. The question of washing dirty village linen in public and losing prestige also deterred them from taking legal action against *Patwari*.

The village informants told me that the entire episode did not pass without consequences. The social prestige of the *Patwari* began to suffer a gradual set-back as the quiet collective social power began to exert. People began to ignore him and withdraw from him. He was neither saluted or wished nor his salutations were responded to. He was simply tolerated as he could not be removed from his office. Once, *Patwari's* house caught fire and as a measure of protest no villager came to his rescue. The *Patwari* family tried to put the fire out but failed and lost the house in fire. Normally, villagers rush to help in such crises, forgetting the differences. But in this case, none went. The *Patwari* became homeless. He took refuge in his in-laws' place in another village and relinquished his office. His elder son was appointed the new *Patwari* of the village.

It was widely believed that the wrath of the God had fallen on him as he was taught a good lesson by God. They reminded themselves of the Gandhian dictum that "purity of means was of equal importance to reach the goal". In the words of Gandhi: "Ends do not justify the means. Means must be as pure as the ends." The unity brought in the village by the first generation was destroyed by one of the leaders of the second generation. The negative solidarity was shown by the villagers when nobody responded in the distress situation of the *Patwari*.

Pardoning the *Patwari*

It was true that the first generation at the time of their departure had seen the second generation maturing along with them. Despite being together for some years, the second generation was not able to imbibe or absorb the values transmitted by the first generation. As we saw village life began to change drastically. The *Patwari* had a change of heart. He confessed to me of his misdeeds and resolve to serve the people by becoming a full time worker of the Congress. He told me to continue my studies as the free country would need officers to run the administration. He recalled the lesson of history as to how the Britishers enslaved the Indians by dividing us in all walks of life. He took a vow to work for the unity, progress and development of the village. He felt that as a Congress worker, he would adopt Gandhi's constructive programme which would bring about all-round development of the individual, village, district, state and the nation. He completely took to *khadi* as he had seen the national upsurge created in the public mind by the *khadi*. As a follower of Gandhi, he believed that *khadi* symbolized self-sufficiency, simplicity and cooperative life, based upon equal justice for all. He also believed that the spinning wheel and *khaddar* would lead not only to political freedom but also to economic emancipation and spiritual self-realization. Besides, the pride of *swadeshi* would induce us to buy only *khadi* cloth which was the main source of employment and neighbourliness.

The villagers were very happy on the change of heart of the *Patwari* and pardoned him for his all past misdeeds. This they did keeping Gandhian principles in mind: "Hate the evil, but hate not the evil-doer." He was invited to come to the village. They all helped him re-build his house. The village once again began to throb with the activities. The influence of the second generation trio became noticeable as village affairs and development were galvanized. My informants told me that *Patwari's* 'home-coming' was not liked by the other two village leaders. They feared his popularity might increase at the cost of theirs as he had linkages with the high-ups in the political circle. They decided to wait and watch him in his new role.

III
PARTICIPATION IN THE QUIT INDIA MOVEMENT

The All India Congress Committee met at Bombay on 8 August, 1942 and passed the "Quit India Resolution". Gandhi declared on the night of 8 August, 1942 that: "I want freedom this moment, this very night, before dawn, if it can be had." He ended his speech with the exhortation: "Do or Die" (Acharya, 1990). The Congress was immediately declared illegal and banned. All Congress leaders were arrested. The rest of the country instantly responded with *hartals* and protests. The telephonic and telegraphic communications were cut. The country was plunged into chaos and disorder. The British government became barbarously repressive (Acharya, 1990:139).

In 1942, I was in the last stage of my matriculation examination. We were active in Congress movement and its various programmes. One of us got arrested while distributing cyclostyled material. He was failed. I received a message to leave Indore immediately to go underground to avoid arrest. The other friend was advised to lie low and avoid visiting arrested friends. The arrested student was very strong in his commitments and convictions. He was told to apologize for his acts so that he could be released. He did not oblige I left for Sanavada, a nearby town, wherein my uncle had become head master of a private school after completing his studies from Ajmer. Contact with local Congress workers was established. I found the activities at a low key. I remained silent and came to Indore only to give examinations. The arrested friend was also allowed to take examinations as he had continued his studies in the jail. Let us now have some idea of the damages done during this period.

The damages done were: 250 railway stations damaged, 550 post offices attacked, 50 post offices burnt, 200 post offices damaged and telephone and telegraph wires were cut at 3,500 places. Firing was resorted to 538 times, 940 were killed and 1,890 were injured. More than 60,000 persons were arrested. Jaya Prakash Narayan escaped from prison and went underground to direct the movement. In fact, it was a leaderless movement and it directed itself. Valour, courage and heroic sacrifice could not make up for the lack of leadership (Acharya, 1990:140). The Muslim League viewed the Quit India Movement as a calculated move on the part of the Congress to compel the British government as well as the Muslims to submit to the Congress rule which means establishment of *Hindu Raj*. At the Karachi session of the Muslim League in 1943, a new slogan "Divide and Quit" was heard (Acharya, 1990:140).

Political Activity in 1943

In 1943, there was lull in political activity due to government repression, famine and war situation. Bengal was struck with a severe famine in 1943. In 1919, India was exporting foodgrains but the output of foodgrains gradually fell. In the first decade of the 20th century, the per capita output of foodgrains was 560 lbs and in 1943 it came down to 399 lbs. In 1942, the Japanese occupied Burma and the rice imports stopped. In 1943, the rains failed. Apart from these natural calamities the war added fuel to the fire in form of the famine. The government purchased large quantities of rice at a fixed price for military consumption. Millions of people died due to the famine. The official estimate put the death at 1.5 million. Prof. Chattopadhyay's estimate was 9.5 million. In rural areas, the people starved silently and died without a groan and growl. Thousands perished in the streets of Calcutta. Nobody tried to snatch a parcel of food from any hotel by force or beg for bread. The government was not ashamed of the scourge for which they could not disown their responsibility. War effort was their first priority. The victims of Bengal famine during the year 1943 outnumbered the total casualties suffered by all the warring nations put together from 1939 to 1945 in the Second World War (Acharya, 1990:144-45).

IV
COLLEGE STUDIES AND VILLAGE WORK

I withdrew from active political work and took to studies as well as "constructive programme of Gandhi". Gandhi often said: "India is a land of villages", and exhorted the people to "go back to the villages and to do the task of national reconstruction". He further said: "Students are the hope of the future. It is from these young man and women that the future leaders of the nation are to rise. Students must not take part in party politics and resort to strikes or agitations. They should also use village products" (Acharya, 1990:89,116,119). A friend of mine and I selected one of the villages approachable by cycle for our work. The village Badi Gawal Toli was three to four kilometres away from Indore. The earlier generation of this village was agriculturalist and kept milch cattle to supply milk to the city. But majority of the present generation have taken to working in a textile mill by selling away their cultivable land to encroaching and spreading city. We began over work in the village by organizing an adult education class. Villagers responded well as we had adopted a teaching method of telling them stories from *Mahabharata* and *Ramayana*. The temple priest found our narration highly stimulating and he became our primary source of support in running this class. Another person called by villagers as *Munshi* (because of having passed elementary education) proved extremely useful. He was a good singer and a natural leader of the village. He continued our classes in our absence as we visited the village twice or thrice. We did spend longer hours on Sundays and holidays.

The supply of pictorial books proved immensely useful. The villagers requested us to get them a regular teacher from the government. The department of education was glad to supply the material, teacher and other facilities to run an adult education centre. Our this success tempted *Munshi* to request us to do something on the health front. He pleaded for the visit of a doctor at least twice a week and to give the village a first-aid box to meet any emergency case. The village did not have a good metalled approach road to connect it with the city. We told our class that before we persuade a good doctor to come to village, we must have a good road so that the doctor can come in his car. The *Munshi* and other villagers decided to call a meeting to discuss the matter. We too were invited in the meeting.

Self-Help Project

In the meeting, *Munshi's* proposal received a very enthusiastic support as a good road would bring a good doctor to treat the ailing children and other villagers. Voluntary labour for constructing an approach road was offered by all. We asked *Munshi* and two other leaders to meet the Collector and the PWD engineer for the advice and help. Both were extremely helpful. The engineer and his staff provided the technical support and the Collector gave some money to buy material for the road. Within eight months the road was completed. A function was organized to felicitate the Director of Health Services, the Chief Engineer and the Collector. The villagers had cleaned their houses, main streets, by-lanes, pond and the temple. The village gave a festive and new look. The entire village participated in the function. The leaders of the village had made one of the oldest men of the village to preside over the function. The village priest recited invocation prayer. The children were prepared to give a short cultural programme. The function was a great success. The officials were happy that the self-help project was completed so well. The Chief Engineer promised to make the road *pucca* by his department. The Director of Health agreed to provide services of a compounder for three days a week. The doctor of the Government Health Centre would visit the village thrice a week. A private doctor had also agreed to give free services twice a week. The Director of Education did not want to lag behind and announced the starting of a primary school in the village from the next session. All the projects were completed within one year.

We felt we had made the villagers sufficiently self-reliant. We had developed a creative and responsible local leadership to take care of their problems by themselves. Whatever was hitherto 'extrinsic' had now become 'intrinsic'. We, therefore, decided to withdraw from the village. We had prepared the village leaders in such a way that the initiative always remained with them. The villagers reluctantly agreed to our withdrawing and in turn extracted a promise from us that we would remain in contact by occasionally visiting each other mutually.

The news of our work in this village reached my native village. The second generation trio of leadership in my village wanted me to take up similar programmes. I declined by admitting my limitation of being 140 kms away to Indore and from such a distance leadership and monitoring cannot be provided. College studies and other work with which I was associated in Indore kept me preoccupied and my visits to the village became rarer. There was no significant event or activity worth mentioning from 1945-47.

V
DAWN OF INDEPENDENCE

Lord Mountbatton, the last Viceroy of India, took charge on 26

March, 1947. His compromise plan was assented by the Congress and the League leaders on 3 June, 1947. The following were the important provisions:

1. Two independent dominions of India and Pakistan were to be carved out.
2. Pakistan would comprise of Sindh-Baluchistan, East Bengal and West Punjab. A British jurist would preside over the boundary commission.
3. Referendum would be held in NWFP and Sylhet. The Legislators of West Bengal and East Punjab would exercise their option for joining either India or Pakistan on behalf of their territories.
4. The princely states could join either side (Acharya, 1990:154).

The Congress was unhappy at the partition. Jinnah was sore at losing East Punjab, West Bengal and Assam and that the two wings of Pakistan would be separated by more than 700 miles. Lord Mountbatton instinctively chose 15 August, 1947 as the date of independence, because it synchronized with the second anniversary of Japan's surrender. He cleverly presented his plans to Gandhi on 4 May, 1947, saying that it combined all possible elements of Mahatma's approach to the tangle. There was grudging admiration as well as admonition in Gandhi's chiding words of reply: "You and your magic tricks" (Acharya, 1990:155).

Congress Committee Passes the Resolution

The All India Congress Committee met at Delhi on 14-15 June, 1947 to ratify the decision of the Working Committee's acceptance of the Mountbatton Plan. P.D. Tandon opposed the resolution saying: "The partition would not benefit either community, the Hindus in Pakistan and Muslims in India would live in fear." Patel supporting the resolution said: "Now the Congress can develop 75 per cent of the country unhampered. The Muslim League can develop Pakistan." Nehru supporting the resolution pleaded: "The most urgent task at present is to arrest the drift towards anarchy and chaos by establishing a strong central government." Gandhi who had proclaimed earlier that "vivisect me before you vivisect India," now advised to accept the resolution. In the latter years, Gandhi was not even a primary member of the Congress. But he was, in the words of Nehru, "the paramount super president of the Congress". The resolution was carried by 157 votes for it, 29 against it and 32 remaining neutral (Acharya, 1990:157). The Muslim League Council met at Delhi on 10 June, 1947 and endorsed partition. Jinnah got the mutilated, maimed and moth-eaten Pakistan that he never wanted. How he reconciled to it was a riddle, wrapped in an enigma (Acharya, 1990:158-159).

The First Independence Day: Gandhi's Relevance Lost

It was celebrated throughout India on 15 August, 1947 with spontaneous enthusiasm. I too joined with great excitement. The people recollected the heroic sacrifices of the freedom fighters and offered homage to the martyrs. Their portraits and photos were taken out in procession by the local people at the flag-hoisting place with patriotic fervour. But Gandhi, the Father of the Nation, venerated as *Bapu* by the populace, was absent at the inaugural ceremony of Indian independence at Delhi, as he was immersed in the invocation of peace at Noakhali (Acharya, 1990:161-162).

Gandhi was not only soon forgotten but his relevance was also questioned by his followers in new India. On many occasions, Gandhian values, ideas and principles were not honoured even by his favourites like Nehru and Patel. To cite a few examples, the Congress accepted ministerial responsibility in 1937 against Gandhi's pronounced dislike. In 1939-40, when Gandhi was pleading for cooperation for British war-efforts, the Congress Working Committee resolved not to give any assistance. And, finally, when Gandhi was trying hard to resist the partition of India, in their haste for transfer of power, the Congress leaders accepted the partition scheme. Rajgopalachari passed the resolution in Madras Legislature, ratifying the partition even before the negotiations at the central level were finalized. Gandhi had to say: "Let me fight my lone battle" (Bandyopadhyay, 1984:359).

Despite negative reaction by his followers, to some of his policies and goals, Gandhi was able to inspire millions by example or practice rather than precept. Non-violence was a creed of the Mahatma but not a policy of the Congress. Gandhi proclaimed: "If some one fired at me point-blank and I faced his bullet with a smile, repeating the name of Rama, then I should deserve congratulations." On 30 January, 1948, Nathuram Godse accosted the Mahatma with a bowing '*namaste*' and shot him thrice. Bleeding Gandhi fell down uttering "Hei Ram" and died. The dastardly crime committed against the nation by Godse was condemned by all. Mercifully, the overwhelming opinion was against Godse's way of thinking. The biography of great man does not end with his death. In fact, it begins with his death. The sparks of Gandhi will illuminate many hearts in the world for generations to come (Acharya, 1990:168-69).

The martyrdom of Mahatma Gandhi has been truly described as the "Second Crucifixion" in the history of mankind. Martyrdom is the only meaningful word to sum up the life of the Mahatma. The whole world mourned the death of Gandhi. To many people world over, Gandhi's death was a personal loss. I did not have personal contact with Mahatma, but I had seen him when he came to Indore, most probably in the 1930s. I am unable to recall the exact date from my memory or the notes I used to keep as a hobby. But I still have very vivid memories of that meeting specially when he appealed for funds, women offered instantaneously their gold chains, ringlets, bangles, etc.----all perhaps out of love, trust and regard for the leader. He left a lasting impression on me. Yet, should I say that I had a close rapport with Gandhi as my devoted *Guru* in social work more or less like Eklavya? As we know from his writings, his magnetic personality and appeals were so inspiring that at Vijayawada Meet 31 March, 1921 the Congress resolved to collect a crore rupees for Tilak Fund, by enlisting a crore of members and introducing 20 lakh *charkhas* before 30 June, 1921. The Fund was oversubscribed and the membership reached 50 lakhs (Acharya, 1990:89 and Krishnamurthy, 1933:15).

VI
SOCIAL WORK IN MY OWN VILLAGE

I had decided that I should now work for my own village as on the eve of independence, I had attained the matured age of 21 years and had also completed my studies at Indore. Henceforth, I would be taken seriously by villagers and not viewed as a village lad who was moving in the streets of the village. I was awaiting response to my application for admission in the Tata Institute of Social Sciences (TISS) for further training in social work.

I found that the unity among the trio and the villagers was of superficial nature. Concern for the village as a whole was missing. The present leadership failed to inspire the villagers. The school headmaster was the only person to enjoy their trust. I found in him a noble person dedicated to the Gandhian ideals and having real interests in rural development.

Third Generation Leadership and Various Campaigns

I went to the school which was now raised to 4th standard. On meeting, I found him to be highly disciplined and a matured person. I gathered from his talk that he was very keen on taking up some constructive work in the village. He was the only person with whom I could communicate comfortably as our mental make-up was of one level, although we belonged to different age-groups. He suggested to clean up the surroundings of four drinking water wells of the village. This work would neither invoke any resistance nor incur any cost. The school children will participate in the campaign. I readily agreed as in my mind also same ideas for self-help project, having demonstrative effect on the villagers were rising. *Guruji,* as the headmaster, was popularly known and referred to, visited some of the households of the village. He talked to the heads of the households and the ladies about his campaign. The ladies immediately welcomed the idea and agreed to arrange brooms and other material needed for the project. *Guruji* was very pleased to bring to school and community together. *Guruji* and I divided the women and children of the village into four groups for four wells. A woman was assigned to lead each group. For the first time in the history of the village, women became active. The men did not interfere much, rationalizing that the work of cleaning the well belonged in the domain of women.

The peer group belonging to my age had been often meeting me to have informed decisions about the city life. The son of the *Lambardar* suggested to me that the programme of cleaning the whole village should be taken up rather than limiting it to only the wells. He was confident that youth of the village would join such a campaign. I happily welcomed the suggestion. *Guruji* too liked the idea as it will galvanize the whole village. He, however, wanted the first project to get over without being disturbed. He assigned the work of cleaning the streets to the boys under the leadership of *Lambardar's* son who readily shouldered the responsibility. He was asked to lead the group and assign the tasks to smaller sub-groups under a team leader to work in different lanes of the village. About seven team leaders were picked up by the son of the *Lambardar*. *Guruji* asked him to bring all of them to draw a detailed plan of work.

The caste composition of leaders made us conscious that lower castes and tribes were going unrepresented. The streets of their locality were also left out. This lapse of the group leader was disapproved by us. This would create caste conflict and may jeopardize village unity and peace. It was impressed upon the young boys that the whole village should be considered as one unit and all sub-units should be involved in the interest of "whole village development." Our point was accepted and two more leaders were selected from the SC and ST groups. They also agreed that the SC/ST boys would clean the lanes of the high caste areas and the high caste boys would clean the lanes of low caste areas. We were happy to bring about such change of attitudes in the young leaders. The work was completed as planned by all the teams including the women's team. The experience in collective working paved the way for taking up self-help projects. The village elders were happy to see the otherwise time-wasting village youth, being engaged in such useful work. They felt that if directed properly, the youth of the third generation is capable of changing the face of the village.

Mobilizing People for Reconstructing the Village Tank

The leaders of the *Panchayat* and other elders became very ambitious. They thought of deploying the robust 'youth power' to reconstruct the village tank. They consulted *Guruji* for direction and guidance. *Guruji* expressed his inability to join such a big project as he lacked expertise and may also be transferred as he was to complete three years within six months. He was assured by the villagers that they will persuade the authorities not to transfer him till the project was completed. The village had full faith in him. He was made the treasurer and authorized to choose chairman of the committee anyone from amongst the members of the village. *Guruji* requested them to call a meeting of the *Gaon Sabha* (Village General Assembly) to decide about the project. He emphasized on complete involvement and participation by all the villagers. He told them that the project would require raising resources in men, money and material. My involvement was also to be solicited. When I was told about the project by the villagers, my only suggestion to them was that the project would need a technical help and hence it should commence only thereafter. The District Irrigation Engineer (DIE) should be consulted after preparing a detailed project proposal, taking into account technical, economic and social aspects.

Problems of Bureaucratic Apathy and Obstacles

Four or five village leaders went to the district headquarters to meet the DIE. They waited for two to three hours. Fortunately, he gave them a good hearing and agreed to depute one of the Assistant Irrigation Engineers (AIE) to visit the village. The AIE did not come. One of the village leaders went to the DIE to remind him of his promise to send AIE. He apologetically explained the reasons and assured to send the AIE on the following working day. Still, AIE did not turn up. The same village leader again went to the DIE. This time, neither the DIE nor AIE were available. From the office he found out that they were not visiting because of no transport. He also warned the village leader not to depend on the engineering staff of the district. The staff would continue to avoid coming to village, unless the palms of the persons whom they wanted to visit were greased.

The villagers ultimately gave up the idea of having a person from the DIE office. They got some private engineer who was willing to help them to prepare the project for a nominal consultation and travel fees. We were happy to know of this development. He told us to organize small meetings in each lane of the village to mobilize people for the project to appraise them of the objectives and the benefits that would accrue from the project. Three benefits were to accrue: (a) drinking water for the village cattle; (b) facility of washing *ghat* (platform) for women; and (c) planting and growing trees for shade/shelter for shepherds and cattle-grazing activity in this area. I could not join the public deliberations on the subject as I was to leave next day for higher studies at Mumbai. *Guruji* and the village leaders asked me to come to village in next summer vacation. They were hopeful of completing the tank project by then. I requested them to keep me informed about the progress of the project by writing letters.

A meeting of *Gaon Sabha* was held after a month of my departure to TISS, Mumbai which I had joined after my Master of Economics. In the first letter, *Guruji* wrote that for the first time elderly women attended the meeting. However, not a single daughter-in-law of the village attended the meeting. Because, the village custom was that the daughters-in-law should not cross the limit of coming to the *Choupal*, as it would mean that they are summoned by the *Panchayat* for having committed some crime. *Guruji* further wrote that it would take some time to break the prejudice. This reminded me of Einstein's words that "... it was easy to break an atom but not a prejudice".

The letter was full of praise for the small sub-group meeting held in the village. It paved the way for a unanimous decision to take up the big self-help project. All the members of this committee were elected unanimously. The village headman (the *Lambardar*) was elected as the chairman, the son of the *Patwari* who had replaced the father as the secretary, and the *Gaon Seth* as the treasurer. A representative from each lane would be its members. Their names were duly approved. Three women also joined as the members of the committee. A sub-committee of the youth was also constituted to support and stand by the main committee. The private engineer and I were requested to serve as consultants to the committee. The work would start on an auspicious day and time as suggested by the village. I wrote back to *Guruji* expressing great satisfaction and joy at the progress and proceedings.

The second letter informed me that the work had started on the project with the chanting of *mantras* (hymns) and by breaking coconut. The sweets were distributed among the villagers who attended the function. Each household was supplying two people to give voluntary labour or deposit wages in cash for two labourers. A roaster had been prepared for deployment of labourers by the secretary. He had been keeping good records. He had proved to be a good manager for the project. The other news was that he had received transfer orders despite villagers' appeal to the authorities to extend his term. He was to leave within a month and thus end his association with the village and the project. It seems the authorities perhaps had not appreciated his involvement and participation in community work in the village. He had no options of alternative means but to resign and serve the community and hence he obeyed the orders to keep his service. The *Patwari* had fully enjoyed his work and satisfied with his involvement in village project. The lessons that he learnt from his work with people of the village could be summarized in social work terminology (Heap, 1979:73) as follows:

1. Stimulating intimate interaction.
2. Facilitating communication about needs and problems.
3. Aiding learning, growth and development.
4. Contributing to physical and social environment change.
5. Preparing for future development and change.

In the end, he wrote that he had asked the secretary of the committee to write to me. My reaction to his transfer from the village was that it would be a great blow to the project as he was respected by all and was a very vigilant and important watch-dog of village interests. His moral authority was accepted by all. He was an outsider and had no vested interest in village politics or group dynamics. He had commenced withdrawing himself from the village by not taking any active responsibility in the work of project committee except as one of the consultants. Thus, we both had to withdraw from the village scene due to the situations beyond our control. I did not receive any letter from the secretary. I was eager and anxious to know about the progress of the project. I, therefore, rushed to the village as soon as the summer vacation commenced.

Upon reaching the village, I found a totally gloomy atmosphere because the project work was suspended. The DIE had stopped the work on the ground that a number of neighbouring villages would be flooded in the event of an overflow in the reservoir of the tank. He had, therefore, rejected the plans prepared by the private engineer as he, being a civil engineer, had no experience in irrigation work. They had to obey the government orders. The work had not progressed an inch since then.

Corruption: The Only Way

The village leaders were of the opinion that bribing the officials was the only way to get this done as they had been doing in British days. They did not expect the bureaucratic culture and system to change with the advent of independence. The villagers suspected the fowl play by AIE as he was not given 'customary money' to visit the village site. They could not oblige him due to the 'moral pressure' created by the *Guruji* and I. They inquired whether I would be agreeable to allow them to deal with the DIE and AIE in the same (bribing) manner as in the past? My emphatic reply was a big no ! The members of the third generation were greatly agitated and wanted to do *satyagraha* in front of the DIE's office. This may attract the public attention and might force the DIE to revoke his orders. I advised them to refrain from it as it would be very difficult to sustain the *satyagraha* due to the distant location of the office. It would not be easy for people to go and come every day to do *dharana* (sitting in strike) at his office. They were convinced of this possibility and in turn asked me to make a representation to DIE on their behalf.

The secretary and I met the DIE but he did not budge. He only advised us to wait for some time as the plans to tap water resources were being made. This would help the villagers to link their project with other projects. I returned very disappointed as the DIE did not revoke his orders. I met other officials but to no avail. Everybody asked us to file a written application if we had any complain against the DIE or his staff. It would be looked into due course. Ultimately, we were left with no alternative but to mark the time and wait for the opportune moment to start the work again.

Scepticism in Approaching the Politicians

The *Patwari*, belonging to the second generation and silently working as a Congress worker, suggested that he could approach the District Congress President and request him to use his influence over the DIE. The *Lambardar* and the *Gaon Seth* were not willing to let the initiative slip into his hands. They suspected his real intentions as he might be wanting to be the leader of the village. They were also not sure about the price that they may have to pay for such a favour from the political bosses. They knew that most politicians were unprincipled and unreliable, since in post-independence the age-old moral and civic values had been completely eroded. Therefore, they did not want intervention of any external person in the village affairs. They had firm faith in 'divine force' and preferred to wait for God's mercy to get the situation resolved.

Recourse to Gandhian Constructive Programmes

I did not want the village to lose its enthusiasm and the unity to break up due to such a set-back. I, therefore, suggested to them to take to Gandhian constructive programmes. Such programmes as village sanitation, adult education, women welfare and agricultural development were accepted by the villagers. They decided that it would be the duty of every villager to make the village a model of cleanliness. The literate and so-called educated villagers belonging to the third generation committed themselves to take adult education classes and wipe out illiteracy from the village. It was decided that the women be given equal opportunity of education and the status of equal partners in village development. In order to improve the agricultural yield per acre, they decided to popularize improved quality of seeds and implements. The other programmes would be developed as and when needed according to availability of resources. Most of these activities became routinized and nothing exciting or worth mentioning happened until the arrival of Community Development Programme (CDP) in 1952. My visits to the village almost became rare and that too of greatly reduced duration. Nevertheless, I managed to remain informed about the 'going-on' in the village.

Advent of the CDP

The Block Development Officer (BDO) was impressed by the level of participation of the villagers in various developmental activities that were organized by themselves. The work done so far was credited to the good officers of the block. As a result, a Village Development Committee (VDC) was constituted by the BDO with the help of the *Lambardar's* son belonging to the third generation. *Lambardar* himself had declined to head the VDC as he was getting old and would not have the stamina to visit block headquarters in connection with the development work of the village. The other leaders also refused to be members of the VDC and nominated their eldest sons as members. Surprisingly, there was not a single woman on the VDC. The third generation *Lambardar* became very powerful as the VDC met very rarely. The BDO directly dealt with the *Lambardar*. Both of them were on friendly terms.

The staff of the BDO claimed the money for public participation for the works already done by the villagers. The *Lambardar* as the chairman of the VDC signed all the documents. The claimed amount was mostly shared by the BDO and the *Lambardar*. The whole deal was kept strictly secret. A very little amount was given to the VDC for the work done in the past. The members of the VDC were happy to receive unexpected amount from the block. This amount was used for repairing village *chaupal*.

In one of the rounds to the village, the BDO saw the incomplete tank. He told *Lambardar* that this work can be taken up as CDP work. The BDO was appraised of the problem of tank project. The BDO assured to tackle the DIE and the villagers should not worry. The fund was available under BDO to renovate the old tanks. The *Lambardar* agreed to take up the work. The *Lambardar* was seeking the permission of the BDO for convening the meeting of the VDC instead of asking him the date of his convenience. The officials were still treated as 'masters' and not as 'servants' of the people. This nexus between the two resulted in a dependency relations for the village. The meeting was called and well attended. The BDO assured the villagers that he would be able to get the DIE's order cancelled. The BDO almost became a demi-God among the villagers as they did not know of the secret nexus between him and the *Lambardar*. The order was accordingly withdrawn and new order was issued by DIE. The explanation offered for this delay was that the clerk of the DIE's office had dropped or misplaced the blueprints of the project. Besides, the objections raised earlier by the office were now adequately clarified by the consulting engineer of the village. The erring clerk was reprimanded and warned to be careful in future. In this matter people proved cleverer. They did not believe that the DIE would agree to give permission to re-start the work without some deal over the booty. However, the villagers were more interested in the tank rather than the manipulations over spoils among the DIE, BDO and the *Lambardar*. The deal was so cleverly struck and executed that it was difficult to catch them. One of the villagers remarked about the developmental funds from government that the "bounties released in the name of people's participation was greatest source of spreading corruption in villages." They in turn made people 'dependent' and the 'self-help projects' were thrown overboard.

The village tank project was completed but instead of its creating a collaborative and cooperative attitude among the villagers, a loss of village unity resulted. The villagers lost faith and trust not only in their leaders but also in themselves. The *bhaichara* phase of life, i.e., mutually depending on each other, had completely disappeared. The modern facilities began to be reaching the village. It was now linked with a bus route to the district headquarters. The arrival of electricity brought with it television and all other ills of urban life. The competitive electoral politics has taken root in the village. The people are divided on caste and party lines. The dominant caste of *Patel* still dominates the village politics and affairs. *Lambardar* belonged to this caste.

First *Panchayat* Election and the Fourth Generation

The third generation is tired and the fourth generation feels that they had become the victims of the lingering third generation.

The third generation was not able to upheld either Gandhian values or village unity which was ushered in by *Guruji* and myself. They attributed the failure of the third generation to the lack of responsible participation and inadequate vigilance. They erred in entrusting the complete responsibility to the *Lambardar* regarding village affairs. It was not enough that he acts responsibly but it was equally essential that we should have made him feel that he was under our constant vigilance and watch. In other words, the members of the VDC should have insisted on calling the meetings to monitor and review the work of the project.

The first election of the head (*Pradhan*) of the village *Panchayat* was most fiercely fought. For other offices and positions very rarely had anyone ever bothered to occupy. Each aspirant candidate for the office of the *Pradhan* had prepared a panel in consultation with his supporters to get his team elected. Two sons---one of the *Lambardar* and the other of the *Gaon Seth*----were in the village political arena, staking their claim to the highest office in the village. One of the Brahmins of the third generation was also prompted by some villagers to stand and fight for the *Pradhan's* office. In reality, the fight was between the two and third generation contestants which had neither numerical strength of their respective castes nor effective support from other higher castes with the exception of Bhils, Chamars and Bhangis who had assured him their support. The whole village was divided into three warring groups. The *Gaon Seth* drew his strength from his clients who belonged to all castes. He felt that his clients would support him.

Finally, the *Lambardar's* son belonging to the fourth generation was elected. The candidates who got defeated sadly decided not to cooperate with the *Lambardar*. He got the votes from his caste fellows, as his caste proved to be a vote-bank for him. They were not ready to lose their traditional hold on the village headship and get humiliated. He could not accomplish anything during his tenure. Corruption in his tenure reached new heights. He would not allow anybody to even raise a compound wall of his house or any other place without paying customary *nazarana*. The villagers who did not pay were harassed. He became very unpopular among the villagers but maintained good relationship with the concerned officials. He did bring some innovative programmes which were mostly taken up by active members of his own caste. In the process, he ended up alienating some of the members of his own caste and the rest of the village. In his own caste, two factions emerged—one supporting him and the other opposing him.

Second Election and the Fifth Generation

The fifth generation was born after mid-1960s. The *Lambardar* belonging to the fourth generation was not sure to win the next election on the strength of the support of his faction alone. As a face-saving device, he nominated his own son belonging to the fifth generation to fight elections. In case the election is lost, the ensuing humiliation would be much less than otherwise. This time five candidates were in the electoral race. Two belonged to the rival factions of the *Lambardar's* caste, a son of *Gaon Seth*, the Brahmin who had fought the earlier election and one each from the barber and the Scheduled Castes. Despite lot of adverse publicity, the *Lambardar's* son belonging to the fifth generation was elected. Unlike earlier times, the defeated candidates did not join together to give a tough time to the elected headman. The individuality had taken over the value of collectivity. Winning and losing elections was like individually won or lost games. The 'community feeling' was fractured.

VII
IMPACT OF MASS MEDIA, WESTERN CULTURE AND POLITICS

The most astonishing fact was that such a situation was prevalent in other villages also. It appears that Indian villages have almost lost their moorings. The communitarian life of the village is replaced by confrontationist and conflict-ridden life as electorally-guided factionalism gradually increased. The political party system has penetrated the village society with a vengeance. The glamour of western culture projected by TV has dazzled villagers to such an extent that they have forgotten the role of their own history and culture in having a united and corporate life. It seems there is a complete obliteration of heroic values from the collective memory of villagers in particular and Indians in general. The creative traditions which have motivated us through the ages to live as members of one single family are getting wipe out from our collective memory.

Besides, even at a national level, the unprincipled, crudely power-centred and populist electoral politics of the post-independence era has led to the loss of India's secular policies. The populist electoral politics has further led to social discrimination, corruption and finally discontent among people. The age-old moral and civil values have been extensively eroded. Consequently, finding no solution into the socio-economic problems, people resort to violence (Nigam, 1993:8).

During the pre-independence days, Mahatma Gandhi practiced and demonstrated renunciation as a core value in national life. The whole nation stood up as one man against the alien rule because there was an ideal and leadership of sterling character before the people. The early days of independence did have some spill-over of the qualities of the erstwhile days. Sardar Patel was a man of steel. Lal Bahadur Shastri's uprightness and other sterling qualities came to be known and recognized after his untimely death. The nation fondly remembers such noble stalwarts and their contribution (Pillar, 1993:8).

Money and muscle have made perfect combination in free India. Those at the helms of national affairs did pretty little to hold aloft a resurgent India with value systems for which Pandit Nehru and Lal Bahadur Shastri toiled all along. Those who uphold values are in a microscopic minority and are relegated to helplessness and eventual ruin. Remedy lies in adopting good electoral reforms, leadership adopting transparent virtue systems, setting examples for others to follow and thus giving out correct signals to the teeming millions. Our countrymen would then see the glimmer of light at the end of the tunnel and a new wave of popular support for national reconstruction will overflow (Pillar, 1993:8). Some of the *satyagrahis* who were still alive told me that when they arrived home after being released from prison, he invariably found the roof of his old house in ruins, parents dead, the where-about of the mentally deranged wife unknown, movable property alienated, children taken away by their poor maternal uncle to his house which was worse than an orphanage and the sky seemed to be the only limit to his sacrifice. Why all these self-effacing sacrifices? It was an era of all making glorious sacrifices for the sake of sacrifices because the goal of *swaraj* was beyond the immediate reach and there were no other rewards or recognitions visible. Still the *satyagrahis* suffered so that India becomes free in future. Patriots died so that India may live (Acharya, 1990:123). It is sad to see our forefathers' sacrifices going in wane.

This situation in which we have landed should remind us of Gandhi's prophetic words: "Man could fly in air like a bird, swim under water like a fish but unfortunately could not live like a man on earth. Man has tamed the elements and conquered space; but could not control his passion. Thus, man also perished in spite of the marvellous and mighty civilization he had built, caught in the whirlpool of his own creation." "Modern science" bemoaned Gandhi, "is able to make all men neighbours but could not make them brothers" (Acharya, 1990:171). Moral bankruptcy of the modern civilizations has brought man to the brink of a bottomless abyss, threatening the very existence of the *Homo Sapiens* on this planet. The greatest problem which India and perhaps the whole world today is facing is the crisis of 'human character.'

VIII
CHALLENGE TO PROFESSIONAL SOCIAL WORKERS

The above discussion poses a great challenge (among others) to professional social workers. They have to think and ponder over their training programmes and activities. They cannot rest by occupying good positions and continue to fight for better emoluments for them. We cannot continue to sing tune of our uniqueness of methods and techniques which till today are heavily dependent on western model.

A comparative study of two villages would lead us to believe that there has been a fewer successes in the work at the micro level. This general inability to arrest macro-level influences or to help people to discern between good and evil has disintegrated the village society in spite of much greater overlap of successive generations. Re-visits to the same villages after a long spell gives a pathetic picture. The village near the Indore city has been eaten away by the city. Most of the villagers were induced to sell their landed properties or the same were acquired by urban development authorities for so called development purposes. They did not get good price for their properties and adequate compensations. All this money was evaporated in gambling and prostitution. They are now living in the slum areas of the city.

If some sort of counselling services about the investment of money that was realized from the sale of land were to be provided to the villagers, they would have been saved from the disastrous situation in which they have now landed. Such a step would require an advanced knowledge of government plans and their implementation schedule. In the absence of such an information, the local level worker would find himself high and dry and would continue to work at micro level without linking it to macro level planning and policies.

In the second village, the village community has been completely disintegrated because of corruption and local leaders' collaboration with officials. The social workers must continuously ask the question and specify their role about the sudden downfall in our moral and social standards. India won her political independence in 1947 and so a period of less than a century is quite insignificant in the history of a nation. This is the time when we could have made joint efforts and developed appropriate strategies to build our nation and enrich our common cultural heritage which has been the cementing force behind Indian unity in the midst of wide-ranging diversities. A series of questions rise and stare at us: What went wrong in our developmental process to change the course of events? Where did we fail? Answering such and other questions must attract our attention. We must apply ourselves to know the reasons for the social unrest and disharmony which are threatening the very existence and solidarity of the nation (Nigam, 1993:6). Would professional workers rise to the occasion and accept the challenges? The social workers should leave their narrow cocoons and address themselves to the issues of national importance.

There is a moral in two case studies detailed here. Sustainable development requires a continuum and an ability to learn from past mistakes with the micro and macro levels. The modest and entirely legitimate aspirations of the people of post-Independence India have suffered a severe set-back because of the nation's disastrous experiment with *Neta-Babu* (politician-bureaucrat) socialism. This brand of socialism has made rich people, including *Neta-Babu* variant, richer and poor people poorer. Now at a time when the nation is being led out of wilderness with the introduction of market-led, deregulatory economic reforms, the last thing it needs is a cultural revolution (Thakore, 1993:6). Let me end this paper by commenting on culture and organization. There are three phases of socio-cultural progression of any social organization. In our two villages we found the evidence of such a progression. The first phase consists of the formulation of values and traditions, the second deals with the stabilization of those values and traditions and the last leads to superannuation, i.e., decay and disintegration. Indian society as a whole is presently passing through the third stage. Let us hope as they say that the night is the darkest when the light is the nearest.

[The author is thankful to Prof. Y. C. Simhadri for providing an excellent opportunity to work in the excellent natural environment of Nagarjuna University, Nagarjuna Nagar, Andhra Pradesh.]

NOTE

The Mahatma knew the pulse of the common people and could comprehend the impulses of the masses. Salt is an indispensable daily necessity of everybody. As per the Indian Salt Act of 1882, the government possessed the monopoly on the collection and manufacture of salt. "The government" proclaimed Gandhi, "has no right to levy tax on salt, a free gift of natural geography and England was not expected to collect tax from the poor peasant of India who earns seven paise per day." Mahatma Gandhi started his march from the Sabarmati Ashram on 12 March, 1930 and the destination was Dandi, a small village on the sea-shore of Gujarat. The distance of 241 miles was covered in 24 days. Gandhi carefully picked up a band of 78 followers from the disciplined disciples of the Ashram. Gandhi and his party reached Dandi on 6 April, 1930 and they defied the mighty British government by picking up natural salt and thus breaking the salt laws. The salt *satyagraha* turned out to be a veritable volcanic eruption. Thousands gave up their jobs and studies and consequently 60,000 *satyagrahis* swelled the British jails.

REFERENCES

Acharya, N.V.R.K. (1990), *The Gandhian Era*. Hyderabad: Cavery Publications.

Bandyopadhyay, Gitasree (1984), *Constrains in Bengal Politics 1921-1941---Gandhian Leadership*. Calcutta: Surat Book House.

Gandhi, M. K. (1992), *The Story of my Experiments with Truth: An Autobiography*. Ahmedabad: Navjivan.

Heap, Ken (1979), *Process and Action in Work with Groups*. New York: Perganeon Press.

Karlekar, Hiranmay (1993), "Politics Without Hope", *Indian Express*, Vijayawada Edition, Friday, 26 November.

Krishnamurthy, B. (1933), "Freedom Fighters of Krishna District: Purna Malikarjunadu a True Gandhian," *Deccan Chronicle*, Vijayawada Edition, Monday, 22 November.

Nayak, G.C. (1993), "Kautilya and Gandhi", *Indian Philosophical Quarterly*, 20(4), October.

Nigam, M. L. (1993), "Need for Cultural Regeneration", *Deccan Chronicle*, Vijaywada Edition, 24 November.

Pillar, A.R.K. (1993), "Combating Corruption", (Letters to Editor) *Indian Express*, Vijaywada Edition, 23 November.

Thakore, Dilip (1993), "BJP's Cultural Revolution", *Deccan Chronicle*, Vijaywada Edition, 25 November.

Venkata Ramanan, K. (1978), *Nagarjuna's History*. New Delhi: Motilal Banarsidass.

10

Age Care Policies and Programmes: Challenges Ahead

by K.V. Ramana

"Winter is on my head; but there is eternal sunshine in my heart."
----Victor Hugo

Ageing of the population is emerging as an issue of great socio-demographic concern to all countries of the world, whether they are developed or developing. Although, the nature of the problems, challenges and situations faced by the countries of northern and southern hemispheres is on the one hand, quite different and on the other hand, somewhat similar too (Krishnan and Mahadevan, 1992). The academic disciplines like social work and sociology are continuously bracing themselves to develop the field of gerontology as part of their responses to the emerging social problems (Mahadevan *et.al.*,1992).

This field focuses on the nature of the relationship that is taking shape between the social institution of family and political institution of the state *vis-a-vis* the issue of caring for the elderly (Walker,1982). In order to obtain correct and deeper insights into the social gerontology, social policy and public policy, a question must be raised as to why does the family care for the elderly. Historically, the family is the main source of care for the elderly. But, in the industrial and post-industrial developed capitalist societies, the values, character and composition of family have changed so much that the elderly somewhat tend to get neglected. Yet, it is firmly established that there is no adequate and comprehensive substitute to family so far as the question of elderly care is concerned (Levin,1986). The state and the politicians are found to be busy in shirking their responsibility as they throw the ball back to the family, neighbourhood or community. They argue that family is the best place where the elderly can be best cared.

This has led the debate to one more point of conflict as to who in family is going to care for the elderly of the family. The feminists are extremely critical as the burden of elderly care falls on women in the family. This is far more true in non-western societies as ratio of male-female carers is shrinking in west. The feminist argument is considerably true as a woman plays three roles of caring in one life. That is, in the first role, she cares for either her's or her husband's parents in their old age. Secondly, she attends to her husband in his old age and finally herself in her own old age (Kitazawa, 1986).

It is against such a theoretical and empirical backdrop that this paper attempts to examine the question of appropriate policies and programmes for the needy aged population in India.[1] In the first section, demographic profile of the elders in the world and in India is briefly attempted. The second section examines the changing role of the elderly by looking into the origin and activities of RSVP movement (Retired and Senior Volunteers Programme). How and what type of welfare services in India are organized and available is briefly discussed in the third section. The fourth section discusses the rationale and relevance of ageing policies and programmes at the global as well local level. The paper ends with a glimpse of challenges lying ahead in the field of social gerontology.

I
DEMOGRAPHIC PROFILE OF THE ELDERLY

Global Perspective

It was widely believed until recently that the world's population has been tending towards being 'young'. However, the trends over time are different. In 1980, the 0-14 years age-group constituted 35 percent of the global population. The 60 plus age-group was only 8.5 percent, while 39 percent of the population in the developing countries was in the age-group of 0.14 years and 6 percent in 60 plus group. Whereas 15 percent of the population in the advanced countries is in the age-group of 60 plus. The United Nations has projected that by the year 2025, 0-14 age-group will come down to 25 percent of the world population and the 60 plus group will move to 14 percent. In terms of absolute numbers, 60 plus group comprising 376 millions in 1980, will jump to 1,121 millions in 2025, of whom 70 percent will be found living in the developing regions. It has further projected that there will be 623 million persons in the Asia and Pacific Region who are in the age-group of 60 plus constituting 56 percent of the world's elderly population. The United Nations also projected that 38 percent of all elderly population will be found in China and India alone by 2025. Again, by the year 2025, the 80 plus population will be 14 percent in developed regions and 8 percent in the less developed countries.

By 2020, it is expected that there will be a serious imbalance in the sex ratio in the developing countries. The scenario in the developed countries is expected to improve. In the developed countries from among the 80 plus age-group which is growing most rapidly, women will form the majority. In terms of urban and rural distribution the 60 plus age-group in the urban area which was 47 percent in 1980 will move to 55 percent and in rural area from 53 percent to 45 percent by the year 2000. The trend towards urbanization of the elderly is unmistakable both in the less developed nations and developed nations. Table 1 provides a summary view of the demographic status of the world population.

The Indian Situation

Coming to India, it can be safely said from decennial demo-

SPACE FOR TABLE 10.1 1/2

Table 1

*Demographic Fact Sheet for Selected ESCAP Countries, 1992**

Countries	Mid-1992 Population (thousands)	Percentage Distribution Aged				Percent urban	Life at birth	Expectancy at 60 a#	Labour Force b#		
		0-14	15-59	60-69	70+				Year	All Ages	60+
ESCAP	3,172,239	32.3	59.6	5.0	3.1	34.9	65.3	16.5	—	—	—
East Asia	1,388,712	25.6	64.4	6.0	4.0	41.7	71.6	18.0	—	—	—
China	1,188,451	26.4	64.4	5.6	3.6	36.4	70.7	17.7	—	—	—
DPR Korea	23,063	28.8	64.5	4.1	2.6	60.4	70.9	18.1	—	—	—
Hong Kong	6,004	20.0	66.6	7.6	5.9	94.5	77.5	20.4	1990	49.5	20.6
Japan	124,921	17.9	63.9	10.1	8.1	77.1	78.8	21.1	1990	51.7	34.0
Mongolia	2,373	40.8	54.0	3.3	1.9	52.7	63.4	16.2	—	—	—
Rep. of Korea	43,901	24.6	67.4	5.1	2.9	74.1	70.6	17.9	1990	—	35.8
South East Asia	470,659	36.0	57.7	4.0	2.3	31.2	62.9	16.2	—	—	—
Cambodia	8,809	37.6	57.3	3.5	11.6	12.1	50.8	14.4	—	—	—
Indonesia	194,600	34.7	58.6	4.2	2.4	32.3	62.4	16.1	1989	42.6	48.9
Laos	4,517	44.0	51.1	3.3	1.6	19.9	50.8	14.3	—	—	—
Malaysia	19,149	37.9	56.2	3.5	2.3	44.7	70.7	17.7	1987	43.8	—
Myanmar	44,377	36.7	56.7	4.3	2.3	25.3	62.2	16.0	—	—	—
Philippines	66,823	39.5	55.2	3.3	2.0	43.8	64.9	16.5	—	—	—
Singapore	2,813	23.2	67.7	5.4	3.6	100.0	74.4	19.0	1989	48.6	18.0

Contd...

SPACE FOR TABLE 10.1 2/2

Contd...

Thailand	58,012	31.3	62.2	4.1	2.4	23.9	66.8	16.8	1988	55.7	38.9
Vietnam	71,259	38.6	54.7	4.0	2.6	22.8	63.6	16.3	—	—	—
South Asia	1,285,697	38.4	55.1	4.2	2.4	28.3	53.9	15.4	—	—	—
Afghanistan	20,231	41.1	54.3	3.2	1.4	18.9	43.3	13.3	—	—	—
Bangladesh	125,299	43.2	52.3	2.9	1.7	17.7	52.7	14.5	1986	30.4	46.4
Bhutan	1,623	39.7	54.8	3.7	1.8	5.8	49.8	14.2	—	—	—
India	**908,094**	**36.3**	**56.5**	**4.6**	**2.6**	**28.0**	**60.1**	**15.6**	**—**	**—**	**—**
Iran	58,007	43.1	50.9	4.0	2.1	58.1	66.9	16.7	—	—	—
Nepal	20,536	41.9	52.9	3.5	1.7	10.5	53.2	14.6	—	—	—
Pakistan	133,637	45.9	49.6	2.9	1.5	33.1	58.7	15.4	1991	28.8	41.1
Sri Lanka	17,881	31.7	60.0	5.0	3.3	21.8	71.4	17.9	1990	43.2	32.2
Pacific	27,172	25.4	61.4	7.0	6.2	70.7	72.3	18.3	—	—	—
Australia	17,482	21.9	62.8	7.9	7.4	85.6	76.8	20.2	1990	63.8	13.1
Fiji	799	35.7	59.0	3.5	1.8	39.8	65.6	16.6	1990	34.2	—
New Zealand	3,477	22.6	62.4	7.6	7.4	84.2	75.5	19.6	1990	—	12.3
Papua New Guinea	4,148	40.3	55.1	3.4	1.1	16.6	55.7	15.0	—	—	—

Notes: This fact sheet is prepared by the ESCAP Population Division, June 1992.
a# Life expectancy at age 60 was estimated from EO using the Coale Demeny West Model Life Tables.
b# *Year Book of Labour Statistics*, 50th Issue, International Labour Office, Geneva.

Source: *World Population Prospects* 1990, United Nations, Department of International Economic and Social Affairs, Population Division, New York, 1991.

graphic data as shown in Table 2 that our population is also tending to have more and more of persons in the 60 plus age-group. As Table 3 shows in 1971, it constituted 7.7 percent of the total population. In 1991, it rose to 55 millions forming 6.5 percent of the total population. By 2000, the 60 plus population will jump to 76 millions, constituting 7.63 percent. In terms of per 1,000 persons, age-group 60 plus has jumped from 137 in 1961 to 164 in 1981 and will be 239 by 2009. It has been observed that there has been progressive decrease in the age of the widowed in the case of both males and females in the 60 plus age-group reflecting the improved life expectancy. The bulk of the females in the 60 plus age-group are widowed and combined with 'never married' and 'divorced'. They constituted 67 percent of female in the 60 plus group in 1981. Only 20 percent of males of this age-group are in this category. Table 4 contains interesting information in terms of rural and urban distribution of 60 plus age-group. It shows that 80 percent of them live in the rural areas. 14.56 percent of males and 7.79 percent of females in the 60 plus age-group are literate.

Table 2

Percentage Distribution of the Total Population by Broad Age-Groups

Census Year	*Age-Group*			
	0-14	*15-59*	*60+*	*All Ages*
1901	38.60	56.35	5.05	100
1911	38.45	56.40	5.15	100
1921	39.20	55.55	5.25	100
1931	40.00	55.95	4.05	100
1941	38.25	56.85	4.90	100
1951	37.50	56.85	5.65	100
1961	41.00	53.36	5.64	100
1971	42.02	52.01	5.97	100
1981	39.54	53.93	6.52	100

Source: For 1901-1971, ESCAP, 1982, Country Monograph Series No.10, Population of India Table No.43. For 1981, *Census of India 1981*, 5 % sample (excludes Assam).

Table 3

Percent of 60 Plus Elderly Population in Some of the States and UTs by Place of Residence During 1961, 1971 and 1981

State/Union Territories	Total			Rural			Urban		
	1961	1971	1981	1961	1971	1981	1961	1971	1981
INDIA	5.6	6.0	6.5	5.8	6.2	6.8	4.7	5.0	5.4
Andhra Pradesh	6.2	6.4	6.7	6.5	6.7	7.1	5.0	5.0	5.1
Bihar	5.6	5.9	6.8	5.7	6.0	7.1	4.6	4.7	5.0
Gujarat	4.9	5.3	6.0	5.1	5.6	6.3	4.6	4.8	5.2
Himachal Pradesh	7.4	7.2	7.5	7.5	7.4	7.7	5.1	2.3	5.1
J&K	5.1	5.6	5.8	5.4	5.9	6.1	3.7	4.0	4.5
Karnataka	5.7	6.1	6.6	6.0	6.3	7.0	4.9	5.1	5.7
Kerala	5.8	6.2	7.5	5.9	6.3	7.6	5.6	6.0	7.1
M.P.	5.2	5.8	6.6	5.2	6.0	6.8	4.7	5.0	5.1
Maharashtra	5.3	5.7	6.4	5.7	6.3	7.1	4.3	4.5	5.1
Nagaland	6.8	6.7	5.9	7.1	7.3	6.7	2.0	1.3	1.7
Orissa	5.7	6.0	6.4	5.7	6.2	6.6	4.7	4.6	4.7
Punjab	6.6	7.5	7.8	6.9	8.0	8.4	5.2	5.7	6.1
Rajasthan	5.1	5.5	6.0	5.1	5.6	6.3	5.1	5.2	5.2
Tamil Nadu	5.6	5.7	6.4	6.0	6.0	6.7	4.8	5.1	5.8
U.P.	6.3	6.7	6.8	6.4	7.0	7.2	5.2	5.5	5.4
W. Bengal	5.0	5.3	5.6	5.2	5.4	5.5	4.5	5.0	5.4
UTs									
Arunachal Pradesh	0.9	4.7	4.8	0.9	4.8	5.0	***	1.2	1.3
Dadra & Nagar Haveli	4.0	4.1	4.0	4.0	4.1	4.0	***	***	3.7
Delhi	4.1	4.3	4.5	5.1	4.9	5.2	4.0	4.2	4.4
Goa, Daman & Diu	8.1	6.6	6.8	8.3	7.1	7.2	6.8	5.2	5.8
Pondicherry	6.9	6.3	6.7	6.7	6.3	6.6	7.3	6.4	6.8

*** No urban area.

Sources: (i) *Census of India*, 1961, Vol. I, Part II C (I).
(ii) *Census of India*, 1971, Sr. I, Part II (ii).
(iii) *Census of India*, 1981, Sr. I, India, Part IV A (Socio-Cultural Tables).

Table 4

Proportion and Growth of Elderly Population in India by Place of Residence 1961, 1971 and 1981

Census Years	*Size of Elderly Population (in millions)*			*Proportion of Elderly Population (in total population)*			*Growth of Elderly Population*		
	Total	*Urban*	*Rural*	*Total*	*Urban*	*Rural*	*Total*	*Urban*	*Rural*
1961	24.7	21.0	3.7	5.6	5.8	4.7	23.3	22.7	26.3
1971	32.7	27.3	5.4	6.0	6.2	5.0	32.3	30.0	45.2
1981	43.2	34.7	8.5	6.5	6.8	5.4	32.0	27.3	55.8

Note: 1981 Elderly Population Data Excludes Assam Population.

Sources: (i) *Census of India, 1961*: Vol. I, Part-IIC(i), India Socio-Cultural Tables.
(ii) *Census of India, 1971*: Series I, Part-IIC(ii) Socio-Cultural Table, 1976.
(iii) *Census of India, 1981*: Series I, India Part IVA. Socio-Cultural Tables, 1988.

Table 5

Labour Force Participation Rates of Elderly Population by Place of Residence and Sex, 1961-1981

Place of Residence/Sex	*1961*	*1971*	*1981*
Hill Area			
Males	76.6	73.8	63.9
Females	22.4	10.5	10.2
Total	49.5	43.2	37.6
Rural			
Males	79.9	77.4	67.8
Females	24.3	11.3	11.3
Total	52.0	45.5	40.2
Urban			
Males	58.4	55.4	47.6
Females	11.4	6.4	5.6
Total	35.2	31.5	26.8

Sources: (i) Census of India, 1961, Part-IIB(i), General Economics Tables, 1964.
(ii) *Census of India, 1971*, Part-IIB(i), General Economics Tables, R.G. India, 1977.
(iii) *Census of India, 1981*, Series -I, India Part-IIIA(i) General Economic Tables, R.G. India, 1987.

II
CHANGING ROLE OF THE ELDERLY

What then would be the new roles of the elderly in the context of the increasing urbanization, nuclearization of the family and the increasing dependence on their children? It would be difficult to provide a simple answer to this very complex question. Also, the answer will differ from the less developed to more developed situations. According to the Retired and Senior Volunteer Programme (RSVP), Western India Chapter, Mumbai, which is an organization dedicated to enhancing opportunities for elderly adults, "the new roles for 'old folks' can be broadly divided into: (1) new roles in the nuclear family; (2) roles in the place of work; (3) new roles in society; (4) role in the field of education; (5) roles in the field of religion and morality; (6) roles in the economic field; and (7) role in the political field" (RSVP, 1992).

The RSVP with a large membership all over the world (its strength in the USA alone is said to be over 4,00,000) enables the elderly to make valuable contributions for the well-being of their communities and the world at large. In India, Rotarian Manohar Advani is the Director General under whose guidance, the RSVP volunteers have been rendering different types of social services particularly for the benefit of the less fortunate members of the community. These include visits to hospitals, destitute homes, orphanages, prisons, borstal schools, leprosy asylums, children's homes, etc. Other activities include: organizing health check-ups for senior citizens; distribution of syringes and needles to patients, welfare projects for the elderly; organizing *mandir darshan* (visits to temples); sight-seeing for the sightless (eye donation) helping senior citizens to organize day care centres; *yoga* sessions; indoor games and sports; accupressure sittings; reading rooms and libraries; athletic meets; lectures and seminars; quarterly bulletins for senior citizens; and marriage information centres for the children and grandchildren of the elderly etc. The RSVP volunteers also conduct pilgrimages, picnics and outings, talent competitions for senior citizens in singing, mono-acting, music, essay-writing competitions etc.

There are 46 Senior Citizens' Associations in Greater Bombay. The RSVP acts as a clearing house as well as a counsellor for these associations/clubs. The list of projects prepared for these associations includes among other things, the RSVP telecare, environmental conservation, inter-generational contacts, consumer guidance, distribution of food and clothing for the needy aged, distribution of old books and magazines, national integration programmes, skill banks, distribution of used toys, dolls and greeting cards among the poor, handicapped and blind children, adult education, helping home-bound elderly, legal advice to seniors, health, recreation, excursions, production of greeting cards on mass scale to be sold as fund-raising project by senior citizens' associations, health fair for seniors, medical camps, organize health clubs/keep fit classes, conduct seminars, symposiums and workshops on the problems of senior citizens, collect the bio-data of well-qualified and experienced citizens and utilize their talents for the welfare of the society in general and of the seniors in particular, provide family counselling, open a library of books and video cassettes, engage the aged in spiritual and cultural activities start a monthly/quarterly magazine for the elderly, to secure identity cards for senior citizens to enable them to enjoy various social security benefits, construction of cooperative housing societies with special facilities for the elders, social security, hostels, homes and *ashrams* for the destitute and the lonely elders, to agitate for grant of maximum amount of tax relief for the retired, persuade the LIC and the GIC to issue special policies for senior citizens, to agitate for representation of elders in different policy-making bodies and to persuade government to start Third Age University.

A majority of the elderly population who live in rural areas continue to play their economic role. This is because they are mostly engaged in agriculture and allied activities. Since they are self-employed, there is no question of their retiring from work. It may be that there is progressive reduction in the hours of work, type and quantum of work done. In the urban areas, the tendency is to retire between 55 and 60 years. The age of superannuation is also fixed at either 55, 58, 60 or 62 years for employees in formal organizations and institutions.

As long as the joint family is fairly stable, the elderly persons are assured of their place in the family, kin group, caste and community. Generally, the oldest living male member in the joint family is the head of the family in whose hands the resources of the family are vested. Decisions in almost all matters pertaining to the family are taken by the patriarch. The elderly are not only source of authority and power but are also respected and revered by the other members of the joint family, particularly the young. With the breakdown of the joint family in the wake of changing values and norms, the traditional roles of the elderly have become tenuous and precarious. Migration towards urban areas and nuclearization of the family which are inevitable consequences of widespread rural poverty and marginalization of large masses of population, have aggravated the already declining status of the elderly. There is also weakening of familial relationships as a result of women's education, urban employment and such other factors of social change.

III
WELFARE SERVICES FOR THE ELDERLY IN INDIA

According to A.B. Bose (1992), former Adviser, Planning Commission, small family norm which now a days is almost universal among the urban middle and upper classes, has contributed to a high degree of dependency of the elderly on their children. There is a definite evidence of neglect of the elderly and apathy towards them on the part of the younger members of the family in the urban areas. Reasons such as lack of adequate accommodation, high cost of living, exorbitant rents, growing individualism and keen desire for privacy and such other forces compel the elderly to remain in the villages while the able bodied and the younger members move into the towns and cities. For all these reasons, the elderly population in the tribal, rural and urban areas has become highly vulnerable.

It is true that the Constitution of India did recognize the responsibility of the state towards the elderly and other vulnerable populations. According to Article 41: "The state shall, within the limits of its economic capacity and development, make effective provision and securing the rights to work, to education, and to public assistance in cases of unemployment, old age, sickness and disablement and other cases of undeserved want." Similarly, Section 125 (d) of the Criminal Procedure Code (1973) makes it obligatory for a person having sufficient means to maintain his parents who are unable to maintain themselves and on production of such proof of neglect or refusal by the son/daughter, the court may order such persons to pay his mother/father a monthly allowance not exceeding Rs. 500. The Hindu Adoption Act of 1957 has recognized the obligation of a person to maintain his/her aged or infirm parents vide Section 30(3).

It is believed in some quarters in the developed countries that dependent, ageing population tends to claim disproportionately large share of the social welfare budget. Such a trend is historically inevitable. In India, the state has not been able to promote social welfare services for the elderly on par with the developed nations for understandable reasons. The chief reason for low budget allocations for social welfare is that these elderly vulnerable are not organized. While they constitute vote banks for certain political parties, they lack lobbying capacity to fight for favourable policies and larger budget allocations. However, thanks to the *United Nations Declaration on Social Progress and Development* (1969) and as a result of the UN sponsorship, the first ever International Conference of Ministers responsible for Social Welfare was held. The deliberations of the later conference have gone a long way in providing a coherent state policy for the care of the elderly. According to Mukunda Rao (1992:3), a UN Consultant, it was for the first time that "a developmental approach to social welfare questions was proposed in addition to the more prevalent remedial and curative approaches". He further says that social welfare policy should elicit and promote widest possible participation of all individuals and groups and these objectives could be best achieved through new partnerships in the field of social welfare policy providing opportunity for greater involvement of beneficiaries, individually and collectively on decisions concerning their needs and implementation of programme including community-based programmes.

IV
AGEING POLICIES AND PROGRAMMES

The Emerging Scenario

New ageing policies and programmes have also started emerging as a result of the World Assembly on Ageing in 1982 and the Vienna Plan of International Action which is the outcome of the World Assembly. *The World Development Report* 1991 states that "vulnerable people must not be forgotten. The social costs of inaction are generally much larger than those of adjusting, but it is necessary to cushion the effect of adjustment on the most adversely affected groups. Cutbacks in public spending can hurt vulnerable groups... [G]uaranteeing food security through food price subsidies, food rations or food supplementation schemes meet basic needs, provided the measures are well-targeted. Carefully targeted income support programmes for the elderly or the infirm provide safety nets for people who are otherwise hard to reach" (1991:7).

The Government of India, in addition to providing grant-in-aid to non-governmental organizations and enacting legislation for the care of the dependent elderly, have also granted tax concessions to the elderly. The Union Budget for the year 1992-93 has provided tax rebate of 10 percent on the net tax payable by persons of 65 years of age and above and whose income is below certain limit. Railways provide 25 percent concession in II class railway fare to persons who are 65 and above for travel beyond certain distance. Similarly, the State Road Transport

Authorities and Undertakings provide concession to elderly persons. There is an Old Age Pension Scheme in almost all states. The pension ranges from Rs. 30 per month in Andhra Pradesh to Rs. 100 per month in Maharashtra.

It is clear from the above analysis that the elderly and the organizations engaged in the care of the elderly have to play a critical role in promoting welfare services for the elderly. The non-governmental organizations have a particularly important role in a country like India. They are already engaged in promoting welfare of the rural masses, urban poor and the remotely located tribal communities. A great many of these voluntary organizations are founded by concerned citizens and staffed by people who are ideologically and emotionally committed to the objectives and goals of these organizations. They draw their resources locally, nationally and internationally. As already pointed out, the state and central governments have schemes of financial assistance for non-governmental organizations engaged in work with different target groups such as the disabled, socially disadvantaged, women, youth, elderly, etc. They are subjected to the government rules and regulations if they receive subsidies or grants from the government.

In recent times, particularly in the last one year, the Government of India has been laying much stress on the role of the voluntary organizations in developmental work. These organizations have inherent strengths such as mass base, public orientation, less rigid and formal procedures, more innovative and experimental and above all they are highly cost-effective. Slowly but steadily, a new type of welfare organization is emerging in India, i.e., 'profit-oriented' or 'for-profit' organizations as different from the traditional service-oriented organizations. This has been the experience of the western societies and it is now becoming increasingly a global trend.

The New Economic Reforms/Policies of the Government of India with emphasis on deregulation and privatization have given a new fillip to this trend. Day-care, adoption, institutional care, housing and health care are some of the areas in which the 'for-profit' organizations are operating. In the nature of things, it is only the affluent that can afford the services offered by such commercially motivated organizations. A large majority of the vulnerable sections such as children, elderly, disabled, etc., have either to depend on the family and community, private charity, or on caring institutions such as orphanages, destitute homes, homes for aged and infirmaries etc. They are an alternative to 'for-profit' organizations. Such caring institutions are grossly and disproportionately inadequate in relation to the need. Therefore, it would be unwise to neglect the already available social institutions and social structures. Further, it should be the endeavour of the governmental as well as non-governmental sectors to strengthen these institutions.

This belief is clearly reflected in the UN monograph on *The Programme for the International Year of the Family* (1994). It states: "...the increasing proportions of elderly in most countries have called to the attention of the governments [regarding] the need to give more considerations to enabling families to provide economic, material and emotional support for the elderly; supporting care-givers; enabling the elderly to remain in the community as long as possible; and extending the productivity and contributions of the elderly to the community" (1994:11).

The UN Principles for Elderly Persons adopted by the UN General Assembly in 1991 are a step forward in evolving global policies on the elderly. Family and community-based age care becomes the new thrust for the care of the elderly. The non-governmental organizations engaged in age care will then have two-fold functions: (i) on the one hand to provide an appropriate package of services for the elderly, and (ii) on the other to organize and mobilize the elderly for self-help and self-assertion. The elderly themselves have to come forward and fight for their rights as provided in the *UN Principles on Ageing and the Global Targets* on ageing set for the decade 1992-2001.

An excellent example of a non-governmental organization playing a significant role in age care policy formulation, age care training and research, provision of welfare services for the elderly and above all playing an advocacy role for the elderly is the Centre for the Welfare of the Aged (CEWA), Chennai (Krishnanair,1991).

The First Global Conference on Ageing (30 August -3 September, 1992) held at Mumbai and Pune, has taken stock of these global trends and situations and commended to the UN for adoption of the Declaration of Rights and Responsibilities of the Elderly and for the implementation of the provisions of the Vienna Programme Action and *UN Principles on Ageing and Global Targets* for the decade 1992-2001.

The organizations of the elderly and the non-governmental organizations engaged in age care services have also to fight ageism which is reflected in various discriminatory policies and practices against the elderly persons. The elderly are subjected to a variety of discriminations and humiliations in the economic, political, social, educational and other areas of life. The elderly also suffer from stigma and negative stereotyping at the hands of the communication media and the cinema in particular. They are discriminated against in the employment sector and work-settings. The state and central governments often dabble with the age of superannuation of its elderly employees for various reasons. The government servants were earlier retiring on attaining the age of 55 years when life expectancy was as low as 32 years. Even though life expectancy has now dramatically changed for the better during the last four decades, the government servants and industrial workers in public sector undertakings in our country are now retiring only at 58 years. In fact, one state government has even brought down the age of retirement to 55 years, though unsuccessfully. However, with the implementation of the Fifty Pay Commission's recommendations, the situation is somewhat changing better.

V

CHALLENGES AHEAD

Mukunda Rao, in his illuminating key-note address delivered at the IFA-First Global Conference on the theme of "New Century, New Hopes, New Thinking About Ageing Policies" has identified a number of challenges facing the elderly population at the national and international levels (1992:17-21). According to him, the biggest challenge is lack of political will in many countries resulting in allocation of meagre resources for the neglected areas of social welfare such as care of the elderly. He goes on to identify several more challenges and these include the need for radical change in the perceptions about the potential strengths, current contributions of their older peoples to their societies. Another challenge arises out of separate and selective advocacies of the situation of different segments of the vulnerable populations. This has resulted in their being distanced and disassociated from broader policy framework and even contributing to competition for public attention and limited resources. Yet, another challenge relates to organizations of older persons as well as those working on their behalf. Private organizations and organizations of older persons should not only place high priority on areas and activities relevant to older persons but should also give attention to wider and broader developmental questions in areas such as improving the environment, reduction of poverty, fighting crime, substance abuse, corruption and development of children, youth and minorities. The elderly have a rightful role to play on all these fronts. Another set of challenges concern the elderly themselves in their life choice, their willingness to take risk and make sacrifices, and their readiness to redefine the goals of their life (as shown in Table 5). The elderly also have to face many dilemma relating to choices of occupation, residence, relations with other family members, changing long-held beliefs and behavioural patterns, adopting a positive stance to social change and adapting to it. The elderly in any society are not a heterogeneous group. Some of them are affluent, better educated and better situated. Whereas, some of their peers like the older women, the poor and destitute and such other sub-groups are not so fortunate. Finally, the biggest challenge is the need to bring about change of the perceptions that the old have about themselves.

[The author acknowledges his special debt to Mukunda Rao for drawing extensively from his Key-Note Address on: "Ageing Policies and Programmes: New Century, New Hopes, New Challenges" delivered at the First Global Conference of International Federation on Ageing at Bombay-Pune during 30 August -3 September, 1992.]

REFERENCES

Bose, A.B. (1992), "Country Report, India: Ageing in India, Societal Responses and Future Perspectives." *Proceedings of the IFA-First Global Conference* held at Mumbai-Pune during 30 August-3 September.

Gangrade, K.D. (1989), "Emerging Conception of Ageing in India: A Socio-Cultural Perspective", *Eastern Anthropologist*, 42(2), April-June.

Kitazawa, Y. (1986), "An Ageing Society: Who Will Bear the Burden?" *AMPO Japan-Asia Quarterly Review*, 18(2&3).

Krishnan, P. and Mahadevan, K. (eds.) (1992), *The Elderly Population in Developed and Developing World: Policies, Problems and Perspectives*. Delhi: B.R. Publishers.

Krishnanair, T. (1991), *Evaluation of Age Care Programmes for Elderly in India*. Unpublished Ph.D. Dissertation, Vishakhapatnam, Andhra University.

Levin, E. *et.al.* (1986), *Families, Services and Confusion in Old Age*. London: Allen and Unwin.

Mahadevan, K. *et.al.* (1992), "Demographic and Social Implications of the Elderly in India" in Krishnan, P. and Mahadevan, K. (eds.), *The Elderly Population in Developed and Developing World*. Delhi: B.R. Publishers.

Nair, T.N. and Ramana, K.V. (eds.) (1989), *Ageing and Welfare of Elderly in India*. Madras: Madras Institute of Ageing.

Pati, P.N. and Jena, B. (eds.) (1989), *Aged in India: Socio-Demographic Dimension*. New Delhi: Ashish.

Rao, Mukunda, M. (1992), "Ageing Policies and Programmes, New Century, New Hopes, New Challenges (Key-Note Address)", *Proceedings of the IFA-First Global Conference* held at Bombay-Pune during 30 August-3 September.

RSVP (1992), *News Line*, 1(2), 30 August.

UN (1996), *World Development Report*, 1996. London: OUP.

Walker, Alan (ed.) (1982), *Community Care: The Family, the State and Social Policy*. London: Oxford.

11

Gender, Market Segmentation and Marginalization in Urban Gujarat

by S.P. Punalekar

CASUAL LABOUR MARKET: AN OVERVIEW

Major cities of Gujarat, namely, Ahmedabad, Surat, Vadodara and Rajkot, are growing at a much faster rate. This growth is not only due to internal factors such as rise in local population, but also substantially due to migration of people from near and distant places from within and outside the state of Gujarat. As a result, demand for physical space within urban centre is exceedingly intense. So also is the situation of labour supply. One notices too many persons chasing too few work opportunities in organized or unorganized sectors of trade, industry and services. The emergence of casual labour in the cities of Gujarat needs to be viewed in this larger context of quite rapid and intense but lopsided growth of urban economy in last few decades.

Principal characteristic of casual labour is casualness or arbitrariness of nature of work and work environment. This is amply reflected through undefined and vague nature of the terms of their employment including work relations. This casual, informal sector largely lacks any definite rules or standards of employment. Employment practices vary from trade to trade, or from place to place for the same trade or economic activity. Another distinguishing feature of casual labour market (CLM) is segmentation. This tendency of market segmentation tends to generate diffused knowledge and ruptured consciousness among the workers. Market intelligence remains to be of a fragmentary nature, compelling the casual workers to rely more on network of patronage or on goodwill of their employers. Primordial ties of village, caste, community, region, etc., are used with full intensity by the workers to gain access to work opportunities and to retain them. The employers too utilize these loyalties to maintain control over the workers. Briefly, the CLM is a lowest link in the entire urban labour market network with all the fluidity and diffusedness one may think of. Casual labourers are face to face with these uncertain and fluid conditions day in and day out. Casual labour activities are quite varied and complex. They include domestic service, hawking and vending, rag-picking, etc. Larger the town or a city, more complex is a network of employment and services. Also, the ways of recruitment, training, retention and dismissal vary from one type of employment sector to another; and it also varies within single sector, say that of construction labour or domestic maid services. In all probability, the casual labourers constitute the lowest segment of proletarian stratum among the urban working classes.

This paper concentrates on female workers working in a specific labour category. They are known as *chakla majoor* in urban Gujarat. *Chakla* means a city square with intersection of three or four roads and *majoor* means a casual labourer. A large number of male and female labourers assemble there daily at 6 or 7 in the morning. At such *chaklas* or city squares, their total number varies from 300 (near Alkapuri Railway underbridge in Vadodara, for instance) to over 3,000 (near Ambawadi in Ahmedabad or Chowk Bazaar in Surat, for instance). A few among them are skilled artisans like carpenters, masons, plumbers, floor and wood polishers, whitewashing hands, repairmen, etc. They come there with their tool kits. Their number is usually small, say less than 10 per cent of the total labourers assembled at any one CLM. In this paper we concentrate on second group, namely, the ordinary labourers. They are without any tools or accessories. They come there to sell their physical labour. They are numerous and include men, women and even children.

Any CLM is sociologically an interesting site to see and usually it makes a lasting impact on any sensitive visitor or academic observer. As soon as the *chakla* labourers notice a familiar face of a contractor and *mukadam* (a sub-contractor), they rush towards him. They jostle with one another with a hope that they can get some work from that contractor and *mukadam*. Even if they see a new, relatively better-dressed person, they crowd around and make inquiries about the nature of work they may find with him. They are always willing to do the work of digging, road levelling, loading, unloading or filling a concrete slab of a building.

And when the labourers and prospective employers meet, then a process of bargaining starts. Some get the job by 8.00 am. or 8.30 am. Some do not get any employment until 10.00 am. Disappointed, some of them go to railway yard or vegetable market to see whether they can get any *majoori* (loading-unloading *ad hoc* work) to make two ends meet. Next day, they come back again at the *chakla* market. According to one estimate, there are four CLMs with a total of over 8,000 labourers in Surat. In Ahmedabad city, there are estimated to be over 15,000 labourers in some 18 CLMs.

Who are these CLM workers? What is their socio-economic background? Where do they live in the city and in what conditions? What are their ways of coping with problems of urban living? What are their occupational conditions? How do they perceive social situation around them? These are some of the questions of sociological and social work interest pursued in this paper. We narrate here the conditions of four female *chakla* labourers. Two of them are from Surat CLM and two from Ahmedabad CLM. Case study material was collected in early 1990s with the help of structured questionnaire and interview guideline. The concluding section attempts to summarize the major themes of the writing and discusses various macro and micro level actions as a social intervention strategies to change their conditions of misery.

LIFE-PROFILES OF THE CASES

(C1) Ramaben: *A Patidar* Woman from Surat City

Ramaben (RM), a 40 year old woman, constitutes our first case from Surat city. She is a Hindu *Patidar* by caste. The *Patidars* or *Patels* are a landowning community in south and central Gujarat with two major sub-divisions among them, namely, *Leuva* and *Kadva*. RM is an illiterate and widow, heading a family of three; one daughter (20-year old, deserted), and two sons, aged 18 and 15. RM values education and hence she has educated her daughter upto 10th standard. Her elder son has taken education upto 5th standard, and the younger one upto 10th standard.

RM goes to the CLM located at Chowk Bazaar daily to find work. Her elder daughter works as a domestic servant in two middle class households. Elder son, Ramu, is employed at a wayside tea-shop for Rs. 150 a month. He works for more than 12 hours a day. He gets tea and snacks free. Her second son, Rohit, works as a whitewasher (painter) with a building contractor who secures bulk contract. Rohit gets job work and earns around Rs. 600 per month. This occupational skill helped him in securing private 'colouring' or white washing contracts. That provides him a chance for extra earnings; bringing in net additional income of Rs. 1,000 to Rs. 1,200 a year. But that also means he has to work extra hours, and use up his holidays. Sometimes, he gets exhausted, falls ill and spends the money on medicines for quicker relief. Extra earnings do not then add up to much.

All four persons in RM's family work. And their total income is Rs. 1,015, i.e., around Rs. 30 to Rs. 35 per day. Per capita income is Rs. 250 per month or Rs. 8 to Rs. 9 per day. Luckily, they have a shelter in Surat city. They live in a neat and clean *zopdi* or hut near Shital Talkies on Rander Road. The hut does not belong to them. It is owned by a person who charges them a monthly rent of Rs. 100. Their dwelling is on an 'unauthorized' land; in other words it is illegally constructed. It may get demolished anytime. Also there is another peculiar aspect, i.e., the greed of a hutowner. He may forcibly vacate the tenant, if he gets another person who promises to pay more. And in Surat, there are competitors among the poor people to get a shelter in a slum locality. RM is feeling such anxiety for last 2-3 years. She said that she has begun inquiring in nearby localities about suitable accommodation. They prefer and are trying for a place (open plot) in Bapunagar slum settlement across Tapi river. This is one of the biggest slums in Surat. Bapunagar slum has over 5,000 huts. Cost of building a hut along with payment for extra favours may be anywhere between Rs. 6,000 to Rs. 12,000. RM is not sure whether she would succeed in obtaining a plot there.

RM's present dwelling is relatively well built, though its roof is thatched with *kachcha* materials. They get water from nearby privately owned waterpost. They have to pay Rs. 5 per month for this facility. In the hut, there is a *chokdi* (an open bathroom), where the female members take their bath. *Chokdi* is also used for washing clothes and cleaning utensils. There is no latrine facility and all of them go out in the open for defecation. Needless to say, defecation in open field surrounding this slum locality and waste water flowing from *chokdis* of several huts have created several stagnant cesspools around. Flies and mosquitoes abound, endangering the health of the community inside and outside this slum. Each slum-dweller does his best to keep his own hut clean to avoid insanitary conditions inside. But right outside his own hut, there is no arrangement to drain out the waste water. RM's hut has no electricity connection. They buy firewood from the local market, spending daily about Rs. 3-4.

RM's family history is interesting. They are the migrants from a village in a Kheda district. Some 25 years ago, i.e., in early 1960s, they had come to Surat city. In village, they had no land and eked out their living on agricultural labour. RM said that now they do not have house in their native place, nor any social connections or linkages. None of them have visited their native place for the last 20 years. They are now residents of

Surat city with whatever prospects they have in store. RM goes to Chowk Bazaar CLM regularly. For the last over 15 years, there is hardly any change in this routine. Why does she go to the CLM? She said that she is not able to get 'regular' work elsewhere. At CLM, she gets work for at least 15 days in a month. She has no other skills either. She gets employed in a gang (team) of construction labourers, recruited by the *mukadams*. There are 4-5 CLMs in Surat city. They are located at a distance of 2-3 kms from Chowk area. But RM visits only Chowk Bazaar CLM. If she does not get work at this CLM by 9.30 to 10.00 am, she returns. If she gets employed, she gets Rs. 18-20 per day. In other words, she gets about Rs. 300 for 15 days, the remaining period being mostly idle. That means her effective earnings are Rs. 10 per day.

For her present conditions, she refused to blame anyone or anything except herself and her fate. She also said that during the last five years, her condition has remained unchanged. There has not been any respite in her struggle for livelihood. Better days have always eluded her, she said. When asked, how would she face and fight her present circumstances? She replied that "only 'other better' work can solve her problems"; meaning "regular, better paid jobs". Neither she believes in placing full trust in the state machinery, nor does she have tall expectations from the labour union. In her view, job that pays better can bring some relief in her life. It is equally significant to note that RM is not totally pessimistic either. She does not say that the conditions can never be altered or improved. But how they can be altered, she does not spell out.

The place where RM stays is quite a large settlement with a cluster of some 3,000-4,000 huts. RM stays in this slum for over 10 years, and yet she does not seem to have very close relationship with her neighbours. Neither she goes out for any social functions/occasions in her neighbourhood, nor does she share or exchange household things with them. She keeps to herself and her family and generally avoids mixing with any of the residents of this locality. "I have no friends with whom I can share my personal feelings", RM said with deep anguish. Why does she remain aloof or isolated from her neighbours? Why does not she cultivate intimate ties with others in the urban slum neighbourhood? She did not reveal her mind on these questions. Her brother's and sister's families live in Surat city. The former lives in a slum settlement in J.J. Market area. He is working in art-silk factory as a weaver. Her sister lives near Bombay Market (also slum area). She works as a bobbin-filler in a textile unit. RM visits them often. These three households help one another in times of difficulty. Closer social ties with one another enable them to overcome moments or times of hardships. RM does feel strongly that because of distances, financial difficulties, etc., she is not able to meet her other relatives living outside Surat city.

RM's daily routine is quite arduous. She wakes up at 4.00 am, and does all the household work including cooking with the help of her daughter. Then she goes to CLM around 7.00 or 7.30 am. When she gets work in the CLM, she is able to return home only around 8.00 pm. She gets rest for about six hours at night. Their daily food is *rotlo ane shak* (loaf and vegetable). There is hardly any variation in this food pattern. No breakfast. If something remains from the early night food basket, they all share it together in the following morning. Only on some religious occasions like *Diwali*, *Holi*, etc., they prepare some sweet dishes, if they have money. RM said, "we do not remain hungry or starved. We do get our minimum food intake." This seems true. Food and other related stock with RM was as follows during our visit to her residence: red *juwar* 40 kgs, wheat 20 kgs, cooking oil 1 kg and kerosene 15 litres. RM has limited household goods, just enough to meet the bare needs. Furniture includes one table, one chair, and one iron cot. Recently, they have purchased a transistor radio and a wall clock. Utensils include a few earthenwares, glasswares and aluminium vessels. The family makes use of readymade garments, but they also buy second-hand clothes from *Shanivaria* market, i.e., a weekly market held on every Saturday at Chowk Bazaar.

RM is quite conscious of the difficulties of the casual labourers as she has spent a good deal of time in this market. She feels that the CLM should be under some regulatory authority to avoid hardships to the labourers. There should be proper system for registration of workers as well as the contractors. She felt that once the number is regulated, there will be some control over the present-day arbitrariness. She also felt that there should be a floor-limit for wages. "For slab-filling the worker must get at least Rs. 25 a day. Other labourers/helpers must get a daily wage of Rs. 20", she asserted. She favoured the idea of a formation of special labour union for the casual labourers. She questioned:

> More than half of us have no knowledge and experience in union activities. We are too many. Also we are not united among ourselves. How can we form our union?

It is indeed encouraging to witness RM's mood of self-reliance and confidence. She said that she would like to do *uchchak* work, i.e., piece-rated or job-work, because "that gives relatively more wages". But she also felt that the workers themselves be resolute in their demands. "The woman should have equal rights in the family property", she asserted. Working conditions should be similar for both, the male and female workers. She did feel that at present the female workers are more at the mercy and goodwill of the *mukadams* and contractors. This situation must change, she emphasized. RM is one of the oldest casual labourers. She began visiting the CLM all by herself, without anyone's help or guidance. She learnt to ask questions to *mukadams* or contractors, who initially succeeded in getting her services at lower wages. But keen observation and self-experience taught her the skills of bargaining, negotiating, etc. In that sense, she is a self-made worker with adequate insights into labour market processes. Even then, occasionally she gets less than the expected wages. The contractor finds some fault in her work and pays her less. That happens once or twice a month. She said:

> Then I decide not to work for that contractor. I also tell my other friends at the CLM to be 'careful' about such 'dishonest' contractors. What else can I do? I cannot forcibly extract my dues from such unscrupulous persons. They are moneyed persons. They have influence and clout. People in authority will believe them, and not us.

RM takes very little interest in socio-cultural or political activities. She does go for voting in local or assembly elections. But that is about all. She does not take active part in meetings, processions, etc. At home, she is busy looking after her household responsibilities. She does not take active part in social or religious activities in her neighbourhood. When in distress, she tries to console herself without anyone's sympathy. When there is food scarcity at home, the whole family would prefer to live on less food than to go to their neighbours for help. So also in other matters.

RM seems to believe in self-reliance even in times of scarcity and distress. Her social contacts are restricted. Her social network includes her close relatives, one or two friends at the CLM and a grocer in her locality who gives upto Rs. 100 worth of daily necessities on credit. But barring this small circle, there is none who can claim to know RM intimately. In other words, she lives in an isolated and socially restricted milieu.

(C2) Reshamben: A Tribal Woman in Surat City

Reshamben Raisingh (RR) is a Bhil (tribal) woman. She migrated to Surat city from Taloda taluka of Dhulia district, Maharashtra. She stays with her husband in a hutment colony near Shital Talkies across Tapi river. RR is 30-year old, illiterate and her husband Raisingh is also illiterate. Both work as casual labourers and wait at Chowk Bazaar CLM. RR gets work for about 20 days in a month with a daily wage of Rs. 15. Raisingh gets work for 15 days in a month with a daily wage of Rs. 25. Together, they earn about Rs. 600-700 per month, i.e., about Rs. 20 per day for two persons together. They came to Surat city in late 1970s, and since then they have settled in this locality, i.e., on the bank of river Tapi. In the early years they had found employment as domestic servant, coolie, helper in a go-down, etc. But all these occupations were temporary. For one reason or another, they could not stick to these occupations. So they decided to go and wait at the CLM for some regular source of earnings. RR was living in a rented hut in Bapunagar slum settlement when they first arrived here. In this area, they lived for about five years. However, she was lucky enough to build her own hut on Municipal Corporation open plot. Now this hutment colony is more or less regularized. There is no danger of eviction or shifting.

RR now has her own dwelling unit. She pays small rent towards land, less than Rs. 20 per year. Her hut is well built with bamboo, mud and tin-sheets. During every rainy season, they spend about Rs. 100 to Rs. 150 for some repairs. There is a small opening on the side walls that serves as ventilation outlet. They get the water from public water standpost for which they pay Rs. 5 per month. There is no private bathroom or a latrine. They use open space around for this purpose. There is no domestic electricity connection either. They use kerosene lamp. They cook the food on a *chulha* (hearth or stove) by using the firewood. They spend between Rs. 30-40 per month on firewood alone, i.e., amount equal to their two days' wages.

In Taloda, their native place, they have their own house. Raisingh's father and mother live there. Both are now in their late fifties, and look after their agricultural holdings. They themselves work on their land. Their holding is too small (less than one acre) and without any irrigation facility. They take only one crop of *juwar* and *tuver* in a year, and whatever is produced is used for domestic consumption. The foodgrains so stored last for about 5-6 months. In the remaining period, this old couple look for some agricultural labour work in and around the village. Raisingh visits them at least twice a year and gives them some money. Indeed Raisingh's parents are surviving on meagre resource. But, because of their presence in the village, the agricultural land has been retained within their family.

Two of RR's immediate neighbours in Surat city are Bhil and *Mochi* (cobbler), both belonging to lower castes. There are some Muslim households also. RR does not much interact with them. RR's brother, Lalubhai, also lives nearby in the same locality. He is a construction worker. RR keeps close relations with her brother's family. RR does visit her relatives settled outside Surat city on occasions of marriage, illness, etc. She does feel that physical distance compels them to postpone visits to their kith and kin. Money is another constraining factor. RR ruefully commented:

> Nowadays, travelling has become costly. When we visit our relatives, we have to take something (sweets, biscuits, etc.) with us. That also costs money. We can not go empty-handed.

RR observes all religious occasions like *Diwaso*, *Holi*, *Diwali*, *Shivratri*, etc. She visits some important temples in the city on festival days.

RR is the first person in her family to get up. She wakes up at 4.00 am. And by 7.00 am, she completes all her household work like cleaning, fetching water, preparation of tea and food, etc. Around 7.00 am, both RR and her husband leave their residence for the CLM. They walk the distance. As they have no child, there is no disturbance in their joint routine. They can lock their hut and leave for work. RR returns home at around 8.00 pm. After arduous manual labour for the full day, she gets physically tired. Yet when she is back home, she has to cook food at night and clean utensils, tidy the room, etc.

She goes to bed at 11.00 pm. She gets rest for only about 5 hours. She said that there are no occasions of scarcity of food in their home. They eat *rotla-shak* daily and some rice on special occasions. They do not remain starved or hungry on any day, she reported. Question of borrowing raw or cooked food from others does not arise. "Who will give us that help anyway?" she quipped. To avoid acute shortage they store some basic necessities. At the time of interview, RR had 8 kgs of *bajra*, 5 kgs wheat, 1 litre of cooking oil, and 2 litres of kerosene. "We always keep about 8-10 days of provision with us. That is just to avoid starvation", she said by pointing towards a tin barrel placed in one corner of her hut.

Her hut symbolized in all respects the living style of a poor household in the city. There was no furniture or fixtures of any kind. Neither table, chairs, umbrella, nor even lantern or *khadio* (small kerosene lamp). The articles like wristwatch, iron cot, etc., constituted items of their dream world. It was an empty hut with bare minimum necessities like a few earthen and aluminium vessels, primus stove, oil cane and a few tin containers. They sleep on the floor. Recently, they have brought three stainless steel plates from the Chowk Bazaar shop. They buy the clothes from Taloda taluka town (native place). Probably, they can keep credit account with traders there.

RR is partially aware of her rights. In some respects, she is still in favour of *status quo* in CLM functioning. She does not want any restrictions to be imposed on the entry of 'new' labourers and even of contractors. She does not intensely feel any necessity of a labour union also. "Union is for other occupations, permanent and factory-like job activities. Not for us", she said. Yet, she pleaded for autonomy for the casual workers on issues like fixation of wages, equal wages for men and women, regulation of working hours, and equal share for women in family property. She thinks that present arrangement of recruitment and allocation of work through the contractors/ *mukadams* is satisfactory and should be continued. As middlemen, they serve useful function of introducing the workers to the labour market and socialize them into its intricacies, she thought. "They do not take their share or 'cut' from labourers' wages", she stated.

Some 10 years ago, when RR first entered the CLM, she had felt utterly confused and also humiliated. Menfolk used to look at her with prying eyes, with doubts, lust and suspicion. "As if my body was for sale", she said. Later, after few days of uninterrupted visits, this atmosphere changed. Also presence of her husband with her in the CLM helped the situation to normalize, she added. On 2-3 days in a month, she gets less than 'stipulated' wages. But she does not complain about this. However, she does feel strongly about 'irregular' work. On some days, she has to return home without work, after 3-4 hours of waiting in the CLM. She is therefore keen in learning about some self-employment skills like soap-making at home. But where she could go for this training and who would teach her?

She gets credit from none; shopkeepers in the locality refuse to give her any commodities on credit. Even tea-shop owner does not give them tea on credit. Knowing this for years, they have realized that if they have some cash money on hand, they can buy things. Otherwise, they have no status to command any goods or services from open market. Hence, the efforts to save and invest in storage of foodgrains. Also, RR has no acquaintance with social workers or do-gooders in Surat city who can possibly help her household in a crisis situation. When they fall ill, they go to a civil hospital for 'free' treatment. They can not afford to go to a private doctor.

They do not have sustained contacts with their neighbours also. RR seems to take very little interest in what goes around at the market place or in their neighbourhood. She does not have even the ration card, because her hut is not 'numbered,' i.e., registered. So, she is deprived of whatever facility that fair price shop can offer. Once she went to an office at Killa Maidan for ration card registration. She was asked to bring papers of registration of hut or electricity bill. She had neither to produce.

(C3) Manjula Palji: Shenva, a Scheduled Caste Woman

Manjula Palji (MP) is a 25-year old woman living in working class locality at Juna Vadaj, Ahmedabad. She belongs to *Shenva*---- a Scheduled Caste. She is illiterate, so also is her husband, Paljibhai. Her household consists of six persons; three sons, one daughter, herself and her husband. Two of her younger sons, aged 3 and 4, are attending *Balmandir*, while her six year old daughter goes to nearby primary school. Both MP and her husband go to CLM at Shahpor *chakla* for *kadia kam*, i.e., construction labour. She gets work for four days, and Palji for eight days in a month. Whenever they get work at CLM, they get a daily wage of Rs. 15. So, together they earn about Rs. 180-200 in a month. For a family of six persons, per capita income is Rs. 30 per month, i.e., one rupee per person per day. This is indeed a low income in a city like Ahmedabad, where cost of living is decidedly very high.

MP lives in a hut near Rampur Tekri. Hut is on a rental of Rs. 50 per month. They feel insecure because if they fail to pay the rent in time, they may be asked to quit. MP said in a pensive tone:

> In such an eventuality, we would shift to any open space in this city. We have to face any consequence including the harassment of anti-social elements or policemen or slum-lords. What can we do except to suffer whatever comes our way?

This family was living in a helpless situation. Some of the basic services like water, latrine facility, etc., are not easily accessible. For water, they have to depend upon nearby middle class family. They use municipal latrine blocks which are unkempt and dirty. They have no electricity connection. They use kerosene lamp, and cook their food on *chulha*. They have to buy firewood from the local market, costing them between Rs. 30 and Rs. 35 per month.

MP and her family originally belonged to Kadi taluka of Mehsana district. However, now there is none in their native place. They were landless and had left the village some 10 years ago in search of livelihood. They came to Ahmedabad and settled down here. From the very beginning, i.e., for last 10 years, MP is going to CLM at Shahpor *chakla* for casual employment. She feels extremely dejected because increasingly she has to face more and more days of unemployment. For most of the days, she waits in the CLM for 3-4 hours, and comes back home disappointed. "In last five years, our condition has progressively deteriorated. Less work and wages, and more mouths to feed", she said gloomily. Over the years, she has grown pessimistic.

She said that they cannot leave Ahmedabad, because they have no other place to go. She also felt that there is no likelihood of better future for their family in this city. "They would continue to slog and struggle for their day-to-day living," she ruefully stated.

Earlier, MP lived in a slum locality at Shankar Bhuvan complex. The Ahmedabad Municipal Corporation demolished that slum settlement two years ago. From there, she shifted to present locality. This is also unauthorized settlement. In her neighbourhood lives one family of *Chamar*, a Scheduled Caste, and two families of migrants from Rajasthan. MP has developed close relations with these three families. They often share one another's burden, and mutually help in times of distress. They sometimes share foodgrains and cooked food also. MP has two close friends: (i) Sharda, who is *Shenva* by caste and also *kadia* worker, and (ii) Nanduben, a *Vankar* (Scheduled Caste) and also *kadia* worker. Besides, her maternal uncle Kalidas also stays nearby. He is a textile worker. Thus, MP has small but fairly dependable network of relatives and friends. Whenever she finds time, she visits them. Also her friends and relatives visit her on social occasions. MP has continued her religious activities, despite tensions of unemployment, overwork, etc. On Sundays, she visits *Bhardrakali* temple near Lal Darwaja area. Also she observes fast on religious days like *Diwali, Janmashtami*, etc.

MP usually wakes up at 5.00 am and does all household work by herself till 8.00 am. That includes cleaning the hut, fetching water, preparing food and attending to school-going children. She does not receive any help from her husband in these *'bairaonu kam'*, i.e., female-specific work. Not only that, her husband often abuses her and occasionally beats her. "All this is on account of frustration arising out of unemployment and shortage of money," MP said. MP's children are very young, the eldest one is only six-year old. MP leaves the children alone at home. The youngest child is just two year old. This boy is left in a custody of her neighbour. MP returns home at 7 pm MP explained her helplessness as follows:

> My heart is always heavy when I leave home. My children are young. They need my presence and protection. But what can I do? I cannot take the child with me in the CLM. That will come in the way of getting me a day's work. Contractors do not prefer women to come with their babies in the market. 'Such women while away their time in nursing their children during working hours,' they say openly.

She goes to bed at 10.00 pm. She gets rest only for 5-6 hours. Whole day's work does have a telling effect on her. She remarked:

> I cannot even manage to stand up in the morning. My whole body aches. But what to do? I look at the faces of my young children, and with great determination get up to do the routine, physically strenuous work. There is no holiday or leisure hours as such for me.

What food do they eat? In morning hours, they eat *rotlas* with tea. In the afternoon food, they have *rotla ane shak*. In the evening, they prepare *khichdi ane shak*. On occasions like *Diwali*, *Holi*, etc., they prepare *shiro* or *sukhadi* (traditional sweet dish). She said:

> Our children look forward to 'good food' as these are the festival days. And that is possible only if we get some regular work and wages on previous days. Otherwise, usual *khichdi-shak* is to be eaten even on festival days.

Luckily, MP's family have not yet suffered very many occasions of hunger or starvation. "There is something to eat at home", she said. She is the last person in the house to eat, after feeding her children and husband. She manages with less quantity of food for herself on many occasions. "I am used to this", she said without any hint of complaint.

MP is very cautious in husbanding her meagre resources. She is a ration card-holder. She always tries to store some foodgrains to avoid dependency on others. At the time of interview, she had the following foodstock: coarse rice 1 kg, *bajra* 5 kg, and wheat 5 kg. She made daily purchases of cooking oil and kerosene. Because of irregular work and frequent days of joblessness, MP has incurred debts. At present, she has a debt of over Rs. 2,000. She owes this amount to her relatives. There is no furniture. She has some aluminium vessels and a few brasswares. For clothes they visit Sunday market near Victoria Garden for second-hand garments.

MP is quite conscious and vocal about her rights as casual workers. She is also sympathetic and broad-minded. She is very much in favour of some control over the arbitrariness of contractors about wagerates, work load, etc. At the same time, she is against imposing any restrictions on entry of new labourers in the market. She argued:

> Because they too have no other source of earning their livelihood, they are compelled to stand in the CLM. How and why should you restrict their entry?

She felt that casual labourers led the most abject and dependent life. According to her, the CLM workers are at the mercy of *mukadams* and contractors and have the lowest social status. She further said in a complaining voice:

> They are regarded as the most illiterate, unskilled and uncouth lot. Anyone can redicule them or boss over them. It is an existence full of indignity and humiliation.

She felt that the CLM workers should come together and launch a struggle on the issues of work-duration, minimum wages, etc. They should not accept work below the collectively agreed upon wages. Labour union alone could exert such pressure on the contractors. But she felt that given the temporary nature of their work and excess labour supply, formation of a labour union is an uphill task. She felt that the rights of casual labourers towards basic minimum needs of survival should be protected. But who would protect these rights? She does not know. She only knows that work can be available at the CLM. For availability of work, she has to depend upon contacts and goodwill of the contractors and *mukadams*. She knows that by bargaining hard, one can increase the wage rate by a rupee or so.

But she also knows that too much insistence on higher wage rate may result into loss of future job opportunity and alienation from known job-givers. The contractors may soon brand her as 'difficult and militant' person. Together they may blacklist her. That meant loss of work opportunity, consequent hunger and starvation at home, increase in debt liability and scolding and beating from her husband. She is aware of these grim prospects. Therefore, she was silent when we asked her about the dealings of the contractors. "I have good relations with them", she would say repeatedly. Does her observation reflect objective situation? One cannot be sure, because her answer was halting and full of caution.

(C4) Savitaben: A Woman from *Chamar* (SC) Community

Savitaben Pitambar (SP) is a 38-year old woman from *Chamar*, Scheduled Caste community. She is a casual labourer attending CLM at Bapunagar Char Rasta, Ahmedabad city. She lives in a hutment colony near Bhidbhanjan Hanuman temple, about 2 kms away from Bapunagar CLM. Her household consists of five persons----herself, her husband and three children. Her eldest daughter is 16 years old. She is illiterate and remains at home for looking after household duties. Her son, Mahesh is 15 and is studying in 7th standard in Municipal School. So also her another son, Naresh, aged 14, is studying in 6th standard. Their education is free, i.e., they have not to pay any fees. But other things like books, notebooks, etc., cost the family some amount. But both parents are keen that their sons should be educated. She said:

> We both are illiterate. We have no decent occupation. Our social status is low. If our sons get educated and secure some regular employment or government job, their future will be different and certainly better than ours.

SP has good deal of aspirations for her children, particularly for school going sons.

There are two earning members, SP and her husband. Both go to Bapunagar CLM for casual labour. SP does mostly *kadia kam* while her husband does any type of job work. They call their work *chhutak majoori,* i.e., casual, unattached labour. She gets work for about 15 days in a month with a daily wage of Rs. 15, while Pitambar gets work for 12-13 days with a daily wage of Rs. 16. In other words, they remain employed for half the month. Together, they earn Rs. 430-450, i.e., a family income of Rs. 15 per day for five persons which works out as per capita income of Rs. 3 per day. Indeed, this income is below subsistence level in Ahmedabad city.

As they live in a rented hut, they have to pay Rs. 60 per month towards rentals. That further adversely affects their purchasing power. SP is living in this hutment colony for last 18 years. Her dwelling is a small unit with some space around. Her hut is 'regularized', i.e., there is no danger of eviction or shifting. But the basic amenities are not easily available to them. For water, they have to depend upon public waterpost which is always crowded with large number of neighbourhood people jostling with one another for their turn. That leads to quarrels, and sometimes physical fights. Latrine blocks are always dirty and present an ugly sight of filth and dirt. There is a constant threat of a health hazard due to these insanitary conditions. But who bothers? SP's hut has no electricity connection. For lighting purpose, they use kerosene lamp. They cook their food on a primus stove. They spend about Rs. 2 per day for kerosene.

SP migrated from a village in Kalol taluka of Mehsana district some 18 years ago. There she lived in Vankarvas. They still have a house there. Pitambar's brother and his family (a total of five persons) live in the native place. They have no agricultural land. They work as *chhutak majoor* in the village, and somehow manage to survive. Pitambar cannot help his brother monetarily because he himself is living at tether's end. But he does go to his village two or three times a year. Each trip costs him between Rs. 30 and Rs. 40. Pitambar and his wife said ruefully:

> We have to think ten times before planning a visit to native place. Not only travel cost, but also we have to take something for our brother's children. So together we have to spend at least Rs. 50 per trip. Also we lose wages for that many days.

SP has to struggle a great deal to make two ends meet. Some 15 years ago, her condition was relatively better. Her husband was then working in a textile mill. But because of severe ill-health, he had to leave the job. Since he was a *badli* (substitute) worker, the management did not allow him to resume the work after recoupment. Since then, the bad days began. SP had to enter the CLM to earn wages to feed the family, and to look after the ailing husband. Children are too small to provide any assistance.

SP gets *kadia* work at the CLM. For the last 8-10 years, she goes to the CLM daily. But she gets work for 10-15 days in a month at Bapunagar CLM. After 10.00 am, there is hardly any chance to get work at *chakla* market. For this reason, SP goes to Maninagar CLM also. But there too, she does not always find work. She is keen to work as unskilled labourer in a factory. "But who will employ me. I have neither the contacts, nor the influence", she said in a pensive mood. SP says that during the last five years, her economic condition has worsened. There is less work and more workers in the *chakla* market. Competition among the labourers has increased and as a result the wages have remained at low level. She said:

> Now there are too many labourers from other districts of Gujarat, and even from Rajasthan, UP and Maharashtra. Obviously, the contractors can pick and choose from amongst us. We have little scope for bargaining.

When SP does not get work at CLM, she goes home, takes the gunny bag and goes out in the streets for picking up rags (papers, plastic bags, bottles etc.). That way she earns about Rs. 5-6. Rag-picking is an alternate job which she has to do to feed the family. She is terribly unhappy about her present status of living. She is also pessimistic about her future. "Our conditions will not change for the better", she asserted.

SP does have some social support base. Her immediate neighbours, *Vankar* and *Chamar* by caste, are quite helpful to her family. One is a textile worker and another is a vegetable vendor. SP's close friend is Jadiben. She is a Hindu *Vankar*, and is a small-time shopkeeper. Also there are 5-6 families of her close relations living near Bapunagar. SP goes to them sometimes. They also visit her house on social occasions. They also try to help one another in times of hardships. SP has continued to observe her religious practices. She goes to Motera, usually on Sundays to offer prayers and *prasad* (food articles offered to God) at Asharam Bapu temple. "That gives me some solace and inner strength", she said.

SP works very hard. She gets up at 5.00 am, and goes to bed at 11.00 pm. Before she goes out for casual labour, she attends to most of the household work. Her elder daughter does help her. Their food is simple: *rotla* and tea in the morning, *rotla-shak* in the afternoon and *khichdi-shak* at night. They store foodgrains that can last for 3-4 days. At the time of interview, there was 5 kgs *bajra*, 5 kgs wheat, 500 gms cooking oil and 2 litres of kerosene. There was no furniture of any kind in the house. They bought 'used' clothes from *Vaghari* (a low caste category) traders, or from the second-hand cloth market near Delhi Gate.

SP felt a sense of humiliation when she first stood in the Bapunagar CLM. People there looked upon her with sense of pity and compassion. She was perplexed, and was not aware about the ways of negotiation or bargaining with the contractors. Within about a month's time, she learnt the modalities of dealing with the contractors and *mukadams*. She is now confident and self-assured. She can decide which work to accept, from whom and for how much wage. By and large, she has mixed experiences with the contractors. "They know their business interests. They are sharp in identifying good and hard-working labourers", she said. SP has liberal views about labour market network. She is keen that the workers themselves should decide about their wage rates, and not to fall prey to pressures of contractors and their henchmen.

She also feels strongly that: (i) wages should be more, about Rs. 20 for female workers; (ii) working should be regularized; and (iii) there should be equal wages for men and women. She also felt that there should be a union of the CLM labourers, and there should be solidarity among them. "Each worker must be assured of at least 20 days of work at the CLM", she asserted.

SP is indeed struggling hard for survival. She works for 10 to 12 hours a day. When she is unable to find work, she goes to her neighbours for help. Also a shopkeeper in the locality extends her credit. So far, she has incurred a debt of Rs. 1,000, mostly to meet domestic needs. When would she repay this debt? She herself does not know. Despite nearly two decades of stay in Ahmedabad, a leading metropolis of Gujarat, her economic condition has not altered. Rather, it has been worsening year after year. Her employment is insecure and wages are pitifully low. There is not enough for healthy survival of the entire family. In such situation, to question her on future plans or prospects is utterly immodest. Yet, SP is not completely distracted or disillusioned. She continues to lead an honest life by working as a casual labourer through CLM. When she fails to get a job through the CLM, she immediately takes up rag-picking work. She can ill-afford to remain idle. How long her spirit and enthusiasm will last? Will she ever experience the life of relative ease and comfort? Will she come out of the vicious cycle of day-to-day struggle? These are difficult questions to answer. SP herself is not very hopeful of a favourable future.

SUMMING UP THE LIFE-PROFILES OF FEMALE CASUAL LABOURERS

In preceding sections we have attempted to outline certain key aspects of living and working conditions of four female casual labourers and their families. Two of them are from Surat and two from Ahmedabad. Both these cities are growing metropolises in Gujarat. They are known for their growth and prosperity; for wealth, industry and luxurious living of elite classes. But how do the poor people live in these cities? And particularly, how do the female casual labourers survive in the urban setting? It is with this view in mind that we concentrate on the socio-economic conditions of these four families. We asked: How do they live and with what level of necessities? What are their occupational conditions? How do they perceive their own work, co-workers, and employers? How do they rate their future prospects? We have been able to document some insights and experiences of these workers. We may now briefly recall the core elements of their existence and perceptions.

All four female workers are within the age-group of 25 to 40. One of them belongs to relatively higher caste, viz., *Patidar*, two to ex-untouchable castes, viz., *Shenva* and *Chamar*, and one to a tribal caste, viz., Bhil. Three of them are married, while one is a widow. Except for one, the remaining three households have relatively smaller family size, i.e. five or less members. There is no education in the older generation, but there are noticeable efforts in some families to educate the younger children. In fact, in one household the highest education is 10th standard (C1). This is a *Patidar* household. In another *Chamar* household (C4), two younger children are attending *Balmandir* in their locality. It is not certain whether these children would go beyond primary school level. Economic compulsions may cut short their educational pursuit, as has happened in the case of their elder brothers and sisters.

How is their housing condition? It is indeed critical beyond words. They live in slum settlements known for their poor hygiene and sanitation level. Three out of four live in the rented huts, paying monthly rent of Rs. 50-100. They are insecure as regards this basic need, i.e., shelter. Insecurity is either due to so-called 'unauthorized' nature of their dwelling/settlement, or the avarice of their landlord for increased rent. Any day they may be asked to leave. Anxieties on this score are quite acute.

We have also noted their household 'possessions'. Most of

them have bare minimum things. List of household assets include stove, tin containers, few utensils, bottles, gunny bags, tattered mattresses, a few clothes, lantern or *khadio*. Some do not have even a footwear. None have electricity connections. All of them get water from public waterposts. They have to pay Rs. 60 per year to get water facility. Two of them have improvised bathrooms, while two households use outside open space for bath. They use public toilet blocks, or defecate in the open space around.

Their economic conditions are pitiable. Except one household (C1), all are living in a hand-to-mouth condition. Whatever they earn is spent on food. Knowing the economic insecurity, they cautiously invest their savings in foodgrains, *bajra*, wheat, cooking oil or kerosene. That is, they immediately buy these things and keep the stock of five to eight days. They know fully well that if on the next day, none in the family gets a job, at least they will have something to eat. Fear of starvation drives them towards such food security measures of short duration. They utilize other low-priced shops or markets in urban areas for buying utensils, foodgrains and even clothes. They buy *utarela* (literally: discarded) or second-hand clothes from *Vaghri* traders. They buy red *bajra*. And their dependence on fair price shops is maximum. When they fall ill, they rush to public dispensary or civil hospital. On rare occasions, they go to private doctors.

These households are perennially embroiled in a cyclical processes of unemployment, underemployment, poverty, ill-health, physical debility, absenteeism and low income. One day they may get the work at *chakla* market. The other day (or for a week thereafter), they may not get the work despite daily wait of 3-4 hours in anticipation. These casual labourers do not have work tools. They have nothing but their labour power to sell. And their number is too large at any one *chakla* market point ranging from 1,000 to 3,000 labourers. And that number seems to be increasing year after year, either due to general increase in impoverishment or drought or such other calamities in the rural areas and consequent migration to the city.

Casual labourers under the study get work for four days (C3) to 20 days (C2) in a month. In rainy season, there is acute unemployment for these labourers. Data on work availability in respect of these four cases give us an average of 12 days per female worker per month. Their daily wage varies from Rs. 15 to Rs. 20. Number of work-days keep fluctuating, and hence the variation in their monthly income, i.e., Rs. 60 to Rs. 300. By 9.30 or 10.00 am, the casual labourer's patience gets exhausted, and they leave the CLM for other pursuits or return home in frustration. We found one female labourer engaged in rag-picking as an alternate source of livelihood. Some go to railway yards or vegetable markets to work as head-load workers. These are days of acute anxieties and frustration for them and their family members.

Female casual labourers have added responsibilities and physical burden. They are the first to wake up and the last to sleep, with average of 5-6 hours of rest. Also they are the last persons to eat. They feed their husband and children first. Physical exhaustion is *kayami* (perennial), they said. Not only that, they have to face the wrath of agitated husband, if they come back home without money. They have to suffer abuses (*galagali*) of their irate husband. Their day-to-day life is so grueling and insecure, it is no wonder that they do not perceive any bright future for themselves. Economic situation is worsening in last few years. Years of struggle for acquiring basic needs of life has not brought about any tangible change in their life and lifestyle.

It is clear that labour market plays a key role in their survival and fulfilment of basic needs. In this context of labour market, they have remained in a disadvantaged position, both in terms of organization or bargaining at individual level. The CLM is dispersed, diffused and composed of too many petty contractors. There are multiple hierarchies between the casual labourers at the lowest rung and the employers at the top, with host of intermediaries. Each category between the two levels attempts to extract the benefit from the total sum of production cost. The lowest level, i.e., the casual labourers, receives the least. These female workers also complained that on some occasions, they were deprived of even 'agreed' wages. But where can they go for redressal of their grievances? They are not organized. There is no labour union to represent their interests or defend their rights.

Thus, the life-profiles of female casual labourers living in two major metropolitan centres of Gujarat show that they are migrants from landless or poor peasant families. They are living here for the last over 10 years. One of them is living here for the last 25 years. Such a long duration of urban existence and yet their long stint of hard labour and production activity has not materially altered their level of living. Even their contacts and communications with the urban institutions and service agencies are minimal as shown in Table 1. Rather, they are slowly moulded into castaway citizens with increased sense of alienation, marginalization and helplessness. If anything, social groups or support linkages such as neighbours, relatives and friends do help them to cope up with the crises like food scarcity, ill-health or such other events. State assistance is negligible and indirect through fair price shops, public dispensaries, etc. *Social workers or their agencies are still farther away.* If shopkeepers in the locality decide to withdraw credit facility and if friends or relatives do not extend a helping hand, many of these families will be on the brink of starvation and hunger. Our case studies illustrate this process vividly.

These case studies broadly indicate some aspects of level and extent of poverty and struggle for survival of female casual labourers in the urban centres of Gujarat. It is necessary that we broaden our canvas and cover larger number of such cases to identify areas of distress and agony of this segment of working class, and to document their perceptions of the conditions in which they are so adversely placed and evolving various survival strategies. These labourers are urban dwellers. They are the workers who contribute their labour in building houses,

Table 1

Socio-Economic Status and Perceptions

		Yes	No
I.	Socio-Economic Status		
	i. Whether migrants	C1, C2, C3, C4	-
	ii. Whether house at NP	C2, C3, C4	C1
	iii. Whether agricultural land at NP	C2	C1, C3, C4
	iv. Years of stay in the city:		
	(a) Less than 15 years	C2, C3	-
	(b) 15 Years or more	C1, C4	-
	v. Whether hut is owned	C2	C1, C3, C4
	vi. Whether feel insecurity of housing	C1, C3	C2, C4
	vii. Whether economic situation in 5 years has remained:		
	(a) As it is	C1	-
	(b) Improved	C2	-
	(c) Worsened	C3, C4	-
	viii. Whether indebted	C3, C4	C1, C2
II.	Occupational Perceptions		
	i. Whether CL should be registered	C1, C3, C4	C2
	ii. Whether contractors should be registered	C1, C3, C4	C2
	iii. Whether wages should vary according to type of work	C1, C3, C4	C2
	iv. Whether labour union necessary	C1, C2, C3, C4	-
	v. Female should get equal wages	C1, C2, C3, C4	-
	vi. Whether equal working hours	C1, C2, C3, C4	-
	vii. Whether you get less than decided wage rate	C1, C2	C3, C4
III.	Help and Assistance		
	i. From government	-	C1, C2, C3, C4
	ii. From social workers	-	C1, C2, C3, C4
	iii. From relatives, friends, etc.	C1, C3, C4	C2
	iv. Credit from shopkeepers	C1, C3, C4	C2
	v. Whether ration card-holder	C1, C3, C4	C2

hotels, plazas, multi-storey buildings, offices, roads, gardens and other physical assets for convenience and comforts of the elitist, well-placed and propertied classes in the urban areas.

CONCLUSION AND THE STRATEGIES OF SOCIAL INTERVENTION

Thematic Recapitulation of the Argument

The principal focus of the paper was on description of living and working conditions of the female CLM workers. It was also intended to know their ideas and perceptions on matters related to their domestic and occupational lives. The information was collected through field observations and questionnaires. Emergence of the CLMs and their incessant growth demonstrates two things: (i) increasing marginalization of lower strata of peasantry and their consequent migration to urban areas in search of livelihood; and (ii) phenomenal growth of secondary labour markets that have come up to cater to the demands of the organized sectors. The CLMs represent this change in creating and sustaining the casual labour sector and thus contributing to the growth of urban economy at lesser costs in terms of wages, social services, etc. The workers at the CLM generate surplus but have less than proportionate share in the total income or output. They have very few options to choose from and thus suffer all inequities and distortions in market network. The labourers coming in search of work gather in the CLM at early morning hours and wait till about 10.30 or 11.00 am. Some get work, some do not. Availability of work depends upon multiple factors. But it is certain that due to influx of large number of labourers, the chances of getting work at the CLM for 10 or 15 days in a month are bleak. When unemployed, they go back home or search for other less remunerative alternatives. Fear of hunger and starvation drive them to take up anything: from rag-picking to begging. Their ways of survival are complex and indeed defies our patience and imagination.

Whatever our assumptions about the city planning or urban renewal, both the CLMs and the residential places of the workers have remained outside the influence of planning perspective and programmes. There are no facilities worth the name at these CLMs, where transactions worth lakhs of rupees in labour costs are negotiated. These CLMs are 'unofficial' open-air spots bereft of any amenities or services—no sheds, no water and no latrine facility.

One can imagine the hardships of the female (and also male) labourers who assemble here daily for all 365 days in a year. Young infants and children of these labourers also share the difficulties of their parents on this score. The CLMs are congested. They are also the sites of frequent traffic jams. The difficulties of the labourers multiply in rainy season. In summer, they have to beg for water at some other places. Most of the labourers coming to the labour markets are migrants from the lower strata of peasantry from villages in Gujarat, Maharashtra and other states. They have left their land, home, families and livestock. Where do they settle in the city? They stay in open spaces in a makeshift huts. Many of them live in slums or *chawls* with perennial sense of insecurity. Some have shifted their huts from one place to another in the wake of municipality's demolition drive. As slum-dwellers, they face problems of drinking water, latrine, electricity, transport and what have you. Health hazards are common due to insanitary conditions around. That further incapacitates them.

The female labourers are largely from the Scheduled Caste and Scheduled Tribes groups, i.e., the most vulnerable sections of Indian society. They are illiterate. Their standard of living is low. One can get an idea of their poverty by looking at their dwelling unit. Most of the dwellings are ramshackle huts with grass-thatched or tinsheet roofs and in need of constant repairs. They are congested and lack proper ventilation. The female labourers are always busy in their own work at household level or at workplace. They are not able to participate in any of the social, cultural, religious and political activities in the city. In native place, some participation was possible. Hence, some of them feel socially isolated or alienated in the urban areas. Some have continued to maintain relations with their native village.

In the city, as many of them do not have their own, i.e., 'authorized' hut or house, their names are not registered in voter's list. Hence, they cannot exercise their voting rights. Because of the same reason, many do not have ration cards. The economic position of the female labourers is deplorable to say the least. While talking with them, one gets an idea about their anxieties, worries, frustrations, fatigue, etc. The female labourers have to carry double burden----domestic as well as outside employment. They have to get up early in the morning, finish their domestic work and then go for their work. Even after coming home in the late evening, they have to do routine household chores including cooking and childcare. Such continuous and mechanical work schedule adversely affects their health. When at home, they are always worried about problems of food, drinking water and fuel. Taking care of children is another responsibility, exclusively their's. Physical and mental strains result in ill-health and psychological tensions.

Their working conditions leave much to be desired. Despite some diversification in their occupational activity, most of them have been working as construction workers. Their place of work is not fixed. Oftentimes, the labourers have to return home as they do not get work. Their wages are low. They do not get other benefits or allowances. These labourers strongly believe that it is not at all advisable for others to join this type of work. The female labourers join this sector and stay in it. The female labourers get lower wages compared to their male counterparts. There is no regulation of wage rates. Because of weak bargaining position of the CLM labourers, they have not been able to force the contractors to pay them fair wages. Even then, the wages in the city are relatively more and chances of employment somewhat better compared to the conditions obtaining in their respective villages. Hence, they prefer construction labour or other casual labour in the city instead of agricultural labour.

The casual labourers cannot aspire for the facilities like medicine, housing, canteen, latrine, urinal, etc., which the labourers in organized sector enjoy. The casual labourers do not have any security of job. Sometimes labourers are dismissed even when the work is in progress. They buy their necessities everyday. So when they do not get work, their position becomes precarious. Therefore, they think it proper to continue the work in spite of heavy odds against them.

There is a lot of harassment by the contractors. Even then they are not able to speak a word against them. They are scared of the consequences of their outspokenness, i.e., immediate blacklisting and retrenchment. They cannot protest openly on most of the occasions. It is unfortunate that so far the government has not paid any attention to this class of labourers. There is no supervision of or control over the labour market processes and transactions. There is no arrangement to compel the contractors to abide by the minimum norms of legal enactments or provisions of labour laws. The CLM labourers are at the total mercy of blind market forces of demand and supply of labour.

Macro and Micro Level Strategies of Social Intervention

Analysis of data on female casual labourers suggest that social interventions in certain areas/sectors can bring about appreciable change in the lives of these labourers. However, it has also to be emphasized that there are larger social forces shaping and influencing the environment in which the labourers find themselves trapped. These larger forces cannot be glossed over. Rather, it should be our endeavour to identify these macro forces and make an attempt to apply correctives. Obviously, the macro social forces are least amenable to short-term measures. That is because they are rooted in political economy of growth and modernization. They have their own intrinsic logic and ideological direction. Keeping in view the above aspects, we attempt to suggest corrective strategies at two levels----macro and micro.

Macro-Level Strategies

1. It is clearly evident that a large segment of casual labour population belongs to SC and ST communities. Secondly,

they belong to lower strata of peasantry. This suggests that emergence of casual labour in the urban CLMs is product of both, displacement of surplus population from rural areas and redundancy or retrenchment of workers in organized sectors like textiles, engineering, etc. It is therefore imperative to review and restructure our rural development policies and our policy on industrialization.

2. The CLM labourers are living in the slums or on pavements. They are victims of arbitrary and anti-poor housing policy. Also, they get affected by various heartless and thoughtless urban renewal programmes which mean demolitions and evictions. Hence, larger policy on the question of shelter to the poor be evolved with proper safeguards in terms of health provision, social service, community interaction, etc.
3. Casual labour is a product of our peculiar development path which encourages capital at an unfair expense of labour. The minimum survival needs are not taken care of within such restrictive framework of growth. It is therefore essential to re-examine our policies on industrial growth and labour as well social defence and social welfare. Issues of labour participation, control and welfare are too vital here. A macro-level review of these parameters is imperative.

Micro-Level Strategies

Macro-level action takes longer time, as it has to mediate through variety of socio-political structures and pressures. Granting this, we need to consider immediate, short-term measures to intervene in the prevailing deplorable situation of the female casual labourers. We suggest the following:

1. Effective implementation of the Contract Labour (Regulation and Abolition) Act, 1970, and also other legislations such as those relating to minimum wages, health insurance, interest of inter-state migrants, etc.
2. Registration of labourers at the CLMs, and encouraging labour cooperatives to effectively protect the interests of

workers in matters of wages, working hours, workload, etc.

3. The labour office of the state government should effectively monitor the transactions between the employers and the casual labourers; and submit monthly reports to the headquarters. At headquarters, there should be monthly review meetings. Corrective steps may be taken up immediately.
4. Setting up of permanent machinery to solve the grievances of casual labourers. Women representatives from the NGOs be associated with this cell/unit/department.
5. Provision of sheds, creche, drinking water facility, latrines and urinals, and health centre at the CLM.
6. To provide transit shelters to the migrant labourers in the city to minimize their hardships. Slum improvement programmes on extensive scale will also help those casual labourers who are living in the squatter colonies.
7. Social (including health and literacy) mobilization with the help of voluntary agencies to generate awareness and build effective leadership among them.
8. Provision of ration cards to the CLM households and registration of their names in the voter's list.
9. The trade unions operating in organized sectors be encouraged to study the situation of the casual labourers; and financial assistance be provided to them to organize the CLM labourers.
10. Extensive documentation and studies on the conditions of female workers in all sectors of employment.

This account of market segmentation and marginalization of female casual labourers in urban Gujarat sounds various warnings. Immediate political and social interventions have to be thought out. The larger social and economic forces have trapped the labourers in a vicious circle. These larger forces cannot be ignored because they are rooted in political economy of growth, modernization and exploitation. As we said, they have their own logic and ideological direction. The task remains to produce counter-logic and counter-ideological direction.

REFERENCES

Acharya, Sarathi (1979), "Employment of Women and Men in India: A Historical Review, 1901-51", *Indian Journal of Labour Economics*, 22(3).

Agarwal, R.C. (1980), "Women Power: The Neglected Factor in Development", *Manpower Journal*, 16(3).

Bardhan, Kalpana (1985), "Women's Work, Welfare and Status: Forces of Tradition and Change in India", *Economic and Political Weekly*, 20(50 & 51).

Desai, Neera and Patel, Vibhuti (1985), *Indian Women: Change and Challenge in the International Decade 1975-85*. Bombay: Popular Prakashan.

Everett, J. (1986), "We were in the Forefront of the Fight: Feminist Theory and Practice in Indian Grass-roots Movements", *South Asia Bulletin*, 6(1).

Halch, Afshar (ed.) (n.d.), *Women, Work and Ideology in the Third World*. London: Tavistock Publications.

Hirway, Indira (1979), "Employment Problem of Rural Women in Gujarat", *Journal of Labour Economics*, 20(3).

ICSSR (1975), *Status of Women in India: A Synopsis of the Report of National Committee (1971-74)*. New Delhi: Allied Publishers.

India (1983), *Statistical Profile of Women's Labour*. Simla: Ministry of Labour, Labour Bureau.

India (1988), *National Perspectives Plan for Women 1988-2000 AD*. Delhi: Department of Women and Child Development, Ministry of HRD.

International Labour Office (1959), "Women's Employment in India", *International Labour Review*, 79(4).

Jhabwala, R. and U. Jumani (1986), *Experiences of Organizing Home-based Workers in India*. Ahmedabad: Gandhi Labour Institute, 29-31 March.

Joshi, Heath (1976), "Prospects and Case for Employment of Women in Indian Cities", *Economic and Political Weekly*, 11(31-33).

Joyce, Libra *et.al.* (1984), *Women and Work in India: Continuity and Change*. New Delhi: Promila and Co.

Kothari, Rajni (1988), "The NGOs, the State and World Capitalism", in his *State Against Democracy: In Search of Humane Governance*. Delhi: Ajanta.

Mehta, Pratibha (1982), *Women Construction Workers With Particular Reference to Legal Security and Social Justice: A Case Study of Delhi*. Delhi: National Institute of Urban Affairs.

Murali Dhar, B. (1984), "Tough Going in Labour Market", *Mainstream*, 22(46).

Nath, Kamala (1965), "Urban Women Workers: A Preliminary Study", *Eco-*

nomic and Political Weekly, 17(37).

---- (1968), "Women in the Working Force in India", *Economic and Political Weekly*, 3(31).

Patnaik, Indu (1989), "Gender Issues in Employment of Women in the Urban Sector", *Other Sociology*, 1(4), June.

Ranade, S.N. and Ramchandran, P. (1970), *Women and Employment: Report of Pilot Studies Conducted in Delhi and Bombay*. Mumbai: Tata Institute of Social Sciences.

Ranade, S.N. and Sinha, G.P. (1975), *Women Construction Workers: Reports of Two Surveys*. New Delhi: Allied Publishers.

Shramshakti (1988), *Report of the National Commission on Self-Employed Women and Women in the Informal Sector*. Delhi: Government of India.

12

Community Mental Health: An Appraisal

by Bharti Sharma

Over the whole universe, it has been increasingly realized that for social development and for happier life, total well-being of all the individuals at all the levels is indeed vital. Besides other components, health is an important social component of total well-being. It is also reflected in our country's declared objective of "Health for All by 2000 A.D.", wherein health is defined as a state of complete physical, mental, social and spiritual well-being. It is more than merely the absence of disease or infirmity. Shah (1982) has stated that mental health is the most essential and inseparable component of health and that it is an integrated component of public health and social welfare programme.

DEFINING MENTAL HEALTH

In 1948, the International Preparatory Commission of the International Congress on Mental Health defined mental health as a condition which permits optimal development of the individual's physical, intellectual and emotional growth—so far as this is compatible with that of other individuals and of the community. The second factor emphasized was that of harmonious development of one's self in a changing environment. Thus, it suggests that the healthy mind can meet with ease all normal environmental situations. Also, the healthy-minded person has the capacities to live harmoniously in a changing environment.

Chaplin (1979) emphasizes the factor of adjustment when he defines mental health as state of adjustment with a subjective state of well-being, zest for living and the feeling that one is exercising his talents and ability. Soddy's (1961) understanding and definition of mental health exuberates the internal balance of the individual, quality of relationship between individuals and the groups and between groups themselves. Soddy (1961) expresses it as a dynamic equilibrium between constancy on the one hand and differentiation growth and change on the other. Barnes' (1989) operational definition describes mental health as a state of psychological maturity and integration, attained by positive striving for self-actualization and a sense of receptiveness to varied environmental stimulations and experiences, which results in a state of well-being and satisfaction of life, free from anxiety and tension. Barnes highlights psychodynamic factors contributing to the maintenance of good mental health. The emphasis is on psychological maturity and integration of personality.

The author of this paper thus derived her understanding of mental health and a mentally healthy person (Sharma,1993) as follows:

> Positive mental health is a balanced and peaceful state of mind. A mentally healthy person is one who is able to think, judge and act rationally, without getting much disturbed or perturbed, emotionally and mentally. Such a person is positively oriented and at peace with one's self, and with other beings in the society. By and large, the person's behaviour denotes smooth interaction pattern with self, with others and with God. Such a person evinces zest for living and has capacities to live harmoniously in changing environment.

Mental health is not so much a matter of freedom from specific frustrations as it is an overall balanced relationship with the world. As long as job and various situations of life facilitate and support feelings of adequacy, inner security and meaningfulness of his existence, it can be presumed that mental health will tend to be good. Poor mental health results when a person feels deprived and frustrated and when he develops anxiety, tensions, emptiness, futility and negative feelings about self. Therefore, a society, dominated by such widespread malaise as poverty, underdevelopment, deprivation and inequality, is more prone to generate poor mental health among its members.

The present trend of thinking and study of mental health also emphasizes the environmental stresses and the ecological factors. They play a significant role in maintaining good or poor mental health. The modern technological advancements which are supposed to be positively and significantly influencing the lives of human beings have actually ended up in setting ecological traps by negatively altering the physical environment. The change is so rapid that it has stretched the pliability of human adjustments. To all these changes in the external environment, the human being usually reacts as an integrated whole.

Mental health can be regarded not as an absolute condition, but a continuum. It ranges from high degree of mental health in its positive aspect to a high degree of mental ill-health in its negative aspect. Parsons (1956) specified six criteria that distinguish mental health from mental illness:

1. Being or not being under psychiatric treatment.
2. Social adjustment as defined by adherence to social norms.
3. Psychiatric diagnosis.
4. Subjective estimate of degree of happiness.
5. Personal adjustment as measured by objectively scored psychological inventories.
6. Evidence of positive striving for self-actualization and successfully coping with normal stress situations.

MENTAL HEALTH AS BIO-PSYCHO AND SOCIO-CULTURAL PHENOMENA

The illustration in Figure 1 provides a bird's eye view of mental health as bio-psycho and socio-cultural phenomena. We shall now discuss each of these phenomena in greater details.

Figure 1
Mental Health as Bio-Psycho and Socio-Cultural Phenomena

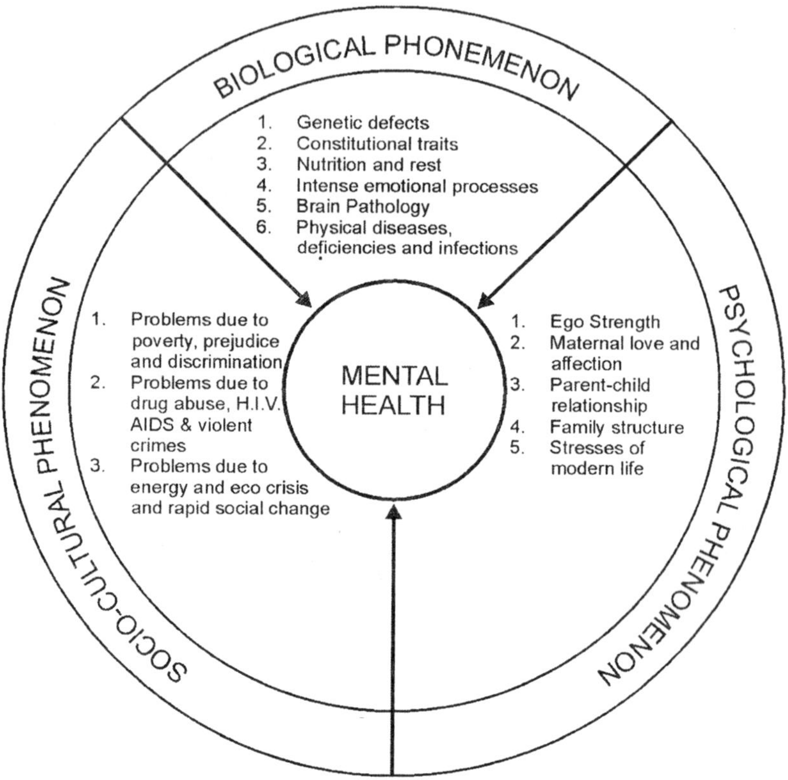

General Health and Mental Health as a Biological Phenomenon

The biological factors and general health influence all aspects of our behaviour. Biological conditions like faulty genes, diseases, endocrine imbalances, malnutrition, injuries and other conditions that interfere with normal conditions, influence the state of mental health. In genetic defects, three defects of major concern are chromosomal aberrations, faulty genes, and inherited predispositions to mental disorders (Coleman, 1976). Abnormalities in the structure or number of chromosomes may cause a wide range of congenital malformations and hereditary disorders. Sometimes faulty genes may also prove detrimental to physical and mental development.

Constitutional traits result from both genetic and environmental influences. They manifest in forms of physique, physical handicaps and vulnerability to stress. Physical impairment is likely to cause emotional aberrations, although much depends upon the way an individual evaluates his adjustive resources. Vulnerability to stress rests on the tendencies such as sensitivity, temperament and activity level. *Malnutrition*, especially during early childhood, not only affects physical development and lowers resistance to diseases, but also stunts growth of the brain. It lowers physical and mental capacities. Similarly, loss of sleep and prolonged fatigue can produce mental disorders. Rest enables an individual to meet his adjustive demands and lowers his physical and mental fatigue, eventually reducing vulnerability to stress.

Intense emotional processes are detrimental to problem-solving and performance of a particular task. As stress increases, behaviour loses spontaneity and flexibility. Severe emotional disturbances also give rise to psychosomatic disorders like peptic ulcers, hypertension and coronary heart diseases. *Brain pathology*, which is one of the biological factors, is due to the organic disturbances that directly affects central nervous system. This condition is caused due to the destruction of brain tissues or interference with functioning of the brain. Thus, brain pathology can also be responsible for maladaptive behaviours.

Physical diseases, deficiencies and infections can cause mental disorders. If the condition of stress is prolonged and severe, it may gradually wear down the individual's adjustive resources and lead to discouragement and even despair. Depending upon one's adjustive capacity, physical handicap can create feeling of inferiority, self-pity and hostility. As a result, an individual may develop psychological handicaps.

Mental Health as a Psychological Phenomenon

Ego is considered responsible for controlling and maintaining the adaptation of the individual to his physical, mental and social environment. It helps in maintaining and defending his sense of personal identity and worth when threatened by failures and frustrations. As stated by Chaplin (1979), the term 'ego-strength' is an important factor in determining whether or not the individual will breakdown under unfavourable conditions. The strength of ego is evident in certain traits of life such as feelings of self-worth, self-autonomy, forthrightness, realistic self-appraisal and positive reactions to frustrations. The ability to control the impulses and thereafter to refine them and fuse them into affective behaviour, indicates the level of psychological maturity and ego-strength (Barnes, 1989). Ego enables the positive belief in one's self as being worthy and effective human being, which is the prerequisite for good mental health. The psychological and interpersonal factors that play significant role in mental health, are:

(a) maternal love and affection;
(b) family patterns and psychological environment during childhood;
(c) interpersonal relationships; and
(d) absorbing the stresses of modern life.

First, let us examine maternal love and affection. Love, warmth and stimulation from mother or mother figure plays an important role in developing a mentally healthy individual. Children deprived of maternal stimulation or mothering have shown faulty development. It may be as a consequence of separation from the mother or lack of adequate mothering at home. Coleman (1976) suggests that the actual nature and damage resulting from maternal deprivation appear to depend on: (i) the extent and duration of such deprivation; (ii) the constitutional make up of the infant; and (iii) the substitute care.

Secondly, during infancy and childhood, the family is the crucial guiding influence in formation of a child's personality. A child growing in the family with healthy patterns turns out to be a well-adjusted and healthy individual. Whereas faulty family patterns are a fertile source of unhealthy development and maladjustment.

The two major issues to be considered here are: parent-child relationships and family structures. Patterns of parent-child relationship play a crucial and responsible role towards developing an emotionally balanced or emotionally disturbed child. Acceptance-rejection, protection *vs.* over-protection, freedom-permissiveness, discipline-lack of discipline, etc., are the indicators of good or poor mental health. Similarly, disturbed family, a social-unsocial family and cohesive-disrupted family render positive or negative experiences as well as construct psychological environment that in turn contributes to mental health or ill-health of the children.

Thirdly, interpersonal relationships, particularly intimate ones, may be conducive either to need satisfaction and mental health or to personal distress and maladaptive behaviour. Healthy, intimate and warm interpersonal relationship is a major source of need-fulfilment. Healthy interpersonal relationship brings marital stability and overall harmony in life. And lastly, the rapid changes, high competitiveness and environmental degradation in the modern life pose new challenges to mental health. In order to maintain a well-integrated and healthy personality, a person has to positively face and sort out frustrations, resolve the value-conflicts and ease the pressures of modern living. He may do so either by absorbing some of them or eliminating all of them.

Mental Health as Socio-Cultural Phenomenon

As a socio-cultural phenomenon, mental health is revealed through overt behaviour which includes performance of social roles and affective behaviour. Prevailing modern-day problems like violence, group prejudices, discrimination, economic and employment problems, rapid social changes and anxiety of day-today living tell heavily on all. Thus, the state of health does not merely consist of individual qualities but rather a function of the interaction between individuals and the whole social structure.

In our rapidly changing world, human beings are confronted with some crucial problems. All are interrelated and all have vitally important implications for our mental health, both as individuals and as a society. Nonetheless, Chakraborty's socio-psychiatric field study of Calcutta (1990), one of the fewer and more recent studies, is quite revealing. The study finds little evidence of poverty giving rise to social disintegration, resulting in poor parental relationship, broken marriages, neglect of children and a weak network of communication. While quoting Finney (1970), Chakraborty reiterates common perception that culture and condition of poverty are basically a psychological problem giving rise to feeling of alienation, cynicism, purposelessness, rootlessness and an anomie. But, as a result of her study, Chakraborty endorses the view of Finney (1970) that the poor in India do not live in a culture of poverty, primarily because the basic religious concept binds them to the whole. However, the study underscores people's belief that a large part of their unhappiness and neurotic complaints were due to the conditions of poverty.

Moreover, the same study reveals that the urbanization *per se* does not give rise to much disorganization, and that the mental health of migrants need not be poor. According to Chakraborty, migrations are of different types and their effects vary, the consequential urbanization cannot be blamed for all psychological ills in developing countries.

Chakraborty (1990) concludes that psychiatric disorders have been found to be more common among women, especially those in older age-groups, widows and economically dependent. However, according to Stanley Yolles (1965), the unresolved major social problems may be the insanitary breeding grounds for chronic mental illness. Taking a lead from these works, an attempt is made here as follows to group the problems into three categories that can influence mental health:

(1) problems arising out of poverty, prejudice, discrimination, social stresses and maladaptive behaviour associated with them;
(2) problems arising out of alarming rise in drug abuse, AIDS and violent crime;
(3) problems of energy, ecological crisis and problems resulting from accelerated and often uncontrolled social change; and
(4) problems emerging as a result of focusing on building a better world for all human beings.

The role of culture in conceptualization of mental health is considered to be a vital factor in determining the standards for normal or abnormal behaviour. Wegrocki (1964) states that normality and abnormality are relative concepts and they differ from culture to culture and are unique to one's own societal configuration. The norms of one cultural milieu for manifestation of different types of behaviour and personality traits may be accepted or criticized by the standards of other cultural setting. Before we begin the discussion on extent of the problem and communitarian approach to tackle it, let us reiterate and round up this part of the discussion on mental health by considering Sathyavathi's (1988) argument.

Sathyavathi (1988) has outlined the shift in emphasis on mental health by stating the following points:

(i) shift "from man and environment to man in the environment". This shift is observable in the study of the personality of the child in the community as well as in understanding of human behaviour during health and ill-health;
(ii) shift from medical model, i.e., from a clinical concentration on illness and disorder to the inclusion of social environmental factors as they impinge on communities and individuals;
(iii) shift from the role of intra-individual or intra-psychic factors to inter personal or psycho-social factors of the family or community; and

(iv) shift from the curative, treatment-oriented or clinic-centred approach to that of prevention, maintenance and promotion-oriented family and community approaches.

COMMUNITY PARTICIPATION AS A PREVENTIVE STRATEGY

According to Shah (1982), the available mental health facilities and the existing trained professionals in the country are too inadequate, especially in view of the needs of the community. Mental health problems are at the rate of 1 per cent in the general population (*National Mental Health Programme*, 1982). Thus, the magnitude of the problem is huge, whereas the available resources in terms of human power, funds and administrative infrastructure are meagre. However, with close coordination of the political will and the team of mental health multi-professionals, the solution is within the reach. The professionals suggest strategy of community participation, training of para-professionals and volunteers in the delivery of mental health care. Such a measure will bring the mental health care facilities to the doorstep of a common person in terms of affordability and availability besides its accessibility. Consequently, minimum care could be provided to a larger section of the community rather than providing maximum care to a few privileged elite persons.

Thus, a vast dormant resource, lying idle in the community itself is to be tapped, which will also create greater involvement and commitment of the community to solve its own problems. An unfortunate tendency of looking upto and depending on government for every solution will be checked and curtailed. The strategy of increased participation of volunteers and para--professionals will fill the lacunae of trained personnel. In addition to that, helping individuals and groups in the community itself has innumerable gains. An outstanding gain is that the mental health becomes the concern of all and no longer that of an individual only or his family alone. The community thus begins to shoulder responsibility of its own mental health.

Community Mental Health Legislation

The fact that the country is undergoing rapid socio-economic and cultural changes and that such changes are likely to increase in magnitude in the coming years, it calls for increased attention of one and all concerned with various issues of mental health. Effects of such changes on individuals, their families, and communities must be properly monitored. The conscientization of the entire population about good mental health needs to be spread at all the levels in order to achieve a healthy and harmonious society. Such an approach, to begin with, can be an important ingredient of communitarian strategy to combat problems of mental health. It should also find expression both in declarations and in allocations of funds for action and research to prevent untoward side-effects and to optimize development.

The Mental Health Act, 1987 registers many advances, yet there is a need for a community mental health legislation. Many advantages can accrue from such a legislation. Some of them are listed as under:

1. Such a legislation may give an official recognition of the fact that mental health is a community health problem.
2. Central legislation can give impetus to states to have necessary infrastructure at state level to begin action on it by providing necessary funds for community mental health. Budgeting of funds for local community mental health activities can go a long way in promoting, maintaining and developing related services.
3. Establishment of local mental health boards can become possible.
4. The agencies for mental health services can derive support from such a legislation. The participation by the community and the non-governmental organizations can be enhanced in this specific area.
5. With the growing thrust to establish services, there would be an increased need for trained personnel. Therefore, there would be a need for allocation of funds for training and re-

search which can derive the impetus from legislation.

6. Legislation can forge an integration of mental health services with general public health services while maintaining the unique character of the former through various means.
7. Legislation can provide community mental health workers the opportunity to work for a positive social change.

Perspectives on Prevention

Three major tasks can be outlined in the field of mental health:

1. Preventive and promotive
2. Curative and therapeutic
3. After-care and rehabilitation

Thus, the goals as perceived in the field of community mental health are: (a) prevention of mental illnesses; and (b) promotion of mental health. The two key tasks to be achieved to reach the goals are: (i) seeking out and eradicating the causes of mental ill-health; and (ii) establishing conditions that foster positive mental health. The three levels of intervention and assistance are as follows: (a) primary prevention, which aims at establishing conditions in the environment that are likely to reduce incidence of maladjustment and behaviour problems; (b) secondary prevention emphasizes the early cognizance and prompt treatment of maladaptive behaviour; and (c) tertiary prevention that will deploy intensive therapeutic measures like that of hospitalization.

It is not possible, of course, to prevent mental disorders altogether or avoid all stresses and challenges resulting from urban-industrial life in modern times. Effective mastery over challenges and crisis is needed for the growth of individual and the group. On the other hand, failure to deal with crisis and problems can lead to a breakdown in functioning of an individual or group. Intervention at such times is a crucial aspect of prevention. However, strictly speaking, early intervention is still corrective instead of preventive. It occurs only after maladaptive behaviour has shown itself. More fundamental prevention would mean trying to keep such behaviour from happening in the first place. Intervention is provided to a member or group of members of a community before they land up in any mental disorder.

Hence, with regard to community mental health goals of prevention and promotion of mental health, three major interventional strategies are found to be playing a vital role, viz., mental health education, supportive services and consultation services.

Mental Health Education

Mental health education aims to provide accurate information and encourage understanding in an effort to replace misinformation as well as fill information gaps. Various studies have shown that most people do not possess enough information about mental illness and mental health. Mental health education gains an added importance when the community is ridden with misconceptions, superstitions, negative attitudes and ignorance in relation to mental health problems. Only when mental health education is target-oriented, that is, aimed at a specific community, keeping in view the socio-cultural factors, that the services will be meaningfully utilized. This also requires dissemination of information regarding the nature and course of mental ill-health for the early detection of the problem with an emphasis on the utilization of available mental health services at an early stage. Mental health education also seeks to help everyone gain knowledge, attitudes and behaviour patterns which will promote and sustain his or her mental health. It is aimed at all ages, educational levels and rural as well as urban population and pursues all available courses to effect action for positive mental health.

To quote an example, Sanjivini, a Delhi-based voluntary organization, lays emphasis on mental health education as well. It has initiated 'Sanjivini Community Education Programme' which plays a significant role in creating awareness about important mental health issues. Their volunteers visit schools, colleges, women's groups, professional bodies to discuss various problems and effective ways to deal with them.

Intervention through Direct Services

Community mental health services can derive great strength by locating the services nearer to the community. An important emphasis of the service should be the community as a whole and not just individuals. Mental health services are also expected to work with other helping agencies to develop mental health networking which is a part of consultation and education function. The community involvement is generated from various angles, which in turn leads to conscientization of community that forestalls and prevents mental health problems. Brij Mohan's (1973) study has been a pointer to the importance of supportive and consultative services in the context of Indian society. Before dealing with supportive and consultative services, key concepts responsible in the service delivery system are highlighted:

(a) *Geographic responsibility*: As in the case of public health, community mental health services too should be provided to the people within their own geographic area. The well-designed services should be responsible for covering a given population, residing in close proximity and thus they can have a catchment area.

(b) *Comprehensiveness*: It would mean providing whatever mental health services needed to anyone residing within the catchment area regardless of age, sex, caste, religion, or the capacity to pay.

(c) *Continuity of care and accessibility*: Continuity of care should be assured by providing mental health services of varying kinds needed by the community located at one place. Accessibility is guaranteed by a limited geographic area. People from catchment area can approach for mental health services according to their requirements.

Various Types of Services

Supportive services that are designed for the total population may provide a base for preventing mental illness and promoting mental health. They involve correction for maladaptive behaviour and supportive as well as educative action to help people in stressful situations. In terms of preventive strategy, it involves timely intervention just before a crisis develops and results in a deep stress. Preventive measure also implies enabling people to develop their potentialities and induce wholesome social climate.

Outpatient services, like physical health services at Primary Health Centres, can be provided to the community members of the catchment area on an ongoing basis. This kind of services will enable the members to obtain adequate help by causing minimum disruption in occupation, social and personal activities of the family members and themselves. This may prove to be lesser of a burden. It will promote and induce greater utilization of services.

Day-care services are necessary for those who may need help to cope with their day-time activities. With the professional help and support such members may gradually become self-dependent. Para-professionals and trained volunteers can form a useful and sound contingent in the total team. The Richmond Fellowship Society (India), Bangalore has successfully ventured into creation of day-care services and half-way homes by adopting therapeutic community approach. Sanjivini at Delhi helps people with emotional problems and even those with schizophrenic breakdown. Like Richmond Fellowship Society, Sanjivini also helps, through the day-care centre, individuals with emotional and psychiatric problems.

Friendly visitors services comprise of dedicated and interested members of both sexes of the community. It can also have separate groups of youth, middle-aged as well as elderly members. Friendly visiting service provided by these groups to the members of the community belonging to their own age-group can go a long way in rendering support. It can be a positive action to help people maintain their balance during stress. They will indirectly play the role of mental health educators also. The friendly visitors can function under the broad guidance and help of the relevant professionals in providing supportive services.

Telephonic services. A stigma is perceived in being associated with mental illness and the use of services in mental health settings. This perception is prevalent in general population and is especially relevant among some of the most high-risk groups, such as adolescents, youths, women and elderly. Telephonic services can bring help to many troubled people who would never present themselves at a mental health facility. Callers can seek help with a wide range of problems including personal relationships, drug, sex, family conflicts, legal questions, loneliness, etc. Such a service has been introduced by the Richmond Fellowship Society at Bangalore which is a boon to those who face initial problem of approaching for consultation and help.

Consultation Services

They would be of prime importance and therefore should form a part of the package. It can assist other agencies providing services in the community to handle potential mental health problems, thereby preventing or avoiding the need for direct mental health services. Another educational function can be in form of assisting people in understanding various mental health problems. It can eventually help the community to improve its coping ability with mental health problems, thus causing lesser strain on the mental health services.

Services for parents: Consultation services for parents are of vital importance for promotion of mental health and prevention of mental ill-health. The importance of parent-child and parent-parent relationship; family structure, and that of maternal love and affection for good or poor mental health is discussed earlier in a sub-section titled: 'Mental Health as a Psychological Phenomenon'. There have been studies indicating mentally ill patients coming from disturbed and discordant fam-

Figure 2
Towards a Healthier Society

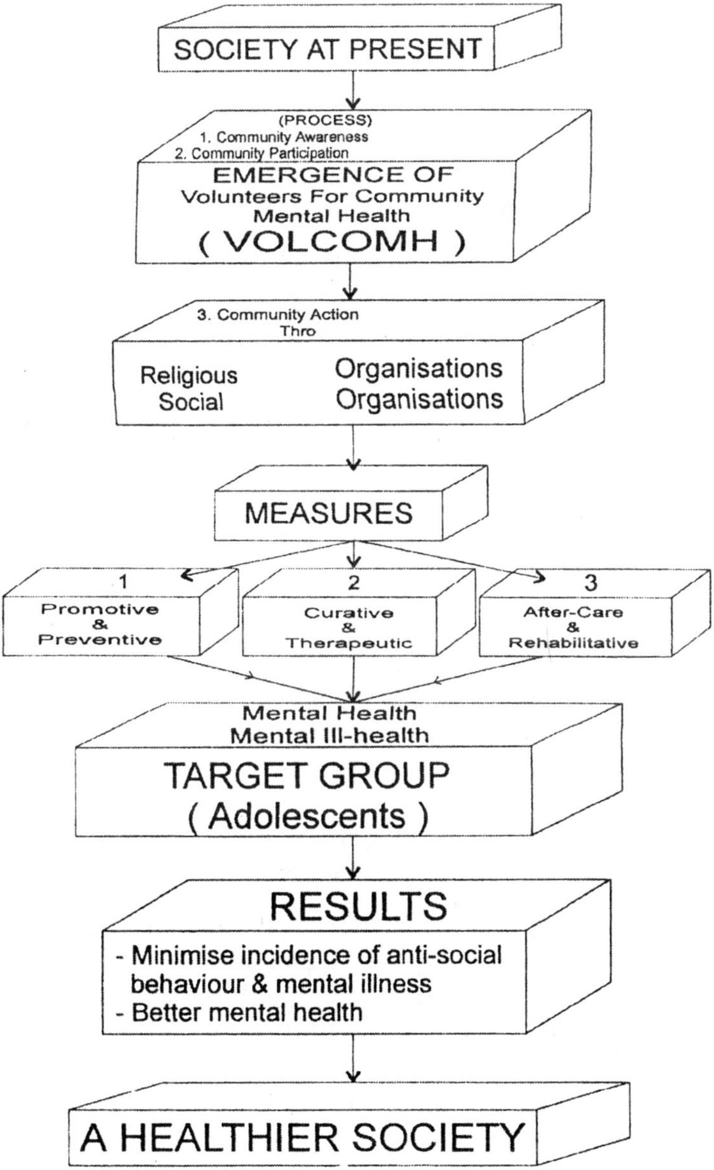

ily climate. All this signifies the importance and need for parent education programmes and consultation services for parents.

School consultation services: The best thing to happen is that each school has social workers who, besides imparting mental health education as preventive measure, can fruitfully be deployed for early detection and treatment of maladjusted behaviour in students and their families. The teachers can be trained as aids in creating and promoting healthier environment. The other alternative is attaching social workers to schools who would cater to mental health services.

Youth consultation services: Adolescents are one of the most vulnerable and high-risk groups in the society. They face problems in day-to-day life due to lack of self-awareness about physical, social, emotional, mental, proper sex education, lack of direction and purpose, poor facilities for guided recreation and lack of proper and healthy avenues to utilize their surging energies in constructive activities. Besides, many times, having a pathological family worsens their case and condition. Youth consultation services can involve itself in awareness-building exercises by designing programmes for educating youths and parents while giving direct consultation services. Similarly, depending upon the need of the community, there could be consultation services for other groups, such as women, senior citizens, migrants, etc.

COMMUNITY MENTAL HEALTH FROM THE GRASS-ROOTS

Figure 2 is suggestive of an attempt being made in Aizawl, the capital of Mizoram, to generate community participation in various issues of community mental health. As a result, Volunteers for Community Mental Health (VOLCOMH) is formed for generating community participation. VOLCOMH is a small band of volunteers of Aizawl town initiated by the Department of Social Work, North-Eastern Hill University with the following goals and aims:

Goals

1. To create awareness among the members of the community with regard to the problems of mental health and mental ill-health.
2. To take promotive measures in the cultural context for accelerating positive mental health for general well-being of the community, and as a means to prevent the vulnerable sections of the community from falling prey to deviant behaviour.
3. To take rehabilitative measures for helping those afflicted with mental ill-health and to lead them to live personally a satisfying and/or socially useful life.

Aims

1. To create awareness among social organizations of Aizawl town with regard to mental health and mental ill-health.
2. To be catalyst to enable social organizations to bring about awareness in the larger community with regard to mental health and mental ill-health.
3. To initiate social organizations to take up activities and programmes in the community to promote mental health.
4. To organize or institute programmes for the rehabilitation of the mentally ill at a time when sufficient ground work is ready.
5. To coordinate activities of social organizations of the town to avoid duplication, to disseminate information about different organizations and to act as a referral agency.
6. To act as nodal agency for organizing training programmes for voluntary or statutory workers to achieve the specified goals.

CONCLUSION

Mental health is no longer an exclusive domain of any one profession. It calls for a collective or a team approach, involving professionals from multi-disciplines like that of medicine, psychiatry, psychology, anthropology, nursing and social work.

Social work can assume a leadership position since basic social work concerns and concepts at micro-level emphasize on family and building ego-strength among its needy members. This ensures better care of the community mental health. Moreover, in the recent times, increased emphasis by social work discipline on macro-level issues of the people and the society blend well with the goals of community mental health as it ensures good scope for making unique contribution so far as preventive and promotive mental health activities are concerned.

As stated by Yolles (1969), community mental health has two primary missions. One is to provide treatment to any person in need. The second is to improve the quality of life for people in a community through a wide variety of courses including the improvement of physical environment and providing the educational and cultural opportunities to the entire community. Thus, community mental health is going beyond one-to-one physician/patient medical model and adopting the prevention-oriented communitarian public health model. From social work perspective, community mental health can even go beyond the latter and opt for a social action model. It would be an added challenge for a social work professionals in the mental health sector to assume the functions of social activists or agents of social change. The social worker may have direct service-giving roles, i.e., the role of orienting other workers to social work skills and methods and imparting mental health education to the community; or the role of mobilizing volunteers for community mental health functions. Such social workers will have to work along with other professionals, sometimes under them, sometimes leading them and sometimes simply as colleagues.

To sum up, as human beings, all of us are concerned with mental health for personal or altruistic reasons. We all want to live in peace and harmony. For being able to do so, we should be honest with ourselves and courageous to admit that we have problems. Cultivation of such an admissive temperament and attitude may prove to be the first formidable step towards its solution.

REFERENCES

Barnes, B.L. (1989), *Mental Health of Indian Sea-Farers*. London: International Transport Workers' Federation.

Chakraborty, A. (1990), *Social Stress and Mental Health: A Social-Psychiatric Field Study of Calcutta*. New Delhi: Sage Publications.

Chaplin, J.P. (1979), *Dictionary of Psychology*. New York: Del Publishing.

Coleman, James C. (1976), *Abnormal Psychology and Modern Life*. Bombay: D.B. Taraporevala.

Finney, J.C. (ed.) (1970), *Cultural Change, Mental Health and Poverty*. New York: Simon and Schuster.

Mohan, Brij (1973), *Social Psychiatry in India: A Treatise on the Mentally Ill*. Calcutta: Minerva Associates.

National Mental Health Programme (1982). New Delhi: Government of India Publications.

Ozarin, L.D. (1982), "Mental Health in Public Health: The Federal Perspective" in M.O. Nagenfeld *et.al.*, *Public Mental Health: Perspectives and Prospects*. New York: Sage.

Parsons, T.S. (1956), *Mental Health Paradox*. Michigan: School of Education Bulleting.

Sathyavathi, K. (1988), "Mental Health" in J. Pandey (ed.), *Psychology in India: The State of the Art*. Vol. 3: *Organizational Behaviour and Mental Health*. New Delhi: Sage.

Sharma, Bharti (1993), *Proceedings of the Workshop on Community Mental Health* (held on September 22-23, 1992). Aizawl: Department. of Social Work, North-Eastern Hill University.

Shah, A.V. (1982), "Integration of Mental Health", *Indian Journal of Psychiatry*, 24.

Soddy, K. ed. (1961), *Identity, Mental Health and Value System*. London: Tavistock Publication.

Wegrocki, M.J. (1964), "A Critique of Cultural and Statistical Concepts of Abnormality" in M. Zax *et.al.* (ed.), *The Study of Abnormal Behaviour: Selected Readings*. New York: Macmillan Co.

Yolles, S. (1965), "Integration of Mental Health Planning." Paper presented at Carribean Seminar on *Mental Health*. Kingston: Jamaica, September.

--- (1969), "Past, Present and 1980: Trend Projections", *Community Mental Health*, I(2).

13

Women's Development, Voluntary Organizations and Social Work Concerns

by Chhaya Patel

ISSUE OF WOMEN'S DEVELOPMENT

It is being rapidly realized that historically, women have been one of the most important but at the same time neglected social groups. This is more so particularly in the developing and underdeveloped or undeveloped countries of the former Third World, i.e., Asia, Africa and Latin America. Even in the developed industrial world, comprising the US, Europe, Japan, Australia, Canada, etc., women's situation is only somewhat 'better' than elsewhere. The women of the industrialized, urbanized countries are far more aware about gender justice and equality in the matters of rights, status and freedom than their counterparts in the Third World and to some extent also in the Second World comprising the former socialist countries. The struggles for women development are launched vigorously mostly in the developed countries of the USA and Europe. In the developing countries also, the issue of women as a focal group for development is receiving far more attention now than a few years ago. Gender justice and equality have become uniform goals of all women's movements.

In countries like India, one often reads about the opening up of numerous centres and cells to specialize in the study of women and various related aspects. This by any account is a welcome and heartening development. As a result of such pioneering institutional efforts, a good deal of focus is levelled on various problems of the women. Because of such multifarious efforts, today a large body of literature has become possible (Barrett, 1984; Patel, 1985; Anant, 1986; Hirway, 1986; Weedon, 1987; Bhagat, 1990; Desai, 1990; Rose, 1992; Thorbek, 1993; Venkateswaran, 1995; Shah, 1996; etc.). This and remaining vast body of literature indicates that the issue of women development has succeeded in drawing the attention of academics, activists, researchers, policy makers, professional social workers and voluntary organizations operating at the national as well as transnational levels. It is generally believed that systematic compilation and documentation of such literature is an inevitable route to valid information, knowledge understanding and finally action. Apart from the recording and taking a note of this appreciable development, we have to address ourselves either as social researchers, social activists or social workers to the questions pertaining to the definitive and qualitative aspects of women development.

From among the wide range and spectrum, the first and foremost question that arises in our mind is: What exactly is women development and it refers to the women of which strata, caste, class, religion and income group of a society? The subsequent questions that follow are: How are we to achieve the goal of women's development? What are various kinds of opportunities available to us? Which options are strategically more sound, viable and effective? How can the structural and systemic obstacles as well as limitations can be overcome? What alternative visions or perspectographies are offered by the social theorists, scholars and the activists of the movement for women's development? Answering to any of these questions satisfactorily requires developing a relevant and realistic perspective on women development. This does not mean that such a vision or perspective necessarily has to be wholly universalistic or spatially comprehensive. Even if it emerges from a particularistic context and conditions, it should be welcome. Because now, as it seems, the days of monolithic, universalistic and all-embracing master/monolithic ideological systems of thought such as nationalism, liberalism, Marxism or socialism are gradually ending. Most of them have become truncated, non-existent, ineffectual or exist only in name. For instance, the ideology of nationalism is fast losing its actual relevance as the nation-state system is gradually becoming porous. Revolutionary changes and quantum jumps in communication technologies have demolished or made holes into national boundaries. However, this is not to deny the existence of nation-states. On the contrary, with the disintegration of the large unions of states, there is actually a process set in motion towards proliferation of new nations. That is to say that nation-states do increase and exist but the nationalistic fervour, ethos and feelings are not the same as it was a few decades ago. Massive standing armies are becoming irrelevant as electronic know-how and technological knowledge are proving superior to physical components of a nation's conventional war-machine. National sovereignty has become weakened in one sense and stronger in other.

Returning to the internal or domestic social realities; it must be stated clearly that the power relations are crucial. They reveal face of an individual or a society. As is known, power perspective is often the basis of wide-ranging social and political analysis. Power analysis reveals the invisible social under-currents. Therefore, in my humble view, the most desirable, concrete and ultimate perspective on women development could emerge from the following words of Weedon (1987:1):

> Feminism is a politics. It is a politics directed at changing existing power relations between women and men in society. These power relations structure all areas of life, the family, education and welfare, the worlds of work and politics, culture and leisure. They determine who does what and for whom, what we are and what we might become.

This passage of Weedon quite sums up the overall theme of this paper, that it is the power relations that in an ultimate sense matters. The existing relations between women and men in a given society are the product of a particularly organized politics. In order to get rid of subjugating, maltreating and exploitative relationships, politics needs to be restructured and reorganized so that the new power relations between men and women on the grounds of gender equality and gender justice can be organized. In the main, two perspectives of women development have emerged. First, the liberal-feminist perspective which aims at achieving full equality of opportunity in all spheres of life without radically changing the existing social and political system. This is typical of liberal thinking. They want change but do not want to battle with the very sources which obstruct change.

Liberal perspective pleads for gradual, slow, passive and superficial or to what we may call reformist social change. Liberal perspective is a sort of an in-house or a particular social order-tailored product. It operates within the limits of a given social system. The second, i.e., the radical feminist perspective, looks forward to a new social order in which women will not be subjugated to men. In other but extreme words, this perspective seeks to procure autonomy from men and recover the true and natural femininity by separating it from the men- dominated structures of society such as economy, polity, culture, business, industry, property, law, etc. This perspective is more forthright and clear in its aims. It does not talk of equality of sex. It talks of autonomy of female self. It seeks to free them from the all-round societal dominance of males. The third point of view is of socialists/feminists who situate women's problem in the context of interaction of caste, class, race, religion and gender relations. Socialist-feminist perspective is more directly aimed at and context-specific. It is rather substantive and well- directed. All these perspectives represent different types of steps and strategies towards completion of women development or liberation. That is to say that the shortcoming of the first is made up in the second and so forth.

However, the context of developing countries is of a fairly different nature than that of the First World. In the developing countries including ours, the socialist-feminist vision is gradually becoming an emerging trend in the women's movement, as the mainstream women movements see a connection between women liberation and human liberation. But this process is by now bound to be somewhat adversely affected by the recent reversals and collapse of socialism in Russia and Eastern Europe. Socialism is becoming a most hated and condemned word. Nevertheless, the essence of its philosophical premises shall continue to remain relevant for all times to come simply because unbridled economic exploitation of natural resources by individuals or business firms is the story of the past. Communitarian and cooperative use of increasingly depleting and unrenewable resources is the only way out. The goal of human liberation and harmonious existence is not possible through any other route. As the goal of women's liberation is linked to overall human liberation, socialist perspective (if not in the same name then in any other name) shall continue to be the only course open to humankind.

As much of the literature on women development informs us, the question of ultimate liberation of women from all kinds of repression, violence, discriminations, harassment, exploitation and conditions of subjugation in society is yet to be adequately taken up. What we are arguing here is about achieving economic and social goals of development in a manner that are (somewhat if not radically) leading to women's development. In the absence of any organized and well-executed governmental drive, voluntary organizations are a chief means to attain such a goal. This is of course an extremely limited and a modest but an interesting proposition. Once set to move ahead in this direction, we shall have to confront with the question of working out approaches and strategies to deal with the women's problems especially in rural areas. As we are particularly concerned here with the role of voluntary organizations in this task, we may also now consider a few theoretical arguments pertaining to the extent of their relevance, efficacy and potential (Kothari, 1987; Roy, 1987).

STATE OF VOLUNTARY SECTOR

A major debate is in motion ever since the publication of Prakash Karat's revealing and sensation-causing article (1984) and the subsequent rejoinders by Harsh Sethi (1985) and Kishen Pattnayak (1985) on the ideological and realistic viability as well as overall assessment of voluntary organizations. The voluntary sector is not the same as it used to be earlier. Some legislative measures by Government of India have further curbed the autonomy and voluntary spirit of this sector. Besides, now, it is a well-discernible trend that the governments are inviting and involving voluntary organizations or non-governmental organizations in so many corrective, developmental and welfarist programmes such as drug abuse control, de-addiction drives, family planning, checking juvenile delinquency, rehabilitation and resettlement of development project affected/ousted people, victims of natural disasters, child development, etc. This obviously raises a crucial question: whether the voluntary sector is capable of influencing the course and outcome of all such goals pursued or intended to pursue by government at various levels. Transformative socio-economic development is primarily a governmental concern. The size of resources such as personnel, fiscal and infrastructural that the government at any level of administration commands is truly colossal, compared to that of any voluntary organization in this sector (Nanavati, 1987). In this, physical or quantitative, sense governmental efforts can never be substituted with howsoever good, honest, service-oriented, committed, effective and useful efforts by any voluntary organizations may be. In my humble understanding, voluntary effort can only be a thin, scattered, oasis-like supplementation to the mainstream governmental effort and certainly not a substitution to it. This is amply clear if we take to empirical evidences. For instance, in the sector of health care, nutrition and community health, voluntary organizations like SEWA-RURAL (Society for Education, Welfare and Action Rural) of Jhagadia in Gujarat has made a pioneering, illustrious and illuminating contribution (Nandedkar, 1987). Howsoever admirable this work may be, it ultimately looks like an oasis in a desert. Its replication or extension to other needy areas often remains an impossible or partially possible dreams. This is in no way to suggest or indicate that such isolated and personalized voluntary efforts do not make any impact (Khanna, Mehta and Bhatt, 1991). In fact, they do so admirably.

With a view to highlighting this point, we may consider one or two empirical evidences here. The history of child development in India makes an interesting parallel of this process. Initial ignorance, unintended policy neglect and inaction on the part of the organized and institutionalized sector of government was well-confronted by the voluntary initiative (Patel, 1990). The rich experience of certain long standing NGOs in the field of child development proved very useful in finally evolving a comprehensive national policy in form of ICDS, i.e., Integrated Child Development Services. The same holds true for the gradual evolution of national policy on tribal development in India (Patel, 1986). Today, there exists a far better organizational infrastructure *vis-a-vis* child and tribal development in Gujarat and in India as a whole than just three-four decades ago. This historical experience holds a mirror to us while we deal with the question of women development through the same route. That is to say that initiation and foundation work is usually to be done by a voluntary organization on a small, pilot-like, experimental scale and subsequent shaping of a national policy and its widespread and comprehensive execution to be done by governmental agencies.

Fortunately, in Gujarat, the urban areas have witnessed pioneering efforts in this direction as SEWA (i.e., Self-Employed Women's Association) of Ahmedabad and Sahiyar of Vadodara have begun the good work in different aspects of the same task. The publication of *Narimukti* and *Shramshakti* (Bhatt, 1989) is one such path-breaking step. Although these voluntary organizations are urban-based, their primary concern is to ameliorate economic conditions of the poor women who migrate to the cities to escape the pangs of poverty in peripheral, underdeveloped rural areas. Sahiyar particularly struggles against the violations of human rights of women. It stands opposed to all forms of oppressions, tortures, harassment and exploitation of women. It can be said that SEWA-Ahmedabad is an instance of a liberal perspective in operation whereas the Sahiyar is a blazing instance of reflecting the mixed operation of a radical and socialist perspectives. However, it is now taking a firm footing as a voluntary organization. Nevertheless, their works and achievements are too well-known to be repeated here.

To sum up, it may be said that in this sub-section an attempt was made to understand various broad advances in the field of women development by looking into a few basic questions. A cursory reference was made to some feminist theoretical/ideological perspectives. In absence of an actual emergence of a desirable perspective on women development, it is imperative to examine what is the next best alternative and what are its strengths and limitations. Voluntary agencies have been playing very important role in two senses. In the one sense, they are filling up the vacuum and void created by the failure of existing efforts and in the second sense, they become fertile soil for breeding appropriate perspectives on women development. From here we move to the final part of this paper wherein it is first intended to define what is social work and then discuss various social work perspectives as they are being evolved and applied. The ensuing discussion involves a slight overlap between the general perspectives of women development and the perspectives which are characteristically representative of social work concerns.

MAJOR CONCERNS AND PERSPECTIVES OF SOCIAL WORK

The profession of social work is sort of a buffer zone, a middle path between gross neglect and inaction, social stagnancy, *status quoistness* on the one hand and revolutionary pursuits, quick actions and radical transformation of entire society through, if need be, a violent struggle on the other hand. Albeit, it has so far admirably functioned within the scope and limits of a liberal perspective. There are some streaks of radical orientations but they have not resulted in substantive and empirically valid outcomes. A few of the student-products of social work training and teaching institutions have indulged in isolated acts of progressive and radical pursuits. But most of the social work schools have operated within the near to self-imposed systemic and structural limits. In order to understand the social work perspective, we shall see what is social work by way of examining a few existing definitional formulations. We may begin to look into it by examining first Sushil Chandra's (1954:13) attempt to define it which is as follows:

> Social work is a dynamic activity undertaken by public or private effort in the implementation of social policy with a view to raising standards of living and to bring about social, economic, political and cultural well-being of the individual family and the group within a society, irrespective of its stage of development.

According to this definition, as it shows, the very act of undertaking any corrective social policy activity by public or private spheres is a sufficient objective of a social work profession. In his view, "stage of social development" or the level of economic development of a given society, community or area is not a determining or a consequential factor in undertaking social work activities, so long as they continue to raise the standards of living of all. This is considered to be a fairly adequate definition of what social work is about. It is simpler but comprehensive. Kher (1950:6) is another social work theorist whose idea of social work is quite relevant, contextual and enriching:

> The aim of social work... is to remove social injustice, to relieve distress, to prevent suffering and so to assist the weaker members of society to rehabilitate themselves and their families, and... fight the five giant evils of (1) physical want; (2) disease; (3) ignorance; (4) squalor; and (5) idleness.

This compact statement on the objectives of social work, as

reflected in Kher's definition, is the most cogent, lucid and comprehensive formulation. Its relevance to current drastically changing socio-economic situations and problems is immense. In other words, it is quite agreeable to define social work as 'dynamic activity' or as 'the art' but it is an extremely necessary precondition to specify the fundamental areas for practising the art of social work. Chandra's definitional formulation affords unlimited, and therefore perhaps overambitious as well as unspecified scope of organizing 'dynamic' activities. This itself is probably the reason why it fails to identify and prioritize the subjects, areas and targets as done in Kher's attempts. Kher pinpoints precise areas and targets such as 'social justice' for 'weaker members' in context to an existing social and economic milieu in India. As we know, these two terms have today become most consequential and current. They have begun changing the socio-economic contours of Indian society.

It is clear that the central concerns or tasks of social work is to tackle the problems of socio-economic backwardness in urban, rural and tribal areas in an organized, planned, coordinated and systematic manner. This shall reduce, abate and abolish the extent as well as the degree of human suffering, injustices, parasitic dependencies and helplessness inflicted on certain social strata by structural and historic contingencies. This is a very timely and immensely relevant perspective of contemporary thinking on social work concerns. Gore's (1985:59-60, 69) following words lend added relevance and emphasis to this perspective of social work:

> The profession of social work would have a more extensive role in defining social policy with reference to welfare needs and problems. The profession would be expected to participate in formulating goals. Working out broad strategies in developing programmes and in implementing them and provide a feedback to planning on the basis of research in implementation of (such) programmes. The broad objective is to meet the special needs of... disadvantaged or unadjusted individuals and groups with a view to enable them to utilize the services... Social work has tended to

neglect or be itself neglected where the basic needs of the larger populations are concerned.... [I]n the case of the Scheduled Castes and Scheduled Tribes, they have failed to... [apply] professional social work... One of the concerns may be to see how the most backward groups and regions can be helped to derive benefits from the services that governmental and other agencies offer.

These three formulations together generate an incisive insight into the definitional and professional concerns of social work. The views of Kher and Gore are of particular importance here as they are more relevant and contextually closer to Indian socio-economic reality. The current trends in social work profession indicate recent phenomenon of reaching out to the remotely located and settled rural as well as tribal society. The frontiers of social work concerns shall extend to such, so far neglected communities, viz., the Scheduled Castes and the Scheduled Tribes. Using Gore's logic and instance, it can be said that reaching out to those neglected tribal, rural and remotely located communities is like reaching out to those hitherto neglected concerns of social work.

This being the main thrust of social work concerns, it is plausible to weigh them against various derived and developed perspectives that are in currency among the professional social workers (Gore, 1985:145-46). These perspectives as contained in Appendices 13.1 and 13.2 and are not exclusive to social work discipline but they are generally of derivative nature and representative of social science domain as a whole. Be it the study of society, economy or polity, any of the three perspectives, referred to in Appendices 13.1 and 13.2 and are used as a general point of reference and premise for this or that justificatory claim. These perspectives have generated very heated debates and controversies in some of the social science disciplines. As we just said, Appendices 13.1 and 13.2 contain a profile of various derived and developed social work perspectives and an index for mutual comparability in form of constituents of respective perspectral formulation (Stein, 1972).

The profession of social work is also aware of three broad

perspectives. In ideological parlance, they can be referred to as conservative (P. 1), liberal (P. 2) and radical (P. 3) perspectives. Since social work as a discipline and as a profession is committed to the training, practice and action part of welfare and development, detailed and rigorous theoretical formulations do not find desirable favour and place. From my subjective judgement, it can be said that the social work perspective has excessive leaning towards conservative and liberal values as well as the approach. The designing of curriculum and conducting of research in social work is directed and organized mainly keeping these two perspectives in mind. This fact is very well borne out in Gore's discussion on this theme which is presented here in an encapsuled form in Appendix 13.2 (1985:144-52). With the result, the development of radical perspective for correcting deep-rooted socio-economic ills is hardly paid any adequate attention.

In the area of rural development, the existing social work perspectives, viz., P. 1 and P. 2, do not make substantive contribution. Although, theoretically, it is fully committed to the 'uplift' of the weaker sections, in practice, it does not go beyond routine and procedural application of social work techniques, skills and methods. The trained social work professionals do acquire capabilities and skills to initiate some such interventions. Sadguru Sevasangh of Dohad, Panchmahals in Gujarat is one such instance of professional social work intervention. The successful application requires rural women to be brought forth by persuasion and demonstration. Income-generating activities need to be strengthened as the first and foremost one-point programme. Economic contribution by women to their family income shall also improve the social and economic conditions of their life and community. Economic independence generates confidence for self-help and self-sustenance. Social work perspectives of P. 1 and P. 2 variants emphasize on this aspect, i.e., teaching, training and orienting them to help themselves in a given situation.

As we saw earlier, P. 1 and P. 2 are generally viewed as

status quoist and reformist perspectives respectively. They conserve the essentials of a society and try to change them in a manner that does not affect those structural essentials in a big way amounting to a complete break with the past and replacements. In other words, their prime goal is to maintain order and stability. Social harmony and cohesion are chief values. Pathetic and trying conditions of human existence do draw sympathetic attentions and even modest ameliorative actions from P. 1 to P. 2 but that is to say "thus far and no further". Social harmony, peace and cohesion are of superior value than the activities motivated by P. 3 to do away with the entire existing social order. Radical methods as advocated by P. 3 are based on conflict and violent means. It is based on the premise of a group or class categorization. It shuns individualistic considerations. It advocates fundamental restructuration of society, polity and economy.

Many social work academics view P. 3 as an undesirable and unviable perspective. They express apprehensions about the havoc that it may bring about if adopted and applied to the social problems. Whereas, a few view P. 3 as an irrelevant to the concerns of social work discipline and profession. If stated simply, it can be said that the differences over the choice of a particular perspective from among these three, as sketched in Appendix 13.1, may actually amount to making a choice over the persistence of social misery, subjugation, injustice or social stability, order and cohesiveness.

APPENDIX 13.1

Various 'Derived' Social Work Perspectives

Sr.No.	Constituent Indicators	Perspectives		
		P.1	P.2	P.3
1.	Status Ideological	Conservative, *Status quoist vis-a-vis* social order and institutions. Democratic governance.	Liberal, humanist reformist and procedurally democratic.	Progressive and radical, seeks basic structural changes in political and economic spheres. Authoritarian.
2.	Goals Structural	Functional stability, social cohesion and value-oriented social concerns.	Persuasive, inter-active, debative, dialogic, exchange of ideas and values.	Conflictive, violent and direct action orientation.
3.	Welfare Model	Residual welfare, re-education, re-sociali-zation, rehabilitation.	Institutionalized welfare programmes for needy groups.	Systemic redistribution of resources. Altering social systems, values, SC/STs, women etc.
4.	Points of Social Intervention Work	Clinical-therapeutic goals, intervention crisis.	Changing adverse social ecology and social milieu by persuasion, dialogue, participative observation.	Activating basic change agents such as workers, peasants, slum-dwellers for rights through struggles and conscientization.
5.	Image of Mankind	Needy individuals/ groups viewed as clients. Social casualties such as deviants, sick etc. to be cured and attended.	Needy individuals /groups' participation as healthy otherwise problems with situations.	Needy individual/ groups viewed as a class, victims of systems' oppression.

Source: H. D. Stein, "Cross-National Themes in Social Work Education", *Proceedings of 16th International Association of Social Work Congress*, The Netherlands, 1972.

APPENDIX 13.2

Approaches to Social Welfare and Social Work

		Religious-Traditional	*Liberal-Reformist*	*Liberal-Missionary*	*Ethical-Revolutionary*
1.	Dominant values	Charity: pursuit of individual and ancestors' salvation.	Democracy, Humanism, Rationalism, etc.	Service, Democracy, Humanism	Humanistic, Spiritual, Ethical
2.	Orientation to existing social structure	Unquestioning conformity	Reforms in social structure	Revivalist, conformist or limited reform	Raising basic issues, redefining traditional social structure
3	Types and level of needs perceived	Primarily basic needs for food and clothing and religio-spiritual need of salvation	Primarily the needs arising out of unfair social arrangements	Needs unmet by existing system such as physical, education and vocational rehabilitation	Primarily needs of groups affected by discriminatory practices
4.	Organization, methods and tools	Direct charity or charity through temples, mosques, etc.	Educational and legislative measures	Establishing residential institutions and orders with full time staff to lead the community	Establishing an order & use of religious symbols such as *satyagraha, lok shakti*

Source: M. S. Gore, *Social Aspects of Development*, 1985, pp.145-46.

REFERENCES

Anant, Suchitra *et. al.* (1986), *Women at Work in India: A Bibliography*. New Delhi: Sage.

Barrett, Michele (1984), *Women's Oppression Today*. London: The Thetford Press.

Bhagat, Varsha (1990), *Gujaratma Streeona Kamot* (Untimely Deaths of Women in Gujarat). Ahmedabad: Setu-Shruti.

Bhatt, Ela R. (1989), *National Commission on Self-Employed Women and Women in the Informal Sector: A Report*. Ahmedabad: SEWA.

Chandra, Sushil (1954), *Social Work in Uttar Pradesh*. Delhi: Indian Conference of Social Work.

Desai, A.R. (ed.) (1990), *Women's Liberation and Politics of Religious Personal Laws in India*. Bombay: C.G. Shah Memorial Trust.

Gore, M.S. (1985), *Social Aspects of Development*. Jaipur: Rawat.

Hirway, Indira (1986), *Denial of Maternity Benefits to Women Workers in India*. New Delhi: Oxford-IBH.

Karat, Prakash (1984), "Action Group/Voluntary Organizations: Factor in Imperialist Strategy", *The Marxist*, 2(2).

Khanna, Renu, Mehta, N.R. and Bhatt, Anil (1991), *Voluntary Efforts in Community Health: Review of the Community Health Project of SEWA-RURAL*. Jhagadia: Society for Education, Welfare and Action-Rural Publication.

Kher, B.G. (1950), *Training of Social Work - An Introductory Survey.*

Kothari, Rajni (1987), "Voluntary Organizations in a Plural Society", *Indian Journal of Public Administration*, 33(3), July-September.

Nandedkar, V.G. (1987), "Voluntary Associations: A Strategy in Development", *Indian Journal of Public Administration*, 33(3), July-September.

Nanavati, Meher C. (1987), "Role of Central Social Welfare Board in the Changing Social Context", *Indian Journal of Public Administration*, 33(3), July-September.

Patel, Chhaya (1990), "Review of Child Welfare Policy and Implementation in Contemporary India", (in Gujarati), *Arthat*, 9(4).

Patel, Priyavadan (1986), *Tribal Development in Gujarat*. Surat: Centre for Social Studies.

Patel, Vibhuti (1985), "Women's Liberation in India", *New Left Review*, No. 153, September-October.

Pattnayak, Kisen (1985), "Non-Party Groups and Their Dependence on Foreign Money", *Economic and Political Weekly*, 20(39), 28 September.

Rose, Kalina (1992), *Where Women Are Leaders: The SEWA Movement in India*. New Delhi: Sage.

Roy, Sanjit Bunker (1987), "Voluntary Agencies in Development - Their Role, Policy and Programmes", *Indian Journal of Public Administration*, 33(3), July-September.

Sethi, Harsh (1985), "The Immoral 'Order': Debate between Party and Non-Party Groups", *Economic and Political Weekly*, 20(8), 28 February.

Shah, A.M., *et.al.* (1996), *Social Structure and Change: Women in Indian Society,* Vol. 2. New Delhi: Sage.

Stein, H.D. (1972), "Cross-National Themes in Social Work Education", *Proceedings of 16th International Association of Social Work Congress*. The Netherlands.

Thorbek, Susanne (1993), *Gender and Slum Culture in Urban Asia*. New Delhi: Sage.

Venkateswaran, Sandhya (1995), *Environment, Development and the Gender Gap*. New Delhi: Sage.

Weedon, Chris (1987), *Feminist Practice and Post-Structuralist Theory*. New York: Basil Blackwell.

Appendices

APPENDIX I

Declaration of Ethics for Professional Social Workers

The Background

This draft of 'Declaration of Ethics for Professional Social Workers' has been prepared by the Social Work Educators' Forum (SWEF) at the Tata Institute of Social Sciences (TISS), Mumbai. The SWEF is a forum for social work educators at the TISS to undertake meetings and activities with a goal to strengthen social work profession and education. In the meetings scheduled by the SWEF in 1991, issues related to values and ethics for social workers were identified and discussed. The SWEF committee then requested Ms. Lata Narayan to prepare the first draft of a code of ethics for social workers which was discussed at an SWEF meeting in September 1991. In 1992, an SWEF sub-committee was formed with the following members to revise the draft: Jeroo Billimoria, Vineeta Chitale, Murli Desai, N.A. Gokarn, Rajshree Mahtani, Vimla Nadkarni, Lata Narayan, M.S. Pawar, and Maveen Soares-Pereira. A drafting committee was formed comprising Ms. Lata Narayan, Dr. Murli Desai and Ms. Jeroo Billimoria. The second draft prepared by the sub-committee was circulated at the National Workshop on Social Work Practice and Education held in May 1993. The third draft was discussed at two SWEF meetings in March 1994. The fourth draft in the form of Indian Declaration of Ethics for Professional Social Workers was discussed at a workshop in February 1995 along with the members of the faculty of the College of Social Work at Nirmala Niketan and the members of the Bombay

Association of Trained Social Workers. The fifth draft, which was an outcome of this workshop, was sent to some senior social work educators. Feedback obtained from them are incorporated in this sixth draft.

The Declaration

Preamble

The Declaration of Ethics for Professional Social Workers is intended to serve as a guide to the members of the social work profession, who have obtained minimally a bachelor's degree in social work and, thus, base their work on recognized knowledge, philosophy and skills. The Declaration is rooted in the contemporary social reality which has a historical background and in the framework of humanistic values, based on the intrinsic worth of all human and non-human life.

The *Bhakti* Movement promoted the value of humanism, that is, every individual has inherent worth and dignity, irrespective of attributes and achievements. Every person, therefore, has an innate capability to run his/her own life. Democracy emphasizes participatory process in the decision-making of an entity and accountability of that entity to its members.

Socialism has promoted the values of equality and legal, judicial, social and economic justice for satisfaction of basic human needs, sharing of natural resources and access to essential services. While equality highlighted non-hierarchy and non-discrimination based on equal worth of every person, the growing value of equity emphasizes recognition of differences, diversity and pluralism.

The ideology of *Sarvodaya* has emphasized the values of *Swarajya* and *Lokniti*, that is, people have to govern themselves in order to obtain equity and justice. This ideology accepts that people are knowledgeable about their situation and the ways to manage them, given the necessary resources. It acknowledges that they have the right to plan their own destinies and determine their lifestyles. It appreciates that local solutions must be congruent with local resource realities.

The social work profession is committed to solidarity with the marginalized peoples. The basic human rights are very often violated for people, who lack economic, physical, mental, social and/or emotional resources. Lack of resources lead to powerlessness and, thereby marginalization of people by the social, economic and political systems. Marginalized people are vulnerable to deprivation and exploitation by those who yield power as they have control over resources.

The profession recognizes that marginalized people need to be empowered so that they themselves play a dominant role for their development and welfare. Empowerment is the process of gaining control overself as well as the resources which determine power. This process aims at reforming the nature and direction of the systemic forces which marginalize the powerless. Systemic change is an imperative for redistributive justice.

The Declaration provides general ethical principles to guide conduct with respect to self and the profession, work with the marginalized and other people in need, the society and the state, coworkers and employing organizations and social work education and research. In its practical application, the entire Declaration and its spirit are of importance, and must be viewed holistically, rather than considering a particular ethical principle in isolation. This also implies that the application of ethical principles must be judged within the context in which they are being considered.

Value Framework

As a professional social worker, I pledge to promote the following values in myself, in the profession and in the society:

1. I pledge to perceive people as having inherent worth and dignity, irrespective of their attributes and achievements and having the capability of continuing development;

   I pledge to perceive myself and other people as part of nature, needing to live in harmony with other non-human existence.
2. I pledge to work towards the overall well-being of people in the spirit of *Sarvodaya*, through the achievement of the following goals:

   Equity, non-hierarchy and non-discrimination of human groups in terms of race, religion, tribe, language, regional origin, gender, sexual orientation and other such factors, and condemning segregation/apartheid/discrimination among them;

   Social, economic, political and legal justice, ensuring satisfaction of basic needs and integrity and security, universal access to essential resources and protective safeguards for the marginalized people; and people-centred development, in the spirit of *Swarajya* and democracy from micro-to-macro-levels, where people participate to determine their life styles and goals for development.

I pledge to work with people, guided by the following values:

* Solidarity and partnership with the marginalized people; and
* Peaceful and non-violent approaches in the spirit of *Ahimsa* for resolving conflicts with self, others and the environment.

Ethical Responsibility to Self and the Profession

As the first essential step to social work practice, I shall constantly seek an understanding of myself and change my attitudes and prejudices which may affect my work.

I shall be sensitive to and respect the feelings and thinking of others, understand behaviours, avoid stereotypes and recognize individuality in every person.

I accept with humility and openness, the need to learn and shall imbibe the spirit of inquiry to constantly update my knowledge base and intervention strategies.

I shall gear my practice upon relevant knowledge and in the changing socio-economic, geographical and cultural context.

I shall use my knowledge, power and status as a professional, for the well-being of all and not misuse these for personal gains.

I shall intervene into the personal affairs of another individual only with his/her consent, except when I must act to prevent injury to him/her or to otherwise, in accordance with the legal provisions.

In order to ensure credibility and integrity of the social work profession, I shall constantly review it and work towards its development.

I shall work towards developing and strengthening of professional associations, which are means for development of the profession.

I shall facilitate development of the new entrants to the profession.

Ethical Responsibility to the Marginalized and Other People in Need

My primary professional response and accountability are to the marginalized and other people in need I work with. My commitment and professional stand shall be with them.

I shall empathize with people's marginalization and thereby respect and give credence/value to their life experiences.

I shall work towards changing the systemic and contextual forces which marginalize people, on behalf of and in partnership with them.

I shall respect people's right for self-determination, and shall ensure that they themselves play an active role in relation to the course of action to be taken about their life situation.

I shall nurture a relationship of partnership with people that promotes mutual reflection on our life situation and our development.

I shall facilitate people's access to opportunities and resources and empower them for work towards their stated goal.

I shall share with people, accurate and relevant information regarding the extent and nature of help available to them, that is, opportunities, rights, strengths, limitations and risks associated with the intervention offered.

I shall enable and encourage people to work with other individuals, organizations and groups, when such collaboration is in the best interest of the well-being for all.

I shall obtain people's consent before recording or permitting third party observation of their activities after informing them about its purpose and utility.

I shall keep confidential, all matters shared by them, and shall inform them fully about the limits of privileged communication in a given situation.

I shall facilitate people's access to official records concerning them, if asked by them. While doing so, I shall take due care to protect the confidence of others covered by these records.

I shall ensure that payment for services by people, if necessary, are fair and commensurate with the intervention provided, and within the capacity for such payment of the people served.

When I perceive the need to withdraw from the helping process, I shall give consideration to all factors in the situation and shall take care to minimize possible adverse effects on the people.

When I anticipate discontinuation of my intervention, I shall notify them promptly and seek transfer, referral or continuation of service, with consideration to their needs and preferences.

I shall not pursue a relationship or use any coercive means to continue services, which the people served wish to terminate, and shall offer suggestions or alternative help that they can avail of.

Ethical Responsibility to the Society and the State

It is my ethical responsibility to promote implementation of the Fundamental Rights and the Directive Principles of State Policy enshrined in the Indian Constitution.

I shall work towards a society and a state that promotes equity, justice, *Ahimsa*, *Swarajya* and *Lokniti*.

I shall advocate changes in social systems and the state policies and legislations to promote the above values.

I shall encourage informed participation by the people in shaping state policies, legislations, and programmes.

I shall respond and offer my professional services in events of emergencies at micro and macro levels.

Ethical Responsibility to Co-workers and Employing Organizations

Respect the inherent worth and dignity of all my co-workers, that include social workers, other professionals, auxiliary workers, volunteers and all those involved in the development process, within and across organizations.

I shall cooperate with my co-workers towards development, accepting and respecting our personal and professional differences.

I shall contribute to the process of collective reflection and democratic decision-making when working as a team.

I shall acknowledge my co-workers' attributes and achievements and will be willing to learn from them.

I shall respect confidences shared by my co-workers in the course of their professional development.

When I am an employer or supervisor to my co-workers, I shall ensure clarity of goals in delegation of roles and responsibilities, provide opportunities for growth, give them due credits and jointly review their performance on the basis of goals and clearly enunciate criteria.

I shall act to promote humanistic values and ethical practices in my employing organization's policies and practice.

I shall ensure that the organization's resources are used judiciously and for the purpose they are intended.

I shall periodically monitor and evaluate the organization's policies and programmes by maintaining records, self-reflection on people's feedback and feedback from the co-workers.

Ethical Responsibility to Social Work Education and Research

When teaching and training, it is my ethical responsibility to be conversant with the learners' needs, readiness and goals.

I shall keep my knowledge update about social work and the subjects I teach through field experience, reading and training.

While teaching and training I shall impart knowledge, inculcate attitudes and develop skills within the value framework of the profession.

I shall recognize the importance of partnership between practitioners and educators for the purpose of social work education and training.

I shall develop a nurturing relationship with the students, encouraging openness and self-study and facilitating sharing and discussions in a learning situation.

I shall, whenever possible, undertake demonstration of people-centered field action projects for the purpose of research and documentation, training and replication.

I shall share the knowledge I gain with other social work educators and practitioners.

I shall contribute to the knowledge base of social work education through my practice wisdom, documentation as well as research.

I shall expose the students to the professional associations and orient them about their role in developing and strengthening them.

When carrying out a research, I shall carefully select the topic for research considering its possible consequences for human beings within the value framework of the profession and towards the goals of people-centred development.

I shall consider the informants of my research as my co-partners in understanding the phenomenon. I shall, therefore, share my research objectives with them and get their informed and voluntary consent, respect their knowledge and attitude about their life situation, and share/interpret the findings with them.

I shall not cause them inadvertent physical or mental discomfort, distress or harm, through my research.

I shall protect the confidentiality of the information shared by them and use the findings for their benefit, by revising policies and programmes concerning them.

I shall provide information services to them, as and when necessary, during the process of data collection.

I shall acknowledge in my paper, the published as well as unpublished material and personal discussions that have directly influenced my paper.

APPENDIX II

Responses of Good Wishes, Appreciation and Regrets

It is intended here to give a glimpse of some of the responses which we got from all those social scientists, social work educators and social work professionals whom we approached for papers as a first step in our effort to bring out this volume in honour of Professor Indira Patel. Some eminent scholars like M.S. Gore (Mumbai), P.D. Kulkarni (Pune), Shanker Pathak (Bangalore), Niranjana A. Gokarn (Mumbai) and K.N. George (Chennai), responded very briefly and expressed their regrets to join the efforts, however they wished the effort well. Whereas some of the scholars such as S.N. Ranade (New Delhi), Suma Chitnis (Mumbai), R.R. Singh (New Delhi), Mirza Ahmed (Lucknow), Dorothy Baker (USA), Meher C. Nanavati (New Delhi) and B.R.K. Raju (Vishakhapatnam) could not get back to us, presumably due to inadequate or lack of proper communications. Some scholars like Ratna Murdia (Mumbai) and Vibhuti Patel (Mumbai) were abroad during this period. The following are some of the select responses which we received either: (a) with a line of encouragement, positive commitment for contributing a paper; (b) initially committed but later unable to do so for quite understandable reasons; or, (c) simply writing a few words of regret while appreciating the effort:

"I am pleased to learn of your efforts to publish Professor Indira Patel Felicitation Volume... I have known Ms. Indira Patel since her student days. I am aware of her ideological leanings and attempts to understand and interpret social work norms in the light of Indian culture and philosophy. I sincerely wish that your efforts to publish this volume in her honour will be a great success... As for my contributing an article, I am afraid the timing and deadline do not fit in with the schedule I have on hand. I expect to be away and I have certain obligations to attend to before I leave. Therefore, you will appreciate I do not have the required time to contribute a studied article on the lines you have indicated. However, considering the years I have known Professor Indira Patel and the regards I have for her, I would like to write a brief foreword/message highlighting her contribution to social work education in India."

— Dr. (Ms.) Parin Vakharia, Secunderabad, Andhra Pradesh
(Founding Dean, Faculty of Social Work, M.S. University, Baroda)

"This has reference to your letter addressed to Dr. (Ms.) A. S. Desai, in connection with the forthcoming Professor Indira Patel Felicitation Volume. Dr. Desai was planning to start working on the paper on her return from the States in September 1993. Unfortunately, on her return, due to the disastrous earthquake in Osmanabad, and our involvement in the relief and rehabilitation operation, she could not do anything on this. The work on the earthquake rehabilitation is still going on which takes most of her time, over and above the normal routine activities of the Institute. In view of all this, though she would have been pleased to contribute a paper, she regrets her inability to do so presently."

— Janaki, P.S. to Prof. (Ms.) Armaity S. Desai
Director, Tata Institute of Social Sciences, Mumbai.

"... I am happy to go through the contents of your letter and am impressed with the contents. The accomplishments of Ms. Indira Patel are outstanding and publication of commemorative volume on social work, welfare and services is befitting. Of course, I have known Indira both as a student as well as a colleague for more than a decade of my tenure at the M.S. University. I have enjoyed it including some of our disagreements.... I congratulate you for launching this ambitious project and wish good luck and good speed. No human being is beyond questioning. We all need our challenges - that is one of the best ways for us to grow and develop our full potential - intellectual, emotional and mental.... However, I regret my inability to contribute an article for publication in this Volume and my reason is *purely personal*.... I can hardly find time to write personal letters leave alone any scholarly contributions. Hope you understand my dilemma."

— Late Dr. Ammu Menon Muzumdar, Little Rock, Arkansa, USA.

"Thank you for your letter regarding the Felicitation Volume that you are planning to bring out in honour of Ms. Indira Patel. I was not able to respond to you earlier due to pressure of work... I am very glad that you have decided to bring out this felicitation Volume. She richly deserves the honour for all the silent yet revolutionary work that she has done for the cause of social work education in the country, particularly making it value based, that too based on the best that is in Indian culture. I shall deem it an honour to be associated with this project of yours. I shall contribute a paper under the section 'Current Issues of Social Work in India.' Wishing you all the best in this project."

— Dr. (Mrs.) Radha Paul, Stella Maris College, Chennai.

"Congratulation for conceiving the plan of a publication in honour of Dr. Indira Patel. I have known her for the past few years and I have great respect for her. Unfortunately, I did not have the fortune of being her student."

— Mrs. Kalindi S. Mazumdar, College of Social Work,
Nirmala Niketan Institute, Mumbai.

"Many thanks for ... the information about the proposed Felicitation Volume. I know Indiraben very well and I am happy about the gesture and your leading role. Please accept my best wishes for your labour of love. My piece on Swadhaya was written on demand... so I must ask for your forgiveness for the present."

— Prof. N. R. Sheth,
Former Director, Indian Institute of Management, Ahmedabad.

"It is heartening to know that Indiraben's unflinching devotion to the field of Social Work, which she never enfolded in the conventional disciplinary boundaries imposed by a perspective alien to Indian conditions, is now being recognised and felicitated. Your initiative for a felicitation volume for her has come not a day earlier.

Much though I would have liked to do a fresh article for the Volume, unfortunately, I cannot do so - despite the extended deadline... Under the circumstances I can give you an article, done jointly... which was published only recently in a newly started foreign journal. Its reach is almost negligible in India. The article fits finely to your

Volume. If your editorial policy permits this, you may include this article."

— Prof. D. L. Sheth, Former Director,
Centre for the Study of Developing Societies, Delhi.

"The plans that you have drawn up for bringing out Prof. Indira Patel Felicitation Volume are really impressive. It gives me pleasure to collaborate with you in this project."

— Dr. Satya P. Agarwal, University of California, Berkeley, USA.

"... I will be happy to contribute an article for the volume being brought out by you in honour of Prof. Indira Patel."

— Prof. K.V Ramana,
Former Vice-Chancellor, Andhra University, Vishakhapatnam.

"May I send greetings and good wishes to Prof. Patel and you who think of honouring her by a well-deserved publication. It is a wonderful idea. I hope to write an article on "Social Action for Social Development" or Social Action by itself because in the section which deals with many issues, I think, one on Social Action will be relevant." (7-4-93).

"... I am not sure whether I can do it as I have got busy with so many small pieces of writing. So sorry, I am to disappoint you. If you can manage with those that are coming to you, anyway, that would be best. In the present condition. I will not be able to do anything..."

— Prof. K.K Jacob, Director,
National Institute of Social Work and Social Science, Bhubneshwar.

"It was kind of you to keep me in touch... regarding the publication in honour of Indira Patel. I certainly appreciate and welcome your initiative... I could consider being a contributor and shall do the best for the same."

"Many things have happened since I last wrote to you increasing the load of responsibility and travel here (20-5-1994). Hence I am sorry to say, I cannot fulfil my desire to contribute an article for Prof. Indira Patel's Felicitation Volume as promised earlier (4-5-1993)."

— Dr. (Ms.) Hazel D'Lima, College of Social Work,
Nirmala Niketan Institute, Mumbai.

"Thank you for inviting me to write an article for Prof. Indira Patel Felicitation Volume. I have an interest in writing but unfortunately will not be able to get time for writing as I would be busy, conducting legal aid courses in South India."

— Fr. P. D. Mathew, Indian Social Institute, New Delhi.

"I feel very guilty for not sending my article though I have agreed to do so. It is becoming increasingly difficult to deviate from my main job. These are hectic days and I am burdened so much with more and more responsibility. I now feel, whether I will be able to write an article.... This being a situation you may have to pardon me if I back out from my commitment to send my article. I have very high respect for Indiraben and I will feel very bad if I do not write on this occasion of her felicitation. I will still try but the chances appear to be bleak."

— Harnath Jagawat,
N.M. Sadguru Water and Development Foundation, Dahod, Gujarat.

"I feel honoured that the editor, Professor Indira Patel Felicitation Volume has asked me to contribute to the volume."

— Dr. C.P. Goyal, Department of Social Work,
Kashi Vidhyapith, Varansi.

" ... congratulations for taking up this project. Your outline is truly impressive. I am pleased to associate with the project and wish you all success for timely publication."

— Dr. S.P. Punalekar, Former Director,
Centre for Social Studies, Surat.

"Congratulation for taking up an excellent job of honouring Professor Indiraben Patel. I am honoured and feel grateful to you to ask me to write the paper.... If I can get the material that I need I will send you the paper. I request you to pardon me if I cannot get the needed resources and fail to send you the paper."

— Dr. H.M Rajyaguru,
(Former Dean, Faculty of Social Work, MSU) Ontario, Canada.

"Thanks for the invitation. It would be a privilege to honour Ms. Indira Patel."

— Gagan Sethi and Dipti Sethi, Jan Vikas, Ahmedabad.

" I am glad you plan to bring out and edit a book to felicitate Prof. Indira Patel. Your outline is quite attractive and I am impressed. This seems to be an interesting exercise.

I wish I can rise to the occasion and write something, perhaps a brief note, on the human being (the human agent) in social work and to bring to bear on social work experience, perspectives from hermeneutics, ordinary language philosophy the newer meaning of social science by Robert [Peter] Winch and the Foucaultian power etc. and all of this to join issues with the objectivist [perspective,] prevailing [in] Parsonian approach to social work. This seems to be an interesting exercise but I doubt if I can do it with all other prior commitments. Without promising anything, I would make an attempt. I know this is all very vague, but I cannot help it."

---- Prof. Sumant Majumdar, Gujarat Vidyapith, Ahmedabad.

"Your plans to bring out Felicitation Volume in honour of Prof. Indira Patel are well-conceived and reflect a good deal of spade-work. I am honoured to be associated and wish you all luck for a speedy completion of the work."

--- Dr. Lancy Lobo,

Social Anthropologist Centre for Social Studies, Surat.

Notes on Contributors

Satya P. Agarwal is a social scientist with a brilliant academic record as well as notable professional achievements in India, the United States and the United Nations. He has won five gold medals and numerous merit scholarships and research fellowships at various universities. He has written pioneering books on the concepts and methodology of manpower supply and demand. While at the United Nations as Chief Technical Adviser, he prepared a large number of technical reports in the socio-economic fields. He has offered various professional help at Centre for South Asia Studies, University of California, Berkeley and at the American Academy of Asian Studies in the USA. He has published a book on *The Social Role of the Gita: How and Why* (1993). As an Honorary Research Associate at the Centre for South Asia Studies, University of California, Berkeley, he is deeply involved in research on *Lokasamgraha* and Ecology.

K.D. Gangrade is former Professor of Delhi School of Social Work and former Pro-Vice Chancellor, University of Delhi. He is an eminent academician and is held in very high esteem by the profession. He has written extensively on conflict resolution, famines, role of values, leadership, *panchayati raj*, rural development, rural community, ideology of social work, social legislations etc. He was closely associated with several NGOs and social welfare bodies. Besides many articles published in various reputed journals, some of his books are: *Community Organization in India* (1971), *Challenges and Responses: A Study of Famines in India* (co-authored, 1973), *Emerging Patterns of Leaderships* (1974), *Crisis of Values: A Study in Generation Gap* (1975), *Social Legislation in India,* Vol. I & II (1978), *Social Work and Development* (1986), and *Conflict Resolution Through Non-Violence: Role of the Universities*, Vol. I & II (co-authored, 1990). He was a Visiting Professor in Sociology and Social Work at Nagarjuna University, Nagarjuna Nagar, Andhra Pradesh.

C.P. Goyal is former Professor and Head, Department of Social Work, Kashi Vidyapeeth, Varanasi. He also worked as Director, National Institute of Social Work and Social Sciences, Bhubaneshwar. Presently, he is associated with the Jain Vishwa Vidyalaya, Ladnu, Rajasthan.

Sandhya Joshi is Reader at the Faculty of Social Work, M. S. University of Baroda, where she is teaching for more than fifteen years. She obtained her M.S.W. degree from Delhi School of Social Work and Ph.D. from M. S. University of Baroda. She is the recipient of the prestigious Council of International Fellowship Award (USA). Her research interest is health and development of poor women and children. She is actively associated with a few voluntary organizations in Baroda city. She has written numerous research articles and a book on *Child Survival, Health and Social Work Intervention* (1996). Presently, she is deputed by the MSU to join a prestigious research project on *To Reduce Barriers to Conceptive Method Availability and Choice*, as Project Coordinator, sponsored by the Population Council, Regional Office, South and East Asia. She is also nominated as a Member of the UGC Panel on Social Work for 1997-2000.

Lancy Lobo is Senior Fellow and Director, Centre for Social Studies, Surat. He obtained his M.Sc. (Anthropology), M.Phil. (Sociology) and Ph.D. (Sociology) from the Delhi School of Economics, Delhi University. He has conducted extensive studies on Scheduled Castes, Scheduled Tribes, OBCs in rural and urban Gujarat. He has published many articles in national and international journals. Three of his articles received Hari Om Ashram Prizes during 1988-90 thrice in succession for the best published research articles, which is a rare honour. His recent book on *The Thakors of North Gujarat* (1995) is widely well-received as a pioneering work in social anthropology. He participated as an Indian co-counterpart in a Six-Nation International Research Project of the United Nations University, Tokyo on *Social and Cultural Supports for the Aging* during 1986-88. He conducted a research study on *Slum as a Habitat: How Do People Cope and the Role of Voluntary Organizations*, sponsored by Indo-Dutch Programme on Alternatives in Development (IDPAD) during 1991-93. He also visited British and Australian Universities during 1995-96. Currently, he is engaged in researches in medical anthropology.

Kalindi S. Muzumdar is former Vice-Principal of College of Social Work, Nirmala Niketan, Bombay University. Her areas of research interest are: Women and Child Development, Family Life, Population Education and Training for Eradication of AIDS. She has edited a book on *Working With the Poor* and the UNICEF has published her books on *ICDS* and *Mobilization of Community Resources.* She visited Yugoslavia and Pakistan for presenting research papers during 1991-92. She has held several prestigious positions in governmental and non-governmental organizations like Bombay High Court, Government of Maharashtra, OXFAM (India) and Bombay Association of Trained Social Workers. Presently, she is given an extension at the college and also practices as a counsellor for cases of familial and marital conflicts. The UGC has appointed her as a member of the DSA Review Committee.

Chhaya Patel is Lecturer at the Faculty of Social Work, M. S. University of Baroda, from where she obtained her Master's Degree in Social Work, a Post-Graduate Diploma in Clinical and Community Psychology and is presently pursuing her doctoral work on *Assessing Social Component of ICDS in Tribal Region of Gujarat* at the MSU. During 1979-84, she co-planned, organized and executed eighty-five youth camps for the university boys and girls in rural areas of the state as Field Organizer of NSS at the MSU. From 1984-86, she worked as Instructor, Social Work at ICDS-MLTC, South Gujarat University, Surat and obtained deep and rich insights into the problems of tribal children and women by extensively touring the interior tribal areas in South Gujarat. She has co-authored a mimeograph titled *From File to the Field* (1995) and written several articles. Presently, she is teaching at the MSU and is actively associated with Sahiyar---a progressive women's democratic rights organization in Gujarat.

S.P. Punalekar is Senior Fellow and former Director, Centre for Social Studies, Surat. He is a renowned sociologist and has written extensively on Tribal and Dalit Studies, Development Policy and Planning, and Interface between Literature and Society. He has worked and held various positions at the Department of Sociology (Bombay University), Sri Ram Centre for Industrial Relations (New Delhi), TISS (Bombay), NIPCCD (New Delhi). His many articles are published in journals of repute. He has authored *School Dropout Among Harijan Children* (1973), *Urban Community Development Programmes in India* (1978) and three books in Gujarati. He has also written 22 monographs. He has visited Melacca, Malaysia and Singapore under the auspices of the APDC---the UN organization.

K.V. Ramana is former Professor in Social Work, Andhra University, Visakhapatnam, from where he also obtained his M.A. and M.S.W. degrees. He obtained his doctoral degree from University of Illinois, USA. During 1988-91, he was Vice-Chancellor of Andhra University. He is the recipient of the Best Teacher Award of Government of Andhra Pradesh. He specialized in social development and worked as chairman and member of several NGOs engaged in rural, urban and tribal development. He has published articles in *Indian Journal of Social Work* and edited several books on social work (in Telegu) for Telugu Akademi. He was President of Association of Schools of Social Work in India during 1977-81. He visited the UK, the USA, Australia, Israel and Indonesia for various academic engagements.

Harsh Sethi is former Fellow, Centre for the Study of Developing Societies, Delhi. He served as Research Director, Indian Council of Social Science Research, New Delhi (1980-84). Earlier he worked as Acquisition Editor at Sage (India), New Delhi. His research is in the area of Grassroots Movements and Sustainable Development. He has contributed numerous articles to professional journals in India and abroad. His articles on "Groups in a New Politics of Transformation" (1984) and "The Immoral 'Other': Debate Between Party and Non-party Groups" (1985) published in *EPW* generated a great interest and widespread debate in the country. His published books are: *Action Research for Development* (co-edited, 1984), *Voices from a Scarred City* (co-edited, 1985), *Rethinking Human Rights* (co-edited, 1989) and *Participatory Development: Learning from South Asia* (co-authored, 1991). Presently, he is the Editor of *Seminar* (Delhi).

Bharti Sharma is Reader in Department of Social Work, Jamia Millia Islamia, New Delhi. She obtained her M.S.W. (1965) from MSU, Baroda and Ph.D. in Sociology (1983) from South Gujarat University, Surat. She worked as Lecturer in MSU during 1966-70, as Research Officer at the BCC, Baroda during 1971-72 and as Professional Field Social Worker at the Wolverhamton Local Authority, England during 1972-74. She also worked at University of Dar-es-Salam, Tanzania as Lecturer in Sociology during 1983-84. Between 1986 and 1993, she initially worked as Lecturer in Department of Home Science at Nirtiri Women's College and then became Reader and Head of the Department of Social Work at NEHU, Aizwal. Mental Health, Social Development, Family and Child Welfare are areas of her research interest. She has written books on *Juvenile Delinquents and their Social Culture* (1990) and *Community Mental Health: Proceedings of a Workshop* (1993) as well as several articles. Recently, she is nominated as a member of the Advisory Committee on DRS in Social Work by the UGC.

D.L. Sheth is Senior Fellow and former Director of the Centre for the Study of Developing Societies, Delhi. He received his M.S.W. degree from MSU, Baroda in 1959 and served there as a Lecturer for a year. He founded (with Rajni Kothari) Lokayan in early 1980s. He was editor of *Alternatives: Human Governance and Social Transformation.* He is founding member of *Lokchintan: Collective Explorations in Democracy* and member, Steering Committee for National Election Study, 1996 (at CSDS). He has published numerous articles in journals both in India and abroad. His books include *Values and the Active Community* (co-authored, 1971), *Citizens and Parties: Aspects of Competitive Politics in India* (edited, 1975) and *The Multiverse of Democracy* (co-edited, 1996). He was appointed as a Member (Social Scientist) to the National Commission for Backward Classes, Government of India in since August 1993. He continues to make major contributions to the study of comparative politics, political sociology, social issues and grassroots movements.

Nitin J. Vyas is a Reader and Officiating Head, Department of Philosophy, M. S. University of Baroda, Vadodara from where he obtained his M.A. and Ph.D. (1979). He is actively associated with philosophical and religious bodies and associations. He has published about twenty-five articles, three edited books and a book on *Evil, Suffering and Salvation: A Comparative Perspective in Religions* (1982). He has participated in numerous national and international conferences. Recently, he visited Indonesia and Singapore.

Index